C is one of the most popular programming languages today. It is flexible, efficient and highly portable, and is used for writing many different kinds of programs, from compilers and assemblers to spreadsheets and games.

This book is based on ANSI C – the recently adopted standard for the C language. It assumes familiarity with basic programming concepts such as variables, constants, iteration and looping, but covers all aspects of C. In general it is as much about learning programming skills as it is about mastering the art of coding programs in C. To this end the text contains a wealth of examples and exercises that foster and test the understanding of the concepts developed in each chapter.

An outstanding feature of this book is the treatment of 'pointers'. The topic is presented in a clear logical and reasoned manner that is easy to follow. Binary files and random access files are also treated in such a manner that the reader can easily become adept at using them.

Anybody who wishes to get to grips with the art of programming in C will find this a most valuable book.

Cambridge Computer Science Texts
Edited by D. J. Cooke, Loughborough University

C by Example

*Also in this series*

29   Cambridge Computer Science Texts

# C by Example

### Noel Kalicharan
*University of the West Indies*

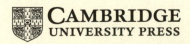
CAMBRIDGE
UNIVERSITY PRESS

Published by the Press Syndicate of the University of Cambridge
The Pitt Building, Trumpington Street, Cambridge CB2 1RP
40 West 20th Street, New York, NY 10011-4211, USA
10 Stamford Road, Oakleigh, Melbourne 3166, Australia

© Cambridge University Press 1994

First published 1994

Printed in Great Britain at the University Press, Cambridge

*A catalogue record for this book is available from the British Library*

*Library of Congress cataloguing in publication data*
Kalicharan, Noel.
C by example / Noel Kalicharan.
p.     cm. – (Cambridge computer science texts: 29)
Includes index.
ISBN 0 521 45023 3 (hc). – ISBN 0 521 45650 9 (pb)
1. C (Computer program language)   I. Title.   II. Series.
QA76.73.C15835   1994
005.13′3–dc20   93-27877 CIP

ISBN 0 521 45023 3      hardback
ISBN 0 521 45650 9      paperback

To my daughters

Anushka Nikita
and
Anyara Saskia

# Contents

# Preface

In the beginning, there was a language called BCPL. This was developed in the 1960s by Martin Richards at Cambridge University. In 1970, Ken Thompson, of Bell Laboratories, developed and implemented the language B on a DEC (Digital Equipment Corporation) PDP-7 computer running the first UNIX operating system. B was strongly influenced by BCPL. When DEC introduced their PDP-11, Dennis Ritchie (also of Bell Labs) modified B to create the language C in order to implement UNIX on the new machine.

Since those early days, C has undergone several changes. Existing features have been modified, new features have been added and some obsolete ones deleted. With the advent and proliferation of microcomputers, several implementations of C emerged. Though compatible to a great degree, there were discrepancies and anomalies in these implementations. In 1983, the American National Standards Institute (ANSI) established a committee to define a 'standard' version of the C language. This standard has been adopted by the major producers of C compilers. This book is based on ANSI C.

C has fast become one of the most popular programming languages today. Perhaps one of the reasons for its widespread popularity is its flexibility – it allows one to program in a 'structured' way yet it permits great 'freedom of expression'. It combines the control structures normally found in high-level languages such as Pascal or Ada with the ability to manipulate bits, bytes and addresses, something usually associated with assembly language. In its early days, C was thought of mainly as a language for writing systems programs – things like operating systems, editors, compilers, assemblers and input/output utility programs. But that view has changed considerably in recent times. Today, C is used for writing all kinds of applications programs as well – things like wordprocessing programs, spreadsheet programs, database management programs, accounting programs, games, educational software, etc. But flexibility is not the only reason.

C lends itself to 'modular programming'. It is easy to create 'modules' which can be treated like the proverbial 'black-box' – we need only know **what** the module does, not **how** it does it. This concept is critical to the writing of a large program, or a program which is being written by several people. A related idea is that, in C, one can create and maintain one's own 'library' of frequently used functions. In this way, duplication of effort can be kept to a minimum.

C is an 'efficient' language. The machine code produced for a C program is comparable to what would be produced if the program were written in assembly language. This is possible because many of C's features (mainly the 'operators' provided) closely resemble features of today's computers, so that translation from C to machine code is straightforward. Another reason is that C is 'small'; for example, there are only 32 keywords (reserved words) and the basic data types are simply character, integer and floating-point. In order to keep down the size of the language, C does not include features considered 'built-in' or 'standard' in other languages. For instance, there are no statements like `read` or `write` for performing input/output and no direct way of comparing two strings. These operations are provided by means of **functions** provided in a standard library.

C is highly portable. This means that a C program can run with little or no modification on different kinds of computers (computers with different processors). This is of crucial importance if, for instance, one wants to change one's computer system. If programs are not portable, then much programming effort on the old system would have been wasted, and changing to a new system would be very costly. A software developer could sell many more programs if they could run on several machines with little or no modification. With the adoption of the new ANSI C standard, C programs have become even more portable.

Finally, and perhaps, most importantly, C is popular because, quite simply, it is a joy to use. And as one's mastery of the language increases, so does the joy.

This text assumes familiarity with basic programming concepts such as variables, constants, looping and iteration, but it covers all features of the C language. It is about the learning of programming in general as much as it is about mastering the art of coding programs in C. It is a truism that learning the syntax of a language is trivial compared with learning programming ideas and being aware of situations in which the syntactic constructs can be used. To this end, there is a wealth of examples and exercises that foster and test the understanding of the concepts developed in each chapter.

One of the main features is the illustration of the use of C constructs in meaningful examples as opposed to their use in contrived examples which serve no purpose other than to illustrate C syntax. In order to develop meaningful examples, certain side topics, such as sorting, hashing and binary trees, are developed. Developing these topics in the text makes the book more self-contained. The student learns a topic that is broadly applicable and so gets to see the C construct used in a wider context. In the conventional approach to teaching a language, features of the language are presented followed by examples illustrating these features. However, in this book, many features are introduced by discussing an example, showing the need for a feature and then presenting the feature. Hopefully, this approach gives one a broader picture of the application of a particular feature.

An important highlight of this book is the treatment of pointers – perhaps the hardest facet of the language but treated cursorily in most books on C. According to one reader of an early draft, 'This book gives a clear, logical and reasoned description of the subject which is quite refreshing to read'. Another topic which is usually glossed over in most books but explored in detail here is file handling. In particular, binary files and random access files are fully treated.

The exercises at the end of each chapter range from those which directly test the understanding of concepts, statements or constructs presented in the chapter to those which require the application of the material to non-trivial problems.

- Chapter 1 presents an overview of the basic features in C – data types, operators, expressions, statements and the basic control structures while and if...else. The treatment is not meant to be complete and many of the ideas introduced are expanded in later chapters.
- Chapter 2 introduces other commonly used control structures – for, do...while, switch and continue as well as a discussion of arrays. The latter includes the use of arrays for storing strings and simple methods for searching arrays.
- Chapter 3 discusses the elementary ideas involved in writing and using functions – the building blocks of C programs.
- Chapter 4 deals with the manipulation of character and string data.

The powerful 'search and insert' technique of hashing and insertion sort are introduced in order to discuss more useful examples.

- Chapter 5 is a more detailed treatment of functions. The flexible and powerful concept of pointers is also introduced here. The chapter ends with a discussion of that very useful (but one that students often find difficult) programming concept – recursion.
- Chapter 6 ties up the loose ends from the previous chapters. In particular, data types, operators, expressions, storage classes and initialization are discussed more fully.
- Chapter 7 starts with an introductory discussion of structures This is followed by some detailed examples illustrating the manipulation of linked lists.
- Chapter 8 continues the discussion of structures, using the versatile binary tree as the main theme. The latter part of the chapter deals with nested structures, unions and bit-fields.
- Chapter 9 covers standard input/output in C in a fair amount of detail. This is deliberate since this is perhaps the area of C that programmers use most often. A number of subtle issues are discussed which are hardly ever treated in most books or even the compiler manual.
- Chapter 10 is devoted to functions which operate on general files. The treatment of binary and random access files rounds off the chapter.
- Chapter 11 discusses the main facilities provided by the C preprocessor and ends with a brief treatment of some of the lesser used features in C.

Welcome to C programming. Though it can be frustrating and difficult at times, it can also be interesting, exciting, fascinating and highly rewarding.

Noel Kalicharan

# 1

# Getting Started With C

In this chapter, we introduce many of the basic features of C. These include the data types, operators and statements most commonly used in C programs. The intent is not to be too formal or complete, but rather to get the reader to the point where he/she becomes familiar with the nature of a C program and can construct non-trivial programs in the shortest possible time. Topics which are glossed over in the interest of brevity and/or simplicity are treated in greater detail in other chapters of the book.

The C programming language is built around a few basic concepts. These include:

(1) **keywords**, e.g., if, while, do, for, int, char, float. Each keyword has a specific meaning in the context of a C program, and may not be used for any other purpose. For this reason, they are usually called **reserved words**. Appendix A gives the complete list of C keywords.

(2) a small number of **data types**, e.g. character (designated by char), integer (int), floating-point (float). Each data type defines constants of that type, for example, 't' is a character constant and 23 is an integer constant. Data types are discussed in more detail later in this chapter (Section 1.3).

(3) **variables**, e.g., sum, count, numStudents. Variables are used to hold data of different types as well as for the names of functions. Variables are discussed in Section 1.4.

(4) **operators**, e.g., = (addition), == (test for equality), | | (logical or), < (less than), = (assignment). One of the hallmarks of C is that it has a rich set of operators, many of which are not found in other languages. An operator specifies the action to perform on its operand(s). An operand can be a constant or a variable. Operators are discussed in Section 1.5.

1

(5) **expressions**, e.g., a + b * c, x = sum / n,
(a == b) || (b == c).

Expressions are formed by combining operators, constants and/or variables according to prescribed rules. Expressions are discussed in Section 1.5.

(6) **statements**, e.g., x = sum / n;
if (a < b) small = a; else small = b;

Statements specify actions to be performed by the program. The commonly used statements are discussed starting from Section 1.6.

(7) **functions** – in C, as in other languages, functions are the building blocks from which larger programs are constructed. In a well-written program, a function performs a single, well-defined task. The dividing of a large job into smaller tasks, each of which is implemented by a function, is a feature of the top-down, modular approach to programming. Functions are discussed in detail in Chapters 3 and 5.

The C language does not contain, among other things, built-in input/output statements. Input/output facilities are provided by means of 'standard' functions provided in the 'standard' library. An integral part of any C programming system is the provision of this library of functions. In addition to I/O functions, the library normally includes

- functions for character and string handling;
- mathematical functions;
- time, date and other system-related functions;
- functions for the dynamic allocation of storage;
- constant definitions for implementation-defined limits, for example, the maximum and minimum values of int variables.

In addition, many libraries on specific systems contain functions for screen-handling or graphics. You will need to refer to your specific compiler manual for details of the library functions provided.

Almost any program one writes will need to perform some input/output. Any such program will therefore need to use at least one of the standard I/O functions. These functions use variable (and other) declarations contained in a special **header** file. (Each class of functions has its own header file). For a user's program to compile and run properly, it is necessary to specify the header file(s) required by the program. The header file containing the declarations for the I/O functions is denoted by ⟨stdio.h⟩. Since it is almost always needed, most users' programs must be preceded by the statement

```
#include <stdio.h>
```

This informs the C compiler to include the declarations in the file `stdio.h` in the user's program.

Other commonly used header files are:

`ctype.h`  – contains declarations for character–handling functions (Chapter 3).

`limits.h` – contains definitions for implementation–dependent limits, for example, minimum and maximum values of various data types.

`math.h`   – contains declarations used by the mathematical functions; these include trigonometric, hyperbolic, exponential and logarithmic functions.

`stdlib.h` – contains declarations for miscellaneous functions, for example, random number functions and functions for searching and sorting.

`string.h` – contains declarations for string functions (Chapter 4).

`time.h`   – contains declarations for system time and date functions.

You will need to consult your compiler manual for the complete list of available header files and library functions.

### 1.1 The first example

Write a C program to print the message

```
Welcome to the World of C
```

One solution is program P1.1.

---

**Program P1.1**

```
#include <stdio.h>

main()
{
   printf("Welcome to the World of C");
}
```

A C program consists of one or more 'functions' (or subprograms), one of which must be called `main`. Our solution consists of just one function, so it must be called `main`. The (round) brackets after `main` are necessary because, in C, a function name must be followed by a list of 'arguments' enclosed in brackets. If there are no 'arguments', the brackets must still be present; `main` has no 'arguments' so the brackets alone are present.

Next comes a left brace (curly bracket); this indicates the start of the 'body' of the function. A matching right brace indicates the end of the 'body' of the function. The braces { and } enclose the statements which comprise the body of the function. The braces are equivalent to `begin` and `end` of languages like Pascal or Algol. The body of our solution consists of a single statement (actually a 'call' to the standard output function `printf`). The 'argument' to `printf` in our example is a **string constant** (also called a **character string**); this is simply a set of characters enclosed in double quotes ("). The effect is that the string (without the quotes) is printed. In general, a statement in C is terminated by a semicolon (;). In the example, a semicolon follows the right bracket (of the call to `printf`) to satisfy this requirement.

In C, a program begins execution at the first statement of `main` and terminates when the right brace (indicating the end of `main`) is encountered. Execution also terminates if a `return` statement (see Section 3.1) is encountered in `main`.

### *1.1.1 Running the program*

Having written the program on paper, the next task is to get it running on a real computer. How this is done varies somewhat from one system to the next but, in general, the following steps must be performed:

(1) type the program to a file. Some compilers require that the name of the file end in '.c', so we could name our file `welcome.c`. Even if the compiler does not require it, it is still good practice to append `.c` to the file name to remind us that a C program is stored in it. Since this program uses the standard output function `printf`, the program is preceded by the line

```
#include <stdio.h>
```

(2) invoke the C compiler to compile the program in the file `welcome.c`. For example, on the VAX/VMS operating system, the command for

doing this is:

```
cc welcome
```

where `cc` specifies that the C compiler is required; it expects to find a file `welcome.c` containing a C program.

Some systems allow you to choose 'compile' from a menu of choices. (You will need to find out the specific command for your compiler).

Assuming there are no errors, the compiler will produce an 'object file', typically called `welcome.obj`, containing the machine code equivalent of the C program. This object file will contain 'place holders' for functions or variables **used** in the program but not **defined** in the program. References to these functions or variables will be resolved in the next step.

(3) invoke the **linker** to resolve references to functions or variables not defined in the program. For example, on the VAX/VMS operating system, the command for doing this is:

```
link welcome
```

Since it only makes sense to link an **object** file, the linker will look for a file `welcome.obj`. But where does it find the functions or variables that need to be resolved? Many systems automatically search the standard library. Others require that the link command specify the library or libraries to be searched. The result of linking is that an 'executable file', typically called `welcome.exe`, is produced. This file contains code which can be executed by the computer. In this example, the linker will find the function `printf` in the standard library and include its code in the executable file being produced.

(4) run the program. For example, on the VAX/VMS operating system, the command for doing this is:

```
run welcome
```

Since only executable files can be 'run', the operating system looks for a file `welcome.exe`. When this program is run,

```
Welcome to the World of C
```

will be printed on the screen.

### *1.1.2 A word on program layout*

C does not require the program to be laid out as in the example. An equivalent program is

```
#include <stdio.h>
main() {printf("Welcome to the World of C"); }
```

For this small program, it probably does not matter which version we use. However, as program size increases, it becomes imperative that the layout of the program highlight the logical structure of the program, thus improving its readability. Indentation and clearly indicating which right brace matches which left brace can help in this regard. We will see the value of this principle as our programs become more substantial.

#### *The newline character (written as* \n, *read as backslash n)*

Suppose we wanted to write a program to print the following lines:

```
Welcome to the World of C
Hope you enjoy it
```

Our initial attempt might be

```
#include <stdio.h>

main()
{
    printf("Welcome to the World of C");
    printf("Hope you enjoy it");
}
```

However, this does not quite give us what we want. When this program is executed, it will print

```
Welcome to the World of CHope you enjoy it
```

Note that the two strings are joined together. This happens because printf does not place output on a new line, unless this is specified explicitly. Put another way, printf does not automatically supply a **newline** character after printing its argument(s). (A newline character would cause subsequent output to begin at the left margin of the next line). In the example, a newline character is not supplied after 'C' is printed so that 'Hope...' is printed on the same line as 'C' and immediately after it.

To get the desired effect, we must tell printf to supply a newline character after printing '...C'. We do this by using the character sequence \n (backslash n) as in program P1.2:

---

**Program P1.2**

```
#include <stdio.h>

main()
{
    printf("Welcome to the World of C\n");
    printf("Hope you enjoy it\n");
}
```

---

The first \n says to terminate the current output line; subsequent output will start at the left margin of the next line. Thus 'Hope...' will be printed on a new line. The second \n has the effect of terminating the second line. If it were not present, the output will still come out right, but only because there is no more output to follow. (This is also the reason why our first program worked without \n).

As an embellishment, suppose we wanted to leave a blank line between our two lines of output. Each of the following sets of statements will accomplish this:

```
(1) printf("Welcome to the World of C\n\n");
    printf("Hope you enjoy it\n");

(2) printf("Welcome to the World of C\n");
    printf("\nHope you enjoy it\n");

(3) printf("Welcome to the World of C\n");
    printf("\n");
    printf("Hope you enjoy it\n");
```

The backslash (\) signals that a special effect is needed at this point. The character following the backslash specifies what to do. The combination is usually referred to as an *escape sequence*. The following are commonly used escape sequences:

\n says to issue a newline character;
\t says to issue a tab character;
\b  says to backspace;
\"  says to print ";
\\  says to print \.

The complete list of escape sequences is given in Section 4.1.

## 1.2 Comments

Comments may be included in a C program to describe what a function is supposed to do, or, perhaps, to clarify some portion of code. A comment begins with the two-character symbol /* and is terminated by another two-character symbol */. It can occur anywhere that a space, tab or newline (so-called 'whitespace' characters) can. For example

```
#include <stdio.h>

main()     /*  This is our greeting program */
{
   printf("Welcome to the World of C\n");
        /* \n — newline character */
}
```

For the purposes of the compiler, a comment is treated as a single whitespace character.

One restriction on comments is that they cannot be nested. Consider

```
/* start of outer comment

   /* inner comment */

end of outer comment    */
```

Here the first */ ends the comment started with the first /*. The second /* is simply part of the first comment. Since, as far as the compiler is concerned, the comment ends with the first */, the word end will cause an error. A way to 'comment out' a portion of a program (which itself may contain comments) is discussed in Section 11.1.4.

## 1.3 Data types

C supports the following data types (among others). Each data type defines constants of that type.

- char — a single character; a character constant is a single character enclosed by single quotes (apostrophes). Examples: 'a', '7', '&'. Characters which are not printable or which have a special use are represented by a backslash (\) followed by another character. For example, '\n' represents the newline character and '\'' (single quote, backslash, single quote, single quote) represents a single quote.
- int — integer (whole number); examples: 25, 0, −1, −247, 32767. C also allows the use of octal and hexadecimal constants. An octal constant begins with a leading zero (0) and a hexadecimal constant begins with a leading 0x or 0X. For example, the decimal number 59 can be written in octal as 073 and in hexadecimal as 0x3b or 0x3B or 0X3b or 0X3B.
- double — double-precision floating point number; a double constant can be written with a decimal point (73.6, −739.31, 1.0, 3.1416), with an exponent using e or E (736 E−1 or 736e−1, whose value is $736 \times 10^{-1}$, that is, 73.6) or both a decimal point and an exponent (0.736 e2 or 0.736 E+2, whose value is $0.736 \times 10^2$, that is, 73.6).
- float — a single-precision floating point number; other languages call this data type real. A float constant is written by adding the suffix f or F to a double constant, for example, 73.6f or 0.736e2F.

The size of these types depends on the architecture of the particular machine. On many machines, an int variable occupies 2 or 4 bytes and a variable of type float gives about 6 or 7 significant digits using 4 bytes. Normally, a variable of type double gives about twice the number of significant digits as a variable of type `float`, and is used when greater accuracy is required.

(The types `char`, `int` and `double` may be preceded by 'type qualifiers' to alter their meaning. These qualifiers are discussed in Section 1.4).

A data type commonly used in C is the **string**. A string constant consists of a set of zero or more characters enclosed by double quotation marks (`"`). Examples:

```
"Once upon a time"
"Pass"
"times 2 ="
"?##$%#)*(_+"
```

C does not allow a string constant to be continued on to another line. In other words, both opening and closing quotes must appear on the same line. However, adjacent strings can be concatenated at compile time. This allows a long string to be broken up and placed on more than one line, as in the following example:

```
printf("Part of a long string can be placed on "
       "one line and the other part could be "
       "placed on the next line. Note that the "
       "pieces are separated by white space, not "
       "commas\n");
```

When this statement is compiled, the five strings are concatenated, forming one string.

In C, a string is stored in an array of characters (see Section 4.4).

For those familiar with the data type `boolean` or `logical` (with constants `true` and `false`) from other languages, it should be noted that C does not have a similar type, at least not explicitly. Rather, C uses the concept of the value of an expression to denote `true`/`false`. An expression can be used any context where a `true` or `false` value is required. The expression is considered `true` if its value is non-zero and `false` if its value is zero. For example, if a and b are integer variables, then it is permissible to write

```
if (a + b) statement1 else statement2
```

`statement1` is executed if (a + b) is non-zero (true); `statement2` is executed if (a + b) is zero (false).

## 1.4 Identifiers

Identifiers are used to denote things like variables, function names (Chapter 3) and symbolic constants (Section 3.5). An identifier begins with a letter or underscore (_ )and may consist of letters, underscores and/or digits. The underscore may be used to improve the readability of the identifier. For example, compare `noofframes` with `no_of_frames`. There is no restriction on the length of a variable name. However, in ANSI C, only the first 31 characters of an identifier are significant. This means that if two identifiers agree in the first 31 positions, they are considered to be the same identifier. (This restriction of 31 applies to **internal** names – names declared and used only in one file. The restriction on **external** names – for example, global variables known in more than one file – is 8. Internal and external variables are discussed in detail in Chapter 6). Both upper and lower case letters may be used in naming identifiers, and an uppercase letter (A, say) is considered different from the corresponding lowercase letter (a, say). So that, for instance, the variable `SUM` is different from `sum` is different from `Sum`. The conventional practice in C is to use uppercase letters for symbolic constants (see Section 3.5) and lowercase letters for variables and function names. In this text, we will use uppercase letters for symbolic constants. Normally, we will use lowercase letters for variables, but for some variables, we will use both upper and lower case in order to improve readability; for example, `noOfFrames` or `maxThrowsPerTurn`.

The C language is built around a number of **keywords** (e. g. `char if`, `do`, `while`, `int`) which are **reserved**. A keyword has a special meaning in the context of a C program and may not be used by a programmer as one of his variables. All reserved words in C must be written in lowercase letters. Thus, for instance, `INT` will not be treated as a keyword; it must be written as `int`. The complete list of keywords is given in Appendix A.

### *Declaring variables*

A variable declaration consists of a data type followed by a variable name. The declaration is terminated by a semicolon. For example,

```
int sum;
```

declares `sum` to be a variable of type `int`. Several variables can be declared in one statement as in

```
int sum, count, numRooms;
```

In this case, the variables must be separated by commas. Other examples of declarations are

```
float deposit, target, interest, total;
char letter, digit, separator;
```

### Qualified integers

In the case of int, a variable declaration can be preceded by the 'type qualifiers' short, long, unsigned or signed. Examples are

```
short int numteams;
long int gross;
unsigned int count;
short unsigned int numstudents;
```

In all of these, the word int can be omitted.

short and long refer to the number of bits used for storing the integer on a particular machine. Typically, short is 16 bits and long is 32 bits; int (by itself) is usually 16 or 32 bits, depending on the machine. You will need to read your compiler manual to find out the sizes on your particular machine. The only guarantee that C makes is that a short int is not bigger than an int which is not bigger than a long int. An integer constant is considered long if it is followed by one of the letters '1' or 'L', e. g. 537L or 8345467L. (The uppercase letter is recommended since the lowercase 'ell' looks too much like the digit 1).

unsigned implies that the value of the variable will never be negative. It can be used to increase the range of positive numbers normally stored. For example, using 16 bits, a variable declared as an int can assume values in the range −32768 to +32767, but a variable declared as unsigned can assume values in the range 0 to 65535.

signed is hardly ever used with int since, by default, an int declaration assumes a signed number.

### Qualified char

The qualifiers signed and unsigned may be used in declaring a char variable. Assuming that a char is stored using 8 bits, an unsigned char can assume values from 0 to 255 ($255_{10} = 11111111_2$), while a signed char can assume values from −128 to 127. In the unsigned case, the bit pattern stored in the variable is interpreted as a positive number. In the `signed` case, the leading bit of the bit pattern is interpreted as a sign bit (0 for positive, 1 for negative).

### *Qualified* `double`

The qualifier `long` may be applied to `double` if greater precision is required. In general, `double` gives about twice the precision as `float` and `long double` gives about twice the precision as `double`. You will need to check your particular compiler for the exact number of digits of precision in each case.

## 1.5 Expressions

Expressions are formed by combining constants, variables and **operators**. The commonly used operators include:

- arithmetic operators
- assignment operators
- relational operators
- logical operators
- increment and decrement operators

The following sections provide a brief discussion of these operators. For a more detailed discussion of the precedence and associativity of operators, see Chapter 6.

### *1.5.1 Arithmetic operators*

These include

| | |
|---|---|
| + | addition |
| − | subtraction |
| * | multiplication |
| / | division |
| % | modulus (remainder) |

For example, the expression

```
n % 4
```

gives the remainder when n is divided by 4. The usual precedence of operators apply. Thus + and − have the same precedence. * , / and %

have the same precedence. The precedence of *, / and % is higher than that of + and −.

When two or more (of the above) operators of the same precedence appear in an expression, they are evaluated from left to right. We say they **associate** from left to right. Thus a / b * c is evaluated as (a / b) * c. As usual, the order of evaluation can be changed by using parentheses, for instance, a / (b * c).

### 1.5.2 Assignment operators

These include (among others)

```
=    +=    -=    *=    /=    %=
```

The basic assignment operator is =. This is used to assign the value of an expression to a variable, as in

```
c = a + b
```

The entire construct consisting of the variable, = and the expression is referred to as an 'assignment expression'. The **value** of an assignment expression is simply the value assigned to the variable. For example, if a is 15 and b is 20, then the assignment expression

```
c = a + b
```

assigns the value 35 to c. The value of the (entire) assignment expression is also 35. The concept of the value of an assignment expression is useful in many situations. Examples will be seen throughout the book.

Multiple assignments are possible, as in

```
a = b = c = 13
```

The operator = associates from right to left, so the above is equivalent to

```
a = (b = (c = 13))
```

In addition to =, there are a number of assignment operators unique to C. These include (among others) +=, -=, *=, /= and %=. If op represents any of +, -, *, / or %, then

```
variable op= expression
```

is equivalent to

```
variable = variable op expression
```

For example, to add num to sum, we could write

```
sum = sum + num
```

However, C allows us to write this more concisely as

```
sum += num
```

### 1.5.3 Relational operators

These include

| | |
|---|---|
| == | equal to |
| != | not equal to |
| > | greater than |
| < | less than |
| <= | less than or equal to |
| >= | greater than or equal to |

Examples:
```
num == 0
ch != 'C'
sum <= (x + y)
```

These operators are used for comparing quantities. == and != have the same precedence which is lower than the (identical) precedence of the others. Operators of equal precedence associate from left to right. To test if a is equal to b, one uses a == b But what if we wanted to test if a is equal to b is equal to c? It is tempting to write

```
a == b == c     /* wrong */
```

However, this is evaluated as (a == b) == c. 'a == b' evaluates to 1 or 0, depending on whether it is true or false; **this** value is what is compared with c, obviously not what was intended. The proper way to write the test is

```
(a == b) && (b == c)     /* right */
```

&& is described next. As the precedence of && is lower than that of == (see Chapter 6), the brackets may be omitted, and the test written as

```
a == b && b == c
```

Nevertheless, in the interest of clarity and readability, it is recommended that you include the brackets.

### 1.5.4 *Logical operators*

These include

```
&&      and
||      or
!       not
```

Examples:   (ch >= 'a') && (ch <= 'z')
            (a < 0) || (a > 9)
            !(n < 1 || n > 12)  equivalent to
            (n >= 1 && n <= 12)

These operators are used for forming compound conditions from simple ones. An example of a simple condition is

```
a < 0
```

This has a straightforward true/false value. The examples above all illustrate compound conditions.

   ! has higher precedence than && which has higher precedence than ||. In a given expression, the operators && and || associate from left to right, and the evaluation of the expression stops as soon as its truth value is determined. As usual, parentheses can be used to force a particular order of evaluation. For example, consider

```
a && b || c
```

&& is performed first; if a is false, && is false and b is not evaluated; c is then evaluated to determine the truth value of || and, hence, of the expression. However, if a is true, b is evaluated; if b is also true, then c is not evaluated since the expression is now known to be true; but if b is false, && is false and c is evaluated to determine the truth value of the expression.

In the expression

```
a && (b || c)
```

the parentheses specify that || is performed first. If it is false, there is no need to evaluate a since the expression must be false. If || is true, then the value of a determines the truth value of the expression.

### 1.5.5 Increment and decrement operators

++      increment by 1
--      decrement by 1

Examples:   ++n and n++ are both equivalent to n = n + 1
            --n and n-- are both equivalent to n = n - 1

In certain situations, the side-effect of ++n is different from n++. This is because ++n increments n **before** using its value, whereas n++ increments n **after** it is used. As an example, suppose n has the value 7. The statement

```
a = ++n;
```

**first increments** n and **then assigns** the value (8) to a. But the statement

```
a = n++;
```

**first assigns** the value 7 to a and **then increments** n to 8. In both cases, though, the end result is that n is assigned the value 8.

### 1.5.6 Mixing operands in an expression

It is permitted to mix the types of operands in an expression. When this is done, C does conversions in the most 'natural' manner. For example, if ch is a char variable, j is an int and x is a float, the following expressions indicate the kinds of conversions performed:

```
j + ch        – ch is converted to int before adding to j;
j * x         – j is converted to float before multiplying by x;
j = x + ch    – ch is converted to float;
                 the addition is performed;
                 the result is converted to int (truncating, if
                 necessary) and stored in j;
x = x + 3.5   – since 3.5 is a double constant, x is converted to
                 double;
                 the addition is performed;
                 the result is converted to float and stored in x.
```

Conversion rules are discussed in more detail in Chapter 6.

### 1.6 Statements

Statements in C can be **simple** or **compound**. In the simplest case, a statement is an expression followed by a semicolon. For example, the assignment **expression**

```
a = b + c
```

becomes an assignment **statement** when it is followed by a semicolon, thus:

```
a = b + c;
```

In C, the semicolon is used to **terminate** a statement. In languages like Pascal or Algol, it is used to **separate** statements. The main point here is that, in C, the semicolon is part of the statement.

A **compound statement** begins with a left brace, {, followed by any number of statements, and terminated by a right brace, }. The left and right braces are similar to begin and end of other languages. An example of a compound statement is:

```
{ count = 0;
    if (a > b) max = a; else max = b;
}
```

A compound statement may itself contain other compound statements, for example,

```
{  overtime = 0;
   if (hours > maxhours) {
      overtime = hours — maxhours;
      regular = maxhours;
   }
}
```

Since the right brace terminates the compound statement, a semicolon is **not** required after it. Inserting one is unnecessary and, in some cases, will give a **syntax** error (for an example, see the end of Section 1.9). If required, the left brace may be followed by declarations; variables declared here will be known only within the compound statement. For example,

```
{   int n;
    char ch;
       .
       .
}
```

Here, the variables n and ch are known only within the compound statement. Their use within the braces does not conflict with their declaration and use outside the braces.

A compound statement can be used in **any** context in which a single statement is required.

## 1.7 Standard input and output

So far, we have not said where printf sends its output or from where a C program gets its input. For the time being, we will assume that output is sent to the standard output device, the screen, and input is supplied using the standard input device, the keyboard.

### Example 2

Write a C program to request two numbers and print their sum.

One solution is program P1.3.

---

**Program P1.3**

```
#include <stdio.h>

main()        /* find the sum of two given numbers */
{
  int first, second;

  printf("Enter first number: ");
  scanf("%d", &first);
  printf("Enter second number: ");
  scanf("%d", &second);
  printf("Their sum is %d\n", first + second);
}
```

---

A sample run of the program is shown below. The numbers 15 and 20 are typed by the user; everything else is typed by the computer.

```
Enter first number: 15
Enter second number: 20
Their sum is 35
```

• The statement

```
    int first, second;
```

declares that `first` and `second` are integer variables. `int` is one of the standard data types available in C. A declaration normally consists of a data type (`int`, in this case) followed by one or more identifiers, separated by commas; the last identifier is followed by a semicolon. **All variables in a C program must be declared before they are used.**

• The statement

```
    printf("Enter first number: ");
```

prompts the user for the first number.

- The statement

```
scanf("%d", &first);
```

gets the next integer typed and stores it in the variable first. scanf is a standard input function. In the example, the first argument is a string which specifies the type of data to be input; %d specifies that an integer is to be input. The other argument specifies **where** to store the integer. The significance of the ampersand (&) will be explained later (Section 5.2), but, for the time being, follow the rule that variables whose values are to be input must be preceded by an &. scanf will be discussed in detail in Section 9.4.4.
- The printf(...) statement prompts for the second number, and scanf(...) reads its value into second.
- Assuming that first has the value 15 and second has the value 20, the statement

```
printf("Their sum is %d\n", first + second);
```

prints the sentence

```
Their sum is 35
```

This printf is a bit different from those we have seen so far. This one contains a **format specification** %d in the string comprising its first argument, **and** it contains a second argument. The effect, in this case, is that the first argument (called the **format string**) is printed as before, except that the %d is replaced by the value of the second argument. Thus, first + second is evaluated (giving 35), and this value replaces %d when the format string is printed.

printf will be discussed in detail in Section 9.4.3.

### *Example 3*

Write a program which requests a user to enter a weight in kilograms. The program converts the weight to pounds and prints the result.

In order to allow weights with fractional parts to be entered, variables which can store floating-point (so-called 'real') values will be used. In C, these variables can be declared to be of type float (other languages, like Pascal or FORTRAN, use the word real). Program P1.4 is one solution.

---

**Program P1.4**

```
#include <stdio.h>

main()        /* convert kilograms to pounds */
{
   float kgs, lbs;

   printf("\nEnter a weight in kilograms: ");
   scanf("%f", &kgs);
   lbs = kgs * 2.2;
   printf("\n\n%6.2f kilograms = %6.2f pounds\n",
          kgs, lbs);
}
```

---

The following is a sample run of this program:

```
Enter a weight (in kilograms): 8

8.00 kilograms = 17.60 pounds
```

- The statement

```
   float kgs, lbs;
```

declares kgs and lbs to be variables of type float. In C, a variable of type float can assume single-precision floating point values.
- The printf statement prompts the user to enter the weight.
- The statement

```
   scanf("%f", &kgs);
```

gets the next number from the input and stores it in kgs. The **conversion specification** %f indicates that a floating point number is expected in the input.
- The statement

```
   lbs = kgs * 2.2;
```

is an example of an **assignment** statement. It is similar to the Basic or FORTRAN assignment statement.

• In the statement

```
printf("\n\n%6.2f kilograms = %6.2f pounds\n",
    kgs, lbs);
```

the values of the two variables kgs and lbs are to be printed. Thus the format string (the first argument) **must** contain two **format specifications** corresponding to these variables. The specification used for both variables is %6.2f. This is interpreted to mean 'a float variable is to be printed in a field width of 6, with 2 places after the decimal point'.

In general, if the value to be printed contains **fewer** characters than the field width specified, it will be padded on the left with blanks (but see Section 9.4.3). If the value to be printed contains **more** characters than the field width specified, C will use whatever field width is necessary for printing the value.

### 1.8 The while **statement**

As written, the above program does one conversion and then stops. If we wanted to do another conversion, the program would have to be re-run. But what if we wanted to convert many weights in one run? We will need some way of getting the computer to repeat the statements of the program. In this case, though, we will need some way of telling the program that we have no more weights to convert. We will use a value of 0 to indicate this.

In C, the while statement may be used to cause a portion of a program to be executed repeatedly. Program P1.5 illustrates how it can be used to solve the problem of converting several weights in one run.

When the while statement is encountered, the expression kgs != 0 is evaluated (! = means 'not equal to'). If it is true (i.e., kgs has a value other than 0), the statement after the expression is executed. In the example, this statement is a compound statement (extending from the left brace to the matching right brace) and includes four 'simple' statements. The expression is then re-evaluated. As long as it is true, the compound statement is executed. When it becomes false (kgs **is** 0), the compound statement is skipped (the while is exited) and the last printf(...)

---

**Program P1.5**

```c
#include <stdio.h>

main()        /* convert kilograms to pounds */
{
  float kgs, lbs;

  printf("\nEnter a weight in kilograms: "
         "(0 to end): ");
  scanf("%f", &kgs);
  while (kgs != 0.0) {
     lbs = kgs * 2.2;
     printf("\n%6.2f kilograms = %6.2f pounds\n",
            kgs, lbs);
     printf("\nEnter a weight in kilograms: ");
     scanf("%f", &kgs);
  }
  printf("\nThat's all for now\n");
}
```

---

statement is executed. The following is a sample run:

```
Enter a weight in kilograms (0 to end): 8.0
8.00 kilograms = 17.60 pounds

Enter a weight in kilograms (0 to end): 10.5
10.50 kilograms = 23.10 pounds

Enter a weight in kilograms (0 to end): 0
That's all for now
```

The general form of the `while` construct is

```
while (expression)
   statementw
```

The word `while` and the left and right brackets are required. The programmer supplies `expression` and `statementw`. `statementw` can be simple, as in

```
while (ch != BLANK) getchar(ch);
/* note the semicolon */
```

or compound, as in

```
while (n > 0) {
   nfac *= n;      /* same as nfac = nfac * n; */
   n -= 1;         /* same as n = n - 1; */
}                  /* no semicolon after } */
```

When a while statement is encountered, expression is evaluated. If it is true (non-zero), statementw is executed followed by another evaluation of expression. As long as expression is true, statementw is executed. When expression becomes false (zero), execution continues with the statement (if any) after statementw. Observe that if expression is false the first time, then statementw is never executed.

As another example, program P1.6 reads a non-negative integer, n, and prints n and n!. For simplicity, we assume that the value supplied is not negative.

---

**Program P1.6**

```
#include <stdio.h>

main()        /* calculate n! */
{
   int n, nfac;

   printf("Enter a number (>= 0): ");
   scanf("%d", &n);
   printf("\n %d! = ", n);
   nfac = 1;
   while (n > 0) {
      nfac *= n;
      n -= 1;
   }
   printf("%d\n", nfac);
}
```

The following is a sample run of this program:

```
Enter  a  number  (>= 0):  5

     5!  =  120
```

As a matter of interest, if the value supplied for n is 0, the while condition n > 0 is false the first time so that the while body is never executed. The result is that

```
0!  =  1
```

(the correct output) is printed by the program.

## 1.9 The `if...else` statement

We illustrate this statement by writing a program which reads two numbers, a and b, and prints the value of a divided by b. If b is zero, the division is not attempted. Program P1.7 is one solution.

---

**Program P1.7**

```c
#include <stdio.h>

main()
{
   float a, b;

   printf("\nEnter two numbers:");
   scanf("%f %f",&a, &b);
   if (b == 0)
      printf("\nCannot divide by zero\n");
   else
      printf("\n%6.2f divided by %6.2f is "
             "%6.2f\n", a, b, a/b);
}
```

---

The general form of an `if...else` construct is

```
if (expression)
   statement1
else
   statement2
```

where the `else` part is optional. The word `if` and the brackets around `expression` are required. `statement1` and `statement2` can be simple or compound. When an `if...else` statement is encountered, `expression` is evaluated. If it is true (non-zero), `statement1` is executed and `statement2` (if there's an `else` part) is skipped. If it is false (zero) and there's an `else` part, `statement1` is skipped and `statement2` is executed.

In Program P1.7, if b is 0 (the test b == 0 is true), then the message

```
Cannot divide by zero
```

is printed and the program terminates. If b is not 0 (e.g. if a is 19 and b is 5), then

```
19.00 divided by 5.00 is 3.80
```

is printed and the program terminates. Note the semicolon that immediately precedes `else`. This is because `statement1` is a simple statement and hence is terminated by a semicolon – the semicolon is part of the statement. However, if it were a compound statement, no semicolon would be required since the right brace serves to terminate a compound statement.

When testing for equality, a common mistake made by C programmers is to write

```
if (b = 0) etc.   /* instead of if (b == 0) etc. */
```

But this does not compare the value of b with 0; rather, it assigns the value 0 to b. The **value** of the assignment expression is therefore 0, and, interpreted as a truth value, this means **false**. The `if` condition would always be **false** and hence `statement1` would **never** be executed.

To illustrate an `if` without an `else` part, consider program P1.8 which

---

**Program P1.8**

```c
#include <stdio.h>

main()      /* find the largest of a set of
               positive numbers */
{
  float largest, number;

  largest = 0;
  printf("\nEnter a number (0 to end): ");
  scanf("%f", &number);
  while (number != 0) {
     if (number > largest) largest = number;
     printf("\nEnter a number (0 to end): ");
     scanf("%f", &number);
  }
  printf("\nThe largest is %6.2f\n", largest);
}
```

---

inputs a set of positive numbers (terminated by 0) and prints the largest. (For simplicity, the program does not check that the numbers entered are indeed positive).

In the statement

```c
if (number > largest) largest = number;
```

if the expression in brackets is true then `largest` is set to `number` and then `printf(...)` is executed; if the expression is false, execution simply goes on to the next statement, `printf(...)`.

The next example illustrates the case where both `statement1` and `statement2` are compound statements. Assuming that `hours` and `rate` have been given values, the statements calculate `regpay`, `ovtpay` and `netpay` based on the following:

If the value of `hours` is less than or equal to 40, `regpay` is calculated by `hours` × `rate` and `ovtpay` is 0. If the value of `hours` is greater than 40, `regpay` is calculated by 40 × `rate` and `ovtpay` is calculated by multiplying the hours in excess of 40 by `rate` times `1.5`.

The above policy is implemented in C as:

```
if (hours <= 40) {
    regpay = hours * rate;
    ovtpay = 0;
}
else {
    regpay = 40 * rate;
    ovtpay = (hours - 40) * rate * 1.5;
}
netpay = regpay + ovtpay;
```

Note again the principle that a semicolon terminates a simple statement and a right brace terminates a compound statement. One implication is that it is almost never required to put a semicolon **after** a right brace. However, it is not necessarily wrong to put one, since C treats an isolated semicolon as a **null** statement (a statement which does nothing). In some cases, though, this may generate a syntax error. For example, if a construct requires a single statement and the right brace (of a compound statement) is followed by a semicolon, C will interpret this as two statements – a compound statement and a null statement – and an error will result. This could happen, for instance in the following situation:

```
if (a == b) {
    .
} ;
else {
    .
}
```

Here, the semicolon will cause an error. The presence of a statement (even though it's **null**) after the first right brace tells the compiler that the `if` statement has no `else` part. Hence the compiler assumes that it has completed compiling the `if` statement. When it sees the word `else`, there will be no `if` with which to match it, and an error will result.

## Exercises 1

(1)   Write a C program to print the following lines:

> There is a tide in the affairs of men
> Which, taken at the flood, leads on to fortune.

(2)   Write a C program which requests the user to enter a number. The number and the square of the number are then printed on the same line. For example, if 4 is entered, the program outputs

```
Number = 4    Square of Number = 16
```

(3)   Modify (2) so that the user can enter as many numbers as required (but one at a time). For each, the number and its square are printed. When the user wishes to stop, 0 is entered. The following is a sample run. The underlined characters are typed by the user; everything else is printed by the computer.

```
Enter a Number: 4
    Number = 4         Square of Number = 16
Enter a Number: 15
    Number = 15   Square of Number = 225
Enter a Number: 0

***End of Session***
```

(4)   Find all the errors in the following:

(a)
```
program main{  }
   (   int n
       begin
   n := 25;
     print("The value of n is "; n)
   end; )
```

(b)
```
main ()
   {
     printf "Mary had a little lamb";
     printf "Its fleece was white as snow"
   }
```

(c)
```
(* The following prints the reciprocals
    from 1 to 20, one per line *)
main ();
   int m; float n;
   {
   printf("The reciprocals from 1 to 20 are: ");
   printf;
   m = 1;
```

```
while m < 20 do
    n = 1/m;
    printf(" %f", n);
  printf("End of listing/n");
}
```

(5) There is no standard data type `boolean` in C. How does C handle true/false values and general Boolean expressions?

(6) Explain the difference between '=' and '=='.

(7) Express `not (a and b) or (b or not c)` in C.

(8) Give an example where a++ has a different side-effect from ++a.

(9) Which statement in C does not require a semicolon after it?

(10) Write a program to request a temperature in °C and convert it to °F.

Modify the program to convert several temperatures. Perform conversions until the 'rogue' value −999 is entered

(11) Write a program to read a positive integer N and determine

(a) whether N is even or odd;
(b) whether or not N is prime;
(c) whether or not N is a perfect square.

(12) A fixed percentage of water is taken from a well each day. Input values for W and P where:

- W represents the amount (in litres) of water in the well at the start of the first day;
- P represents the percentage of the water in the well taken out each day.

Write a program to print the number of the day, the amount taken for that day and the amount remaining in the well at the end of the day. The output should be terminated when 30 days have been printed or the amount of water remaining is less than 100 litres, whichever comes first.

(13) On the first day, a store gives d% discount off the price of a certain item. On day 2, it gives d% off the day 1 price. On day 3, it gives d% off the day 2 price, etc. Write a program to input the original price of an item and d, and determine on what day the price drops to less than half the original price.

(14) Each line of data consists of an item number, the unit price of the item and the quantity sold. Data is terminated by an item number of 0. Write a program to determine which items earned the most and least revenue.

# 2

# More Control Structures and Arrays

In Chapter 1, we discussed the fundamental 'nuts and bolts' for creating a C program. Two important control structures – while and if...else – were introduced. It was mentioned that these are all one needs for expressing the logic of any computer program. However, this does not mean that they are always the most convenient ones to use. There are many situations in which the logic could be expressed more smoothly and elegantly with other control structures. In this chapter, we discuss these additional control structures available to the C programmer. The latter part of the chapter is devoted to a discussion of arrays – a fundamental data structure that is an almost indispensable part of most programming languages. Two methods of searching for a value in an array – sequential and binary search – conclude the chapter.

## 2.1 The for statement

The for statement in C is similar to the for statement in Pascal or Algol, the DO statement in FORTRAN or the FOR...NEXT construct in Basic. However, there are important differences in that the C version is much more powerful and flexible. To illustrate a simple use of the for statement, consider a variation of the weight conversion program discussed in Sections 1.7 and 1.8.

We want to write a program which, when run, will ask the user to enter the number of weights, numweights, to be converted. The program will then allow that many to be converted. Program P2.1 will do the job.

The general form of the for statement is

```
for (expr1; expr2; expr3)
   statementf
```

**Program P2.1**

```
#include <stdio.h>

main()        /* convert kilograms to pounds */
{
   int j, numweights;
   float kgs, lbs;

   printf("How many weights to convert?");
   scanf("%d", &numweights);
   for ( j = 1; j <= numweights; j++) {
      printf("\nEnter a weight in kilograms: ");
      scanf("%f", &kgs);
      lbs = kgs * 2.2;
      printf("\n\n%6.2f kilograms = "
             "%6.2f pounds\n", kgs, lbs);
   }
   printf("\nThat's all for now\n");
}
```

It consists of

- the word `for`
- a left bracket, (
- `expr1`, called the initialization step; this is performed when the `for` is about to be executed.
- a semicolon, ;
- `expr2`, the test or condition which controls whether or not `statementf` is executed.
- a semicolon, ;
- `expr3`, called the re-initialization step
- a right bracket, )
- `statementf`, called the **body** of the loop. This can be a simple or compound statement.

When a `for` statement is encountered, it is executed as follows:

(1) `expr1` is evaluated.

(2)  `expr2` is evaluated. If it is false (zero), execution continues with the statement (if any) after `statementf`. If it is true (non-zero), `statementf` is executed, followed by `expr3`, and this step (2) is repeated.

This can be expressed more succinctly as follows:

```
expr1;
while (expr2) {
   statementf;
   expr3;
}
```

In the program above, the `for` construct is simply used for counting the number of weights to be converted. Suppose `numweights` is 3. The effect of the `for` statement is as follows:

(1)  `j` is set to 1 (initialization expression is `j = 1`).
(2)  the test `j <= numweights` is performed. It is true, so the body of the loop is executed (one weight is converted). The re-initialization step `j++` is then performed, so `j` is now 2.
(3)  the test `j <= numweights` is again performed. It is true, so the body of the loop is executed (another weight is converted). The re-initialization step `j++` is then performed, so `j` is now 3.
(4)  the test `j <= numweights` is again performed. It is true, so the body of the loop is executed (another weight is converted). The re-initialization step `j++` is then performed, so `j` is now 4.
(5)  the test `j <= numweights` is again performed. It is now false, so that the `for` loop is terminated and execution of the program continues with the statement

```
printf("\nThat's all for now\n");
```

It should be noted that on exit from the `for` loop, the value of `j` is available and may be used by the programmer if required.

In C, the `for` statement can be used for a lot more than just counting the number of times a loop is executed. This is because `expr1`, `expr2` and `expr3` can be **any** expressions; C does not even require them to be related in any way. So, for instance, `expr1` can be `j = 1`, `expr2` can test if a is equal to b and `expr3` can be `k++` or any other expression the programmer desires. Thus the following is perfectly valid in C:

```
for (j=1; a == b; k++) statement
```

It is also possible to omit any of `expr1`, `expr2` or `expr3`. However, the semicolons must be included. Thus, to omit `expr3`, one can write

```
for (expr1; expr2; ) statement
```

In this case,

(1) `expr1` is evaluated.
(2) `expr2` is evaluated. If it is false (zero), execution continues after `statement`. If it is true (non-zero), `statement` is executed and this step (2) is repeated.

This is equivalent to

```
expr1;
while (expr2) statement;
```

If, in addition, we omit `expr1`, we have

```
for ( ; expr2 ; ) statement   /* note the
                              semicolons */
```

Now, `expr2` is evaluated. If it is false (zero), execution continues after `statement`. If it is true (non-zero), `statement` is executed, followed by another evaluation of `expr2`, and so on. The net effect is that `statement` is executed as long as `expr2` is true - the same effect achieved by

```
while (expr2) statement
```

As another example, we write a program to print multiplication tables. The program requests a value for type of table (7, say), a starting value (11, say) and an ending value (15, say) and prints a multiplication table from the starting value to the ending value. For the above values, the following table will be produced:

```
11 × 7 =  77
12 × 7 =  84
13 × 7 =  91
14 × 7 =  98
15 × 7 = 105
```

Program P2.2 will do the job.

---

**Program P2.2**

```c
#include <stdio.h>

main()       /* print a multiplication table */
{
   int type, start, end, j;

   printf("Type of table? ");
   scanf("%d", &type);
   printf("Start of table? ");
   scanf("%d", &start);
   printf("End of table? ");
   scanf("%d", &end);

   for ( j = start; j <= end; j++)
       printf("\n%2d × %2d = %3d", j, type,
                                 j * type);

   printf("\n\n**End of table**\n");
}
```

---

## 2.2 The do...while statement

The general form is

```
do
    statement
while (expression);
```

The words do and while, the brackets and the semicolon are required. The programmer supplies statement and expression. **When a** do...while is encountered,

(1) statement is executed.
(2) expression is then evaluated; if it is true(non-zero), repeat from (1). If it is false (zero), execution continues with the statement (if any) after the semicolon.

Thus as long as expression is true, statement is executed. It is important to note that because of the nature of the construct, statement is **always executed at least once**. The program for the following problem illustrates a use of do...while.

*Problem:*  A man deposits $1000 in a bank at an interest rate of 10% per year. At the end of each year, the interest earned is added to the amount on deposit and this becomes the new deposit for the next year. Write a program to determine the year in which the amount accumulated first exceeds $2000.

The solution given in program P2.3 is written in terms of

| | |
|---|---|
| initialDeposit | (1000, in the example) |
| interestRate | (10, in the example) |
| targetDeposit | (2000, in the example) |
| deposit | the deposit at any given time |

The program does not cater for the case when the initial deposit is greater than the target deposit. If this is required, a while statement may be used (exercise!).

*Example – greatest common divisor*

Consider the problem of finding the greatest common divisor (gcd) of two positive integers, *m* and *n*, say. This can be done by using Euclid's algorithm, thus:

(1) Set *r* to the remainder of *m* divided by *n*
(2) If *r* is 0, the gcd is *n*. Stop.
(3) Set *m* to *n*
(4) Set *n* to *r*
(5) Repeat from (1)

---

**Program P2.3**

```
#include <stdio.h>

main()
{
    int year;
    float initialDeposit, interestRate,
            targetDeposit, deposit, interest;

    printf("\nInitial deposit? ");
    scanf("%f", &initialDeposit);
    printf("\nRate of interest? ");
    scanf("%f", &interestRate);
    printf("\nTarget deposit? ");
    scanf("%f", &targetDeposit);

    deposit = initialDeposit;
    year = 0;

    do {
        year++;
        interest = deposit * interestRate / 100;
        deposit += interest; /* same as
                        deposit= deposit + interest */
    } while (deposit <= targetDeposit);
    printf("\nDeposit first exceeds %7.2f at the  "
        "end of year %2d", targetDeposit, year);

}
```

---

This algorithm can be implemented using a do...while statement. Program P2.4 requests two positive values. Observe that the first do...while keeps asking until two positive values are entered. When this occurs, the program continues with the calculation of the gcd. On exit from the second do...while, the value of r is 0, the value of n is also 0 (since this was just assigned the value of r) and the value of m is the gcd.

---

**Program P2.4**

```
#include <stdio.h>

main()
{
    int m, n, r;

    do {
        printf("\nEnter two positive integers: ");
        scanf("%d %d", &m, &n);
    } while (m <= 0 || n <= 0);

    /* At this point, both m and n are positive */

    printf("\nThe greatest common divisor of "
            "%d and %d is ", m, n);

    do {
        r = m % n;
        m = n;
        n = r;
    } while (r > 0);

    printf("%d", m);
}
```

---

Note that it does not matter whether m is greater or smaller than n. If it is smaller, the first execution of the do . . . while simply interchanges m and n, so that m now has the larger value.

The following is a sample run of program P2.4:

```
Enter two positive integers: 88 −9

Enter two positive integers: 67 0
```

```
Enter two positive integers: 100 16

The greatest common divisor of 100 and 16 is 4
```

## 2.3 The `switch` statement

This statement allows multi-way branching. For example, suppose the type of a variable is stored in an integer `type` and that the valid values of `type` are 0 (undefined), 1 (int), 2 (float) and 3 (double). Consider

```
switch (type) {
  case 0:   printf("undefined variable\n");
            break;
  case 1:   printf("an integer variable\n");
            break;
  case 2:   printf("a floating point variable\n");
            break;
  case 3:   printf("a double precision variable\n");
            break;
  default:  printf("illegal variable type\n");
            break;
} /* end switch */
```

When the `switch` statement is encountered, the value of `type` is compared with all the values after the word `case`. If any matches, control is transferred to the statement labelled by that case. Normally, execution continues until the end of the `switch` unless an exit is forced by a `break` or `return` statement. In the example, `break` causes control to be transferred out of the `switch` statement. In general, `break` is used to cause immediate termination of the execution of a `switch`, `while`, `for` or `do...while` statement. For another example of its use, see Section 2.5.2. The `return` statement is used within a function to return control to the 'caller' and is discussed in Chapter 3.

In the above program, if `type` does not have a legal value (one of 0, 1, 2 or 3), then execution begins with the statement labelled with `default:`. If there was no statement labelled with `default:` and no case matched the value of `type`, then no action occurs. If present, `default:` does not **have** to be the last label in the switch – it can appear anywhere. However, if control is transferred to it, then all statements up to the end of the

switch are executed, regardless of their labels, unless an exit is forced by
`break` or `return`.

Sometimes the same action must be performed for several cases. In such
situations, we could label the same statement with several case constants.
For example, suppose we wanted to count the number of vowels and
non-vowels in some input. If the current character is stored in `ch`, we
could use

```
switch (ch) {      /* caters for lowercase vowels only */
   case 'a':
   case 'e':
   case 'i':
   case 'o':
   case 'u': vowels++;
             break;
   default :
             nonvowels++;
             break;
}
```

Strictly speaking, the last `break` is not necessary since the end of the
`switch` has been reached anyway. But it is included for uniformity as
well as to cater for the possibility that another case may be added at the
end at a later stage. If this happens, then we will not have to remember
to put in `break`.

The general form of the `switch` statement is

```
switch (expr) statement
```

where `expr` is an expression which evaluates to an `int` and `statement`
is almost invariably a compound statement. Any statement within the
compound statement may be labelled as follows:

```
case <constant expr> :
```

where <constant expr> is also an `int`. Within the same switch, no
two <constant expr> can be the same, that is, case labels must be
unique. At most one statement can be labelled with `default:`.

It must be emphasized that once control has been transferred to a given
statement (because its label matches the value of `expr`), all statements up

to the end of the switch are executed unless a break or return transfers control out of the body of the switch.

## 2.4 The continue statement

This statement can be used within a while, do...while or for to terminate the current iteration of the loop and begin the next.

In the cases of

```
while (expr) {
    .
    continue;
    .
}
```

and

```
do {
    .
    continue;
    .
} while (expr);
```

control is transferred to the closing right brace, in effect causing expr to be evaluated immediately. The loop is then executed or not, depending on whether expr is true or false.

In the case of

```
for (expr1; expr2; expr3) {
    .
    continue;
    .
}
```

control is transferred to the closing right brace, in effect causing expr3 to be evaluated immediately. expr2 is then evaluated and the loop is executed or not, depending on whether expr2 is true or false.

continue is useful in cases where one does not wish to invert a condition and indent another level. In the following,

```
for (j = 0; j < max; j++) {
    .
    scanf("%d", &n);
    if (n <= 0) continue;

    /* processing for positive n */
    .
}
```

if n is less than or equal to zero, control goes to the closing right brace of the `for` statement. The logic could also have been expressed as:

```
if (n > 0) {
    /* processing for positive n */

}
```

but now the code controlled by the `if` has to be indented an extra level.

### 2.5 Arrays

An array is a data structure consisting of several elements all of which are of the same type. An array in C is declared by specifying its type, its name and its size as in

```
int number[100];
```

This declares an integer array called number of size 100. The **elements** of number are number[0], number[1],..., up to number[99]. In C, arrays are subscripted starting from 0. Also, **square brackets** (as opposed to round brackets) are used to enclose the size (in the declaration) and the subscript (in specifying an element).

As another example,

```
char name[25];
```

declares 'an array of characters' called name of size 25. The elements of name are name[0], name[1],..., up to name[24]. One character can be stored in each element of the array.

*Problem*:   Write a program to read N integers (N <= 100), find the
average and print the amount by which each number differs
from the average.

In order to find the average, all the numbers must be read, and to print the
differences, the original numbers will be needed. The numbers will be stored
in an array as they are read. Program P2.5 is one solution to the problem.

Points to note:

(1) It is possible for `scanf ("%d", &n)` to return without assigning a
value to n. If this happens, `(n < 1) | | (n > 100)` would be undefined.
To guard against this, n is initialized to 0.

(2) The `do...while` ensures that only when the amount of numbers lies
between 1 and 100 (inclusive) that processing continues. If a value which
is less than 1 or greater than 100 is entered, the user is asked to re-enter.

(3) Because the precedence of `| |` is lower than that of `<` or `>` (see Section
6.2), the expression after `while` could have been written as `(n < 1 | |`
`n > 100)`. We have included the extra brackets for clarity, and to
save us the trouble of having to remember the relative precedence of
the operators.

(4) Strictly speaking, the variable `temp` is not required. The first `for` loop
could be written as:

```
for (count = 0; count < n; count++) {
    scanf ("%d", &number [count]);
    sum += number [count];
}
```

(5) In the expression `sum / n`, n is converted to `float` (since `sum` is of
type `float`) before the division is performed. However, if both `sum`
and n were `int`, an integer division would be performed.

### *Example – family size survey*

Arrays are convenient for preparing the results of surveys and popularity
contests. Consider a survey done to determine the number of persons who
come from 1-child, 2-children,..., up to 10 or more-children families. Each
person in the survey indicates the number of children in his/her family.

**Program P2.5**

```c
#include <stdio.h >

main()
{
    int number[100], count, temp;
    float sum, average;
    int n = 0; /* see Points to note (1)
                   on opposite page */

    do {
        printf("\nHow many numbers (1 - 100)? ");
        scanf("%d", &n);
    }while ((n < 1) || (n > 100));

    sum = 0;
    for (count = 0; count < n; count++) {
        scanf("%d", &temp);
        sum += temp;              /* sum = sum + temp */
        number[count] = temp;  /* put the number in
                                     the array */
    }
    average = sum / n;
    printf("n\n\nThe average is %7.2f\n", average);

    /* 'Step through' the array, printing the
       differences from average */
    printf("\nThe numbers and the differences from "
        "the average are\n\n");
    for (count = 0; count < n; count++)
        printf("%8d %7.2f\n", number[count],
                  number[count] - average);
}
```

Thus the data for this might look like:

2 3 1 4 1 3 7 8 6 2 12 10 4 3 1 5 2 3 ...

We will use 0 to terminate the data. {Why is 0 a good value to use?} Note that a family of 12, say, will be counted in the 10 or more category.

Since there are 10 categories, we will need an array of size 10. We could use an array declared as

```
int family[10];
```

to hold the counts for the 10 categories. But, then, we would have to assume that:

family[0] holds the count for families with 1 child;
family[1] holds the count for families with 2 children;

    .

     .

family[9] holds the count for families with 10 or more children.

While this could work, it seems more logical and readable to assume:

family[1] holds the count for families with 1 child;
family[2] holds the count for families with 2 children;

    .

     .

family[10] holds the count for families with 10 or more children.

To this end, we declare

```
int family[11];
```

and use only elements family[1] to family[10]. Program P2.6 reads each item of data and increments the appropriate family count by 1 until all the data has been read. Then, it prints the result of the survey.

Point to note: It is possible that in attempting to read data, scanf may encounter problems such as end-of-file being reached or a disk being damaged. If this happens, no value would be assigned to numchild and scanf would return a value of 0 or the value of the symbolic constant EOF (defined in ⟨stdio.h⟩) if the end-of-file was reached. However, if a value is successfully assigned then scanf returns a value of 1 (one value

**Program P2.6**

```
#include <stdio.h>

main()
{
    int family[11], j, maxchild, numchild;

    maxchild = 10;

    for (j = 1; j <= maxchild; j++)
        family[j] = 0; /* set the counters to 0 */

    /* read and process the data until
        numchild = 0 */
    scanf("%d", &numchild);
    while (numchild > 0) {
        if (numchild > maxchild) numchild = maxchild;
        family[numchild]++;
        scanf("%d", &numchild);
    }

    printf("\nResults of Survey\n");
    printf("\nChildren    Number of Families\n\n");
    for (j = 1; j <= maxchild; j++)
        printf("%5d        %9d\n", j, family[j]);
    printf("\nEnd of Table\n");
}
```

assigned). Just in case the read is unsuccessful, one should use code such as

```
if (scanf("%d", &numchild) != 1) numchild = 0;
```

which, in this case, assigns a value of 0 to numchild if the read was unsuccessful.

Assuming the following sample data:

1 2 3 4 5 6 7 8 9 10 9 8 7 6 5 4 3 2 1 2 2 7 7 8 2 2 3 12 15 13 1 1 2 2 3 3 4 6 5 6 5 4 4 4 5 0

program P2.6 produces the following results:

```
Results of Survey

Children    Number of Families

    1                4
    2                8
    3                5
    4                6
    5                5
    6                4
    7                4
    8                3
    9                2
   10                4


End of Table
```

### 2.5.1 Strings

In C, a string is stored in an array of characters. Each character in the string occupies one location in the array. The null character ' \0 ' (the 'character' whose numeric value is zero) is put after the last character. This is done so that programs can tell when the end of a string has been reached. For example, the string

```
"Marsha Charran"
```

is stored as follows (◇ denotes a space):

| M | a | r | s | h | a | ◊ | C | h | a | r | r | a | n | \0 |

Since this string has 14 characters (including the space), it requires an array of, at least, size 15 to store it since we must cater for the terminating \0.

A string can be read from the input using the specification %s in scanf. For example, given the declaration

```
char name[20];  /* caters for 19 characters
                    plus \0 */
```

we can read a string into name with

```
scanf("%s", name);   /* observe no & before
                        name */
```

Beginning at the next non-whitespace character, characters are stored starting at name[0] until the next whitespace character is encountered. The terminating \0 is added automatically. Thus, the string read cannot contain a blank and it is the programmer's responsibility to ensure that the array is large enough to hold the string. For the time being (until Chapter 5), take it on faith that an array name is not preceded by & when a value is being read into it using scanf. For reading a string containing blanks, the function gets (Section 9.4.2) can be used. To print a string, we can also use %s in printf, as in:

```
printf("My name is %s", name);
```

%s is replaced by the string stored in name, excluding the terminating \0.

### Example – finding the first name

We illustrate some simple string handling by writing a program to read a set of names and print the first one in alphabetical order. We will use scanf to read the names; hence the names may not contain spaces. The general idea is that when a new name is read, it is compared with the first one in order, so far, and replaces it, if necessary. Strings are compared in C using the standard function strcmp (string compare). If str1 and str2 are two strings, then

```
strcmp(str1, str2)
```

returns a negative value if str1 is less than str2, zero if str1 is equal to str2, and a positive value if str1 is greater than str2. The comparison is done on a character by character basis until the value to be returned is determined. For example, if str1 is "herd" and str2 is "heaven", the comparison will proceed up to the third letter. Since 'r' is greater than 'a', strcmp returns a positive value (in fact, the value of 'r' – 'a'). For letters, 'less than' means 'comes before in the alphabet' and 'greater than' means 'comes after in the alphabet'.

To assign one string to another, the standard function strcpy (string copy) must be used. The string in str2 can be copied to str1 by using

```
strcpy(str1, str2)
```

Note that the assignment is in the same order (right to left) as in a normal assignment statement.

In order to use strcmp and strcpy, our program must be preceded by the line

```
#include <string.h>
```

string.h is a header file containing declarations for standard string functions.

Program P2.7 shows one solution to this problem. The variable firstname is used to hold the first name in alphabetical order. The variable name is used to hold each name, in turn. The name 'end' is used to terminate the data. The maximum length of a name is 24. The program assumes that at least one name is supplied before 'end'.

Further examples involving arrays of characters are discussed in Chapter 4 and two-dimensional arrays are discussed in Section 11.3.

### 2.5.2 *Sequential and binary search*

Consider the problem of searching for a given value in an array of values using a sequential search. To be specific, suppose we are searching for an integer value, key, in an integer array number of size max. (Thus the elements of the array are number[0], number[1], ..., up to number[max − 1]). We can use a for loop in which key is compared with an element of number each time through the loop. However, if key matches an element, no further comparisons are necessary and execution of the loop must be terminated. This can be accomplished by using the break statement. The following code does the search; it assumes that values have been stored in key and the array number.

```
for (j = 0; j < max; j++)
    if (key == number[j]) break;
if (j == max) /* loop was exited in the normal way */
    printf("\n%4d was not found\n", key);
else       /* exit was forced by 'break' */
    printf("\n%4d was found at position %3d\n", key, j);
```

---

**Program P2.7**

```
#include <stdio.h>
#include <string.h>

main()
{
    char name[25], firstname[25];

    printf("Type a list of names terminated "
            "by 'end'\n");
    scanf("%s", firstname);

    scanf("%s", name);
    while (strcmp(name, "end") != 0) {
        if (strcmp(name, firstname) < 0)
            strcpy(firstname, name);
        scanf("%s", name);
    }

    printf("\nThe first name in alphabetical "
            "order is %s\n", firstname);
}
```

---

As another example, suppose the elements of number are arranged in ascending order, and we are searching for key using a binary search. A binary search is based on the following:

(1) key is compared to the middle item, number[mid], say, of the array.
(2) If key is equal to number[mid], the search is successful.
(3) If key is less than number[mid], then if it is in the array at all, it must be before position mid (since the numbers are in order). Subsequent searching can be confined to this portion of the array.
(4) If key is greater than number[mid], then if it is in the array at all, it must be after position mid (since the numbers are in order). Subsequent searching can be confined to this portion of the array.

The variables lo and hi are used to define the portion of the array which remains to be searched. The following assumes that values have already been stored in `key` and the array `number`, and that the variables `lo`, `hi` and `mid` have been declared as `int`.

```
lo = 0;
hi = max - 1;
do {
    mid = (lo + hi)/2;
    if (key == number[mid]) break;
    if (key < number[mid])
        hi = mid - 1;
    else /* key > number[mid] */
        lo = mid + 1;
} while (lo <= hi);

if (lo > hi) /* loop was exited in the normal
                way */
    printf("\n%4d was not found\n", key);
else  /* exit was forced by 'break' */
    printf("\n%4d was found at position %3d\n",
            key, mid);
```

In the above, the `do...while` loop is used to control the search. If the key is found, the loop is immediately terminated with `break`; otherwise, the loop is terminated when the pointers `lo` and `hi` 'pass' each other, indicating that the key was not found.

## Exercises 2

(1)  Write a program to convert several temperatures from °C to °F. The program first requests the number of conversions to be done.

(2)  Give the declarations for the following. For each, indicate the valid range of subscripts.

(a)  an array of 75 real (floating point) values;
(b)  an array capable of storing a name of maximum length 30.

(3)  Write a program which requests two integers, $m$ and $n$, and produces a table of squares from $m$ to $n$, inclusive.

(4)  Write a program to input an integer, $n$, between 1 and 9, and print a line of output consisting of ascending digits from 1 to $n$, followed

by descending digits from $(n-1)$ to 1. For example, if $n=5$, produce the line

123454321

(5) Write a program to read an integer from 1 to 999 and print the integer in words. For example, if 437 is read, the output should be:

four hundred and thirty-seven

(6) Write a program which converts an integer into Roman numerals.
(7) Write a program to read a set of non-zero numbers into an array of maximum size 100. Data is terminated by 0 and the amount of numbers is unknown beforehand.

- find and print the largest;
- find the sum of the numbers;
- arrange the numbers in ascending order.

(8) Write a program to read a set of names and print the last one in alphabetical order.
(9) A retail store has 10 departments which submit their daily sales to the store manager. Management wants a report which includes the department name, daily sales and what percentage of the daily sales each department contributes. The total store sales is also printed at the end of the report. Write a program to produce the report, given the department name and daily sales for each of the 10 departments.
(10) The Sieve of Eratosthenes can be used to determine all primes less than a given integer $n$. The method can be described as follows:

(a) store 1's in elements $P[1]$ to $P[n]$ of an array;
(b) set $f$ to 2;
(c) set to 0 any element of $P$ whose subscript is a multiple of $f$;
(d) set $f$ to the subscript of the next element of $P$ which contains 1.

Repeat steps (c) and (d) until $f$ reaches or exceeds the square root of $n$. The subscripts of those elements containing 1's are prime numbers.

Write a program to determine all primes less than 1000.
(11) There are 500 light bulbs (numbered 1 to 500) arranged in a row. Initially, they are all OFF. Starting with bulb 2, all even numbered bulbs are turned ON. Next, starting with bulb 3, and visiting every third bulb, it is turned ON if it is OFF, and it is turned OFF if it is ON. This procedure is repeated for every fourth bulb, then every fifth bulb, and so on up to the 500th bulb. Write a program to determine which bulbs are OFF at the end of the above exercise.
(12) Write C code to read an integer value for score (0–100) and print

the correct letter grade based on the following:

below 50    –   F
50 to 59    –   C
60 to 69    –   B
70 to 79    –   B+
80 to 89    –   A
90 to 100   –   A+

(13) Write a program to read integer values for month and year and print the number of days in the month. For example, 4 1990 (April 1990) should print 30, but 2 1992 (February 1992) should print 29. (A leap year, $n$, is divisible by 4; however, if $n$ is divisible by 100 then it is a leap year only if it is also divisible by 400).

# 3

# Functions – the Basics

In this chapter, we discuss the basic features of functions – how they are defined, how they return values and how they are used. These ideas are discussed using several examples – the factorial function, searching an array using sequential and binary searches and the simulation of the One-Zero game – a game involving dice. More involved issues pertaining to functions are discussed in Chapter 5.

In general, a C program consists of one or more functions. Our programs so far have consisted of a single function called main. However, we have made use of predefined C functions such as printf, scanf, strcmp and strcpy. Functions enable a large task to be broken down into smaller subtasks, each of which is handled by one function. In this way, a complex problem can be divided in such a way that each individual portion becomes manageable. A function in C is similar to a procedure or function in Pascal, or a subroutine or function in FORTRAN.

Usually a function is written to perform a task and return a value to the function which called it. Sometimes a task is performed but no value needs to be returned.

In this text, functions are written to conform to the new ANSI C Standard. Appendix B cites the differences between the new standard and traditional C.

### 3.1 An example – factorial

As a first example, let us write a function which, given $n$, calculates and returns $n!$ where

$$0! = 1,$$
$$n! = n(n-1)! \qquad \text{for } n > 0$$

For example $5! = 5 \cdot 4 \cdot 3 \cdot 2 \cdot 1 = 120$

The following is one solution:

```
int factorial(int n)      /*function definition;
                              no ';' after ')'*/
{
    int nfac;    /* local variable declaration */

    if (n < 0) return 0;    /*return 0 for an
                              invalid argument*/
    for ( nfac = 1; n > 0; n-- )
        nfac *= n; /* equivalent to nfac = nfac * n */
    return nfac;         /* value returned to the
                              calling function */

}
```

In the example,

- the statement

  ```
  int factorial(int n)
  ```

  declares the type of the result (int) the function returns, the name of the function factorial, and the type (int) and name (n) of the parameter which will correspond to the actual argument when the function is called. When the function is called, an integer argument must be supplied. Note again that there is no semicolon after the right bracket.
- the left brace, {, indicates the start of the **body** of the function.
- after the left brace comes the declaration of variables used only within this function, i. e., **local** (also called **automatic**) variables. In this function, there is one such variable, nfac, which will hold the value of *n*! When a function is entered, storage is allocated for all local variables. This storage is released (hence the local variables cease to exist) when the function returns.
- after the local variable declaration(s) come the statements to be executed by the function.
- The statement

  ```
  if (n < 0) return 0;
  ```

says that if n is negative, the function will return a value of 0 to the caller. The caller can decide what to do in this case.

- The for loop calculates the value of *n*! for valid values of *n* ($n>=0$). You should verify that it returns the correct value for $n=0$ and $n=1$.
- The for loop leaves the value of *n*! in nfac. The statement

```
return nfac;
```

says that the value returned to the caller is the value of nfac.

To illustrate how the function may be used, we write a complete program (P3.1) to print the values of *n*! for $n=0, 1, ..., 7$.

---

**Program P3.1**

```
#include <stdio.h>

main()
{
    int factorial(int n), num;

    printf(" n     n!\n\n");
    for (num = 0; num <= 7; num++)
        printf(" %2d     %4d\n", num, factorial(num));
}


int factorial(int n)            /* function definition;
                                   no ';' after ')'. */
{
    int nfac;                   /* local variable
                                   declaration */

    if (n < 0) return 0;        /* return 0 for an
                                   invalid argument */
    for ( nfac = 1; n > 0; n-- )
        nfac *= n; /* equivalent to nfac = nfac * n */
    return nfac;                /* value returned to the
                                   calling function */

}
```

Note that, in `main`, we declare the properties of `factorial` in a similar manner to the function definition. This is accomplished by

```
int factorial(int n);
```

and is called a **function prototype**. A function prototype specifies the type of value returned by the function, the name of the function and the type(s) of argument(s) expected by the function. This enables the compiler to check that, when the function is used, the correct number and type of arguments are supplied. It is not necessary to use the same variable in the prototype as in the function definition; **any** variable may be used, for example,

```
int factorial(int x);
```

This variable will be used by the compiler only if it needs to generate an error message. (In more formal terms, the scope of such a variable extends only to the end of the prototype). In fact, it is not necessary to use any variable at all – the type alone is enough. Thus the following is valid and acceptable as a function prototype:

```
int factorial(int);
```

Finally, if you wish (but it is **not** recommended), you may omit the type (of argument) as well, and use:

```
int factorial();
```

However, in this last case, the compiler will be unable to check the number and type of arguments supplied, and will be less helpful in detecting an erroneous use of the function.

Another important reason for using a function prototype is that if the function is called with an argument which is a different type from the corresponding formal parameter, the argument is automatically converted to the required type. Without the prototype, an explicit cast (see next) may be needed or an error could result. A **cast** is a construct used for converting an expression to a specified type. For example, if n is int, the construct

```
(double) n
```

converts the value of n to double. The actual content of n is unchanged. The effect is the same as if n were assigned to a variable of type double and this variable used in place of the construct.

It is **highly recommended** that the **full** function prototype always be used in your programs. A function prototype is declared in the same manner as the header line of a function definition, except that the prototype is terminated by a semicolon. The function definition is discussed in more detail in Section 3.2.

In C, a program begins execution with the first statement in main, and execution normally terminates when control reaches the right brace indicating the end of main. In the above program, execution begins with the first printf(...) which prints a heading. The for loop is then executed with the variable num assuming the values 0, 1, 2, 3, 4, 5, 6, 7. For each value of num, the function factorial is called with num as its argument. (Note that, in C, a function is 'called' simply by using the name of the function with the appropriate argument(s). What actually happens is that the **value** of num is stored in some temporary location and it is this location that is passed to the function and associated with the parameter n. Thus n is associated with the **value** of num but not with the original variable num. In C, we say that arguments are passed 'by value'. Thus it is impossible for a function to alter the original value of an actual argument, but see Chapter 5 for a discussion of 'call by reference'.) The function then calculates the factorial and returns it to the place in the printf(...) statement from where it was called. printf(...) then prints the values of num and its factorial. When run, the above program will print

```
n           n!

0            1
1            1
2            2
3            6
4           24
5          120
6          720
7         5040
```

If it were required, the value of the factorial could have been assigned to a variable as in

```
numfac = factorial(num);
```

The value of `numfac` could then be used as and when needed.

### 3.2 Function definition

The general form of a function definition is

```
type name(formal parameter list, if any)
{
    declaration of local variables

    statements
}
```

**Caution**: there is no semicolon after the right bracket of the formal parameter list.

In this text, we will use the term **formal parameter** (or, simply, parameter) in reference to the function definition, and the term **actual argument** (or, simply, argument) in reference to a **use** of the function.

If the parameter list contains two or more items, they are separated by commas. Each item in the formal parameter list consists of a type followed by a variable name. It must be emphasized that **each** variable name is declared with its own type identifier. For example,

```
float average(int a, int b)     /* right */
```

is correct, but

```
float average(int a, b)      /* wrong */
```

is not.

If the function has no parameters, the brackets must still be present, as in

```
int fun()    /* no parameters */
```

However, it is permitted (and recommended) to use the word **void** to make it clear that there are no parameters, as in

```
int fun(void)
```

A special ellipsis notation – a comma followed by 3 periods (, ...) – allows the programmer to specify that the function may take a variable number of arguments. For example,

```
int fun(int a, float b, ...)
```

declares a function fun which takes at least two arguments – an int and a float – and returns a value of type int. The ellipsis notation can be used only if the parameter list contains at least one other parameter. If used, it must appear as the last item in the list. The function is expected to be called with at least as many arguments as there are parameters preceding the ellipsis notation.

'type' specifies the type of value returned by the function. If the function is being used for effect only (and not to return a value), 'type' is specified as void. A function returns a value to the caller by using a return statement, where an expression may be written after return. The expression may be enclosed in brackets, if desired. Also, a return statement with no expression causes control, but no useful value, to be returned to the caller. If no return statement is present, control returns to the caller when the terminating right brace of the function is reached.

Usually, when a function returns a value, it is either assigned to a variable or is used in an expression. If neither is done, then the return value is simply discarded. For example, scanf returns a value (either the number of assigned items or EOF, see Section 9.4.4 for details) but it is common to use a statement such as:

```
scanf("%d %d", &a, &b);
```

where the return value is not used. Of course, it is good defensive programming always to test the return value of scanf to ensure that it has worked.

### 3.3 Sequential search

The next example relates to the searching problem discussed in Section 2.5.2. Suppose we wish to search for a given number, key, in an array called number of size max. Thus the elements of the array are number[0], number[1], ..., up to number[max − 1]. We can delegate the search to a function. Of course, when the function is called, it must return to the caller some indication of the result of the search. One common approach is to return the location of the given number if the search was successful and to return –1 if the search was unsuccessful.

So far, we have said what the function must do and what it must return. What we have not said is **how** the function must accomplish the task. Herein lies the beauty of using functions. The rest of the program can look upon this function as a 'black box'; it knows what the function must be given and what it returns, but it need not be concerned with the inner workings of the function. In this particular example, we can use a sequential search if the numbers are in arbitrary order, but we can decide to use a binary search if the numbers are sorted. First, here is the function based on a sequential search.

```
/* this function searches for key from number[0]
   to number[max—1] */

int sequential(int key, int number[], int max)
/* function definition */
{
    int j;    /* local variable declaration */

    for (j = 0; j < max; j++)
        if (key == number[j]) return j;
                            /* search successful */
    return —1;
    /* search unsuccessful */
}
```

Note the declaration of the array parameter number. It is not necessary to specify the size in the function; all that is necessary is to indicate that it is an array. This is accomplished by the square brackets [] after the name. The reason is that, in the function definition, no storage is allocated to the formal parameters (or local variables). It is only when the function is called that actual arguments (arguments for which storage has been allocated) are provided to correspond to the formal parameters. (Also, storage is allocated to local variables only when the function is about to be executed. This storage is released when the function is about to return). Since the size is not specified, the function is more general in that it will work, whatever the size of the actual argument. To illustrate, suppose `main` contains the declaration:

```
int scores[50], grade, found;
```

Assume that values have been stored in the array, and `grade` has a certain value. It is required to determine if `grade` occurs in the first 25 locations of `scores`. This can be achieved by the statement

```
found = sequential(grade, scores, 25);
```

The program can then test the value of `found`. If it is –1, it means that `grade` was not found; otherwise, the value of `found` is the (first) location in which `grade` appears. If we wanted to know if `grade` appeared anywhere in the array, this could be done with

```
found = sequential(grade, scores, 50);
```

As written, the function searches locations 0 to `max-1` for `key`. As an exercise, modify the function to search from locations `first` to `last`.

## 3.4 Binary search

Next, we present a search function based on a binary search. Note that a binary search can be performed only if the numbers are sorted. In the function, we assume that they are sorted in ascending order. As a variation from the previous binary search, a `while` loop is used instead of `do...while`. This is slightly better since an invalid value of max (0, say) will be caught at the 'top' of the loop, and the function will return –1, a reasonable thing to do.

```
/* does a binary search for key from number[0] to
   number[max-1] */

/* function definition */
int binary(int key, int number[], int max)
```

```
{
    int lo, hi, mid;    /* local variables */

    lo = 0;
    hi = max - 1;
    while (lo <= hi) {
        mid = (lo + hi)/2;
        if (key == number[mid]) return mid;
                                        /* search successful */
        if (key < number[mid])
            hi = mid - 1;
        else /* key > number[mid] */
            lo = mid + 1;
    }
    return -1;    /* search unsuccessful */
}
```

This function can be used in exactly the same way as sequential, above. For instance, searching for grade in the first 25 locations of scores is accomplished by

```
found = binary(grade, scores, 25);
```

and the value of found tested to determine the result of the search.

### 3.5 The One-Zero game

One-Zero can be played by several players using a six-sided die. Each person takes turns at throwing the die. On each turn, a player may throw the die as many times as desired and the score for that turn will normally be the sum of the values thrown. However, the catch is that, if ever a 1 is thrown, the player's turn ends and the score for that turn is 0. Obviously, the longer one keeps throwing the die, the greater the chance of throwing a 1. A game consists of a predetermined number of turns, say 10, for each player. The winner is the person who accumulates the most points.

There are a number of strategies one can adopt for playing a turn.

(1) Playing it by 'feel'; whenever one feels it is time to stop, then stop (unless, of course, forced to by throwing a 1).

(2) Setting a maximum number of points, say 15, for each turn. If one's points tally for a turn reaches or exceeds 15, then stop.

(3) Setting a maximum number of throws, say 5, for each turn. If one makes 5 throws (without throwing a 1), then stop.

We will develop a C program to test strategy (3) for the maximum number of throws (maxThrowsPerTurn) ranging from 1 to 20. For each value of maxThrowsPerTurn, we will play a game of 100 turns; the total score for the 100 turns will be calculated and printed. The program will be developed based on the following pseudocode outline:

```
for maxThrowsPerTurn = 1 to 20
    play a game (100 turns)
    print maxThrowsPerTurn, gameScore
endfor
```

'play a game (100 turns)' can be expanded to

```
gameScore = 0
for turn = 1 to 100
    play one turn, using maxThrowsPerTurn
    add scoreThisTurn to gameScore
endfor
```

'play one turn' can now be expanded to show the details of playing a turn and obtaining the score for that turn.

In our program, we will use separate functions to 'play a game' and 'play one turn'.

One question here is how do we simulate the throwing of the die? Unfortunately, this varies somewhat from one system to the next. In order to present a uniform solution, we assume that a function random is available and is declared as follows:

```
int random(int first, int last)
{
  /* this function returns a random integer from
     first to last, inclusive */
}
```

Thus to simulate the throwing of the die, we will use random(1,6).

This program also allows us to illustrate the use of **symbolic** (also called **manifest**) **constants** in C. A symbolic constant is simply an identifier used in place of a constant. For example, in the above outline, the constants 1, 20 and 100 are usually referred to as 'magic numbers' because they seem to appear for no good reason. There is no reason why the maximum throws must range from 1 to 20, and no reason why there must be 100 turns per game. In order to make the program flexible, we will use symbolic constants in place of these numbers. In C, symbolic constants are usually defined at the start of the program, so that if changes are required, they can be easily located. Symbolic constants are declared using def ine as in:

```
#define LOWMAX 1
#define HIGHMAX 20
#define TURNS_PER_GAME 100
```

Note that there is no semicolon after a definition. Also, it is conventional in C to use uppercase letters for symbolic constants to distinguish them from variables. #def ine is explained in more detail in Section 11.1.1.

Program P3.2 gives a listing of all the functions. It simulates 20 games (each with a different value of maxThrowsPerTurn) of 100 turns each. It is complete except for the details of the function random. An implementation of random is discussed next.

---

**Program P3.2**

```
#include <stdio.h>

#define LOWMAX 1
#define HIGHMAX 20
#define TURNS_PER_GAME 100

main()
{
    int maxThrowsPerTurn;
    int playOneGame(int turns, int throws);

    for (maxThrowsPerTurn = LOWMAX;
            maxThrowsPerTurn <= HIGHMAX;
            maxThrowsPerTurn++)
```

```
      printf("%2d %5d\n", maxThrowsPerTurn,
        playOneGame(TURNS_PER_GAME, maxThrowsPerTurn));
}


int random(int first, int last)
{
  /* this function returns a random integer from
       first to last, inclusive. For an example, see
       comments following program */
}


int playOneGame(int maxTurns, int maxThrows)
    /* returns score for the game */
{
    int gameScore, turn, playOneTurn(int throws);

    gameScore = 0;
    for (turn = 1; turn <= maxTurns; turn++)
        gameScore += playOneTurn(maxThrows);
    return gameScore;
}


int playOneTurn(int maxThrows)
/* returns score for the turn */
{
    int scoreThisTurn, throw, dieValue;
    int random(int low, int high);

    scoreThisTurn = 0;
    for (throw = 1; throw <= maxThrows; throw++) {
        dieValue = random(1,6);
        if (dieValue == 1) return 0;
        scoreThisTurn += dieValue;
    }
    return scoreThisTurn;
}
```

*Comments on the program*

- The declaration of the function prototype (in `main`)

  ```
  int playOneGame(int turns, int throws);
  ```

  says that `playOneGame` is a function which, given two integer arguments, returns an `integer` value. Similar remarks apply to the declarations:

  ```
  int playOneTurn(int throws);
  int random(int low, int high);
  ```

  in the other functions.
- The program can be made even more flexible by allowing the user to enter the values for `lowMax`, `highMax` and `turnsPerGame` when the program is run. Since these are now variables rather than symbolic constants, they are written using lowercase letters as well (following our convention for naming variables).
- In `playOneTurn`, note the use of `return 0` to cause a 'break' in the `for` statement and return a score of 0. This is what we want; if ever a 1 is thrown, the turn ends immediately with a score of 0. If a 1 is never thrown, the `for` loop terminates normally and the accumulated score is returned.
- As indicated earlier, the function `random(...)` may vary somewhat from one system to the next. The following version is written using the ANSI C standard functions `rand` and `srand`. In order to use these functions, the statement

  ```
  #include <stdlib.h>
  ```

  must precede the program. The function prototypes are

  ```
  int rand(void);
  /* returns a random integer between 0 and the
  predefined constant RAND_MAX. The value of
  RAND_MAX is also defined in <stdlib.h> */

  void srand(unsigned int seed);
  /* uses seed to set a starting point for the
  sequence generated by rand */
  ```

The following is the function r andom. However, before it could be used, we would need to 'seed' the random number generator. This could be done in main( ), thus:

```
unsigned int seed = 53;  /* an arbitrary integer */
srand(seed);  /* 'seed' the random number generator */


int random(int first, int last)
/* this function returns a random integer from
    first to last, inclusive */
{
    int offset;

    offset = rand()/(RAND_MAX + 1.0) * (last − first + 1);
    return(first + offset);
}
```

In the second to last statement, it is important to use 1.0 instead of 1. Since r and returns an integer and (RAND_MAX + 1) is also an integer, if 1 is used an integer division would be performed, always giving 0 (since the maximum value of r and is RAND_MAX). However, using (the double constant) 1.0 causes (RAND_MAX + 1.0) to be evaluated as double, in turn causing the value returned by r and to be converted to double and a floating-point division to be performed. The value of (last − first + 1) is also converted to double and the multiplication performed. The result obtained is truncated before being assigned to the integer variable offset. In effect, the construct

```
rand()/(RAND_MAX + 1.0)
```

returns a random value between 0 (inclusive) and 1 (exclusive).

Another reason for using 1.0 is that, on many systems, the value of RAND_MAX is the largest integer on the system (typically, 32767 for 16-bit ints). If we tried to add the integer 1 to it, overflow would occur since we would be trying to exceed the largest value which can be stored.

As a final embellishment, let us modify the program to tell us which value of maxThrowsPerTurn gave the highest score. This can be done simply by modifying main as shown in the (now) complete listing of program P3.3.

**Program P3.3**

```c
#include <stdio.h>
#include <stdlib.h>

#define LOWMAX 1
#define HIGHMAX 20
#define TURNS_PER_GAME 100

main()
{
    int maxThrowsPerTurn, scoreThisGame, bestScore,
        bestStrategy;
    int playOneGame(int turns, int throws);

    unsigned int seed = 53;   /* an arbitrary
                                        integer */
    srand(seed);   /* 'seed' the random number
                        generator */

    bestScore = 0;
    for (maxThrowsPerTurn = LOWMAX;
         maxThrowsPerTurn  <= HIGHMAX;
          maxThrowsPerTurn++)
    {
        scoreThisGame = playOneGame(TURNS_PER_GAME,
                                     maxThrowsPerTurn);
        printf("%2d     %5d\n", maxThrowsPerTurn,
            scoreThisGame);
        /* new part - determine best strategy */
        if (scoreThisGame > bestScore) {
            bestScore = scoreThisGame;
            bestStrategy = maxThrowsPerTurn;
        }
    }
    printf("\nHighest score obtained was %d using "
        "a maximum of %d throws per turn\n",
        bestScore, bestStrategy);
}
```

```
int random(int first, int last)
/* this function returns a random integer from
   first to last, inclusive */
{
    int offset;

    offset = rand()/(RAND_MAX + 1.0) *
                (last - first + 1);
    return(first + offset);
}


int playOneGame(int maxTurns, int maxThrows)
/* returns score for the game */
{
    int gameScore, turn, playOneTurn(int throws);

    gameScore = 0;
    for (turn = 1; turn <= maxTurns; turn++)
        gameScore += playOneTurn(maxThrows);
    return gameScore;
}


int playOneTurn(int maxThrows)
/* returns score for the turn */
{
    int scoreThisTurn, throw, dieValue;
    int random(int low, int high);

    scoreThisTurn = 0;
    for (throw = 1; throw <= maxThrows; throw++) {
        dieValue = random(1,6);
        if (dieValue == 1) return 0;
        scoreThisTurn += dieValue;
    }
    return scoreThisTurn;
}
```

Point to note: in the last `printf` statement of `main`, the first (string) argument is too long to fit on one line. However, as discussed in Chapter 1, C does not allow a string constant to be continued on to another line. In cases like these, it can be broken up as shown (with no intervening comma). When the program is compiled, adjacent strings will be concatenated and treated as a single string.

A sample run of this program produced:

```
 1          351
 2          550
 3          743
 4          714
 5          721
 6          736
 7          886
 8          914
 9          712
10          523
11          826
12          382
13          387
14          670
15          402
16          262
17          354
18          281
19          299
20           88
```

```
Highest score obtained was 914 using a maximum of
8 throws per turn
```

### Exercises 3

(1)  Find all the errors in the following:

```
/* The following function returns the sum of
its arguments *\
    int sum(a, b);
```

```
{    int a, b;

     sum = a + b;
}
```

(2) What is a 'function prototype' and why is it important? Why is it advisable to use the full function prototype in one's programs?

(3) Describe two ways in which the word 'void' can be used in one's programs.

(4) Write a C function 'shakespeare' to print the following lines:

> There is a tide in the affairs of men
> Which, taken at the flood, leads on to fortune.

(5) Write a function which, given three integers `initial`, `final` and `increment`, prints a table of temperature conversions from Celsius to Fahrenheit. The table ranges from `initial` to `final` in steps of `increment`. $\{F=32+9C/5\}$

(6) Write a function which, given a positive integer $n$, returns TRUE if $n$ is even and FALSE if $n$ is odd.

(7) Write a function which, given a positive integer $n$, returns TRUE if $n$ is prime and FALSE, otherwise.

(8) Write a function which, given a positive integer $n$, returns TRUE if $n$ is a perfect square and FALSE, otherwise.

(9) Write a function which, given $n$, returns the sum $1+2+...+n$.

(10) Write a function which, given an integer, prints it digit by digit, with one blank after each digit.

(11) Write a function which, given the number of a month, prints the name of the month. For example, given 5, it prints 'May'.

(12) The integers 1, 1, 2, 3, 5, 8, ... are known as Fibonacci numbers. If $F_n$ denotes the $n$th Fibonacci number, then F can be defined as:

$$F_1=1, \ F_2=1$$
$$F_n=F_{n-1}+F_{n-2}, \ n=3, 4, 5, ...$$

that is, each member of the sequence is the sum of the preceding two. Write a function which, given $n$, returns the $n$th Fibonacci number.

(13) The exponential function is defined by

$$e^x=1+x/1!+x^2/2!+x^3/3!+...+x^n/n!+...$$

Write a function which, given $x$, returns the value of $e^x$. Assume the existence of the function `factorial`.

(14) Write a function which, given an array of characters containing digits, returns the integer value of the digits.

(15) Write a function which, given an array of characters containing digits and possibly including a decimal point, returns the `double` value of the number.

(16)  Write a function which, given an array of characters and an integer max, returns TRUE if the first max characters form a palindrome (the same spelt backwards and forwards, e.g. civic), and FALSE, otherwise.

(17)  Write a function which, given an array of characters and an integer max, reverses the first max characters in the array. For example, 'unusual' is converted to 'lausunu'.

(18)  Write a function which, given a double number $x$ and an integer $n$, returns the value of $x^n$.

(19)  Write a function which, given an integer $n$ and a base $b$ ($\leq 10$), prints the base $b$ equivalent of $n$.

(20)  Write a function which, given three values representing the sides of a triangle, returns:

- 0 if the values cannot be the sides of any triangle. This is so if any value is negative or zero, or if any length is greater than the sum of the other two.
- 1 if the triangle is equilateral.
- 2 if the triange is isosceles.
- 3 if the triangle is scalene.

(21)  Write a function which, given an integer $n$, classifies it as 'perfect', 'abundant' or 'deficient'. A number is perfect if the sum of its divisors (excluding the number itself) is equal to the number, e.g. 6. A number is abundant if the sum of its divisors (excluding the number itself) is greater than the number, e.g. 12. A number is deficient if it is neither perfect nor abundant.

(22)  Write a function which, given $n$, prints $n$ blank lines.

(23)  Write a function which, given an integer array and its size, returns TRUE if all the elements of the array are 0 and FALSE, otherwise.

(24)  Write a function which, given an array and its size, determines if the array contains any value which is repeated at least once. Decide what the function should return.

(25)  Write a function which given num, first and last, where

num is an integer array;
first and last are integers

returns the location of the smallest element from num[first] to num[last].

Using this function, write a function to sort num in ascending order.

(26)  It is required to print a set of random integers on each of several pages. Given the following:

amtperpage – the amount of numbers on each page
firstnum, lastnum – the random numbers are taken from the range firstnum to lastnum, inclusive.
numpages – the number of pages on which random numbers are to be printed. The pages are numbered consecutively starting at 1.

No number is to be repeated on the same page or on any other page. If a number is generated which has already been used, the next unused number (in sequence) is used. (Assume that the number after `lastnum` is `firstnum`). Write a program to read values for the above variables and print the required number of pages.

Your program must cater for the case where the amount of numbers in the range is not enough to fill the required number of pages.

# 4

# Character Handling

In this chapter, we discuss several aspects of the manipulation of characters and strings. {The manipulation of strings using pointers is quite common and is discussed in the next chapter.} The 'function' getchar is used for reading characters from the standard input, usually the keyboard. The 'function' putchar is used for sending characters to the standard output, usually the screen. (Strictly speaking, getchar and putchar are not functions, but macros; however, the distinction does not really matter. Macros are discussed in Section 11.1.1). In order to use these functions, your program must be preceded by the statement

```
#include <stdio.h>
```

Our sample programs use certain character-testing functions such as isupper (test for uppercase), islower (test for lowercase) and isalpha (test for alphabetic). To use these functions, your program must be preceded by the statement

```
#include <ctype.h>
```

The sample programs also use certain string-handling functions. Among these are strcpy (copy a string) and strcmp (compare two strings). To use these functions, your program must be preceded by the statement

```
#include <string.h>
```

The character-handling concepts are illustrated using a letter-frequency count program.

The string-handling concepts are illustrated using a word-frequency count program. In order to fully appreciate this program, the programming techniques of hashing and insertion sort are discussed in some detail.

## 4.1 Character sets

A character can be any one of the following:

- a digit from 0 to 9;
- an uppercase letter from A to Z;
- a lowercase letter from a to z;
- a special symbol like $, *, /, #, (, +, ), etc.

Characters are the symbols we use to express, in writing, whatever we wish to say. Since we would like to communicate our programs and data to the computer which, in turn, would communicate its results to us, the computer must be able to represent all the characters we may wish to use. We thus speak of the **character set** of a computer, meaning the set of characters which the computer can represent and manipulate.

The characters mentioned above are usually referred to as **printable** characters. In addition to these, there are what are known as **control** characters.

To illustrate what is meant by a control character, consider how the two lines

Leila Jones
525 Fern Ave

can be stored in computer memory. We need some way of telling the computer where a line ends and another begins. We can do this by introducing a special character (called the NEWLINE character, say). If we denote the NEWLINE character by Δ, we can imagine the above data being stored as (◊ denotes a space):

| L | e | i | l | a | ◊ | J | o | n | e | s | Δ | 5 | 2 | 5 | ◊ | F | e | r | n | ◊ | A | v | e | Δ |

(Inside the computer, of course, each character is represented by its 'character code').

Suppose the data in memory is being printed. When Δ is encountered, the computer will not try to print this character, but will start a new line. Thus Δ is used to control the format of the output; it is **not** printed. It is an example of a control character.

Another example of a control character is one which is used to tell the computer when to start a new page; this is called the NEWPAGE (or Form Feed, FF) character. If the computer is printing a report and it comes across this character, it will tell the printer to 'advance to a new page'. The NEWPAGE character is not printed, but instead causes an action (paging) to take place.

Consider what happens as you type on a computer keyboard. Assume that, as you type, the information is being stored in a file on disk. Each key that you press generates the code for that character on that machine, and it is this code that is stored in the file. When you press the 'RETURN' or 'ENTER' key, the code for the NEWLINE character is stored in the file.

A file created as above is usually referred to as a **text** file, or a file of characters. Since text files are commonly used, C provides facilities for manipulating information in a text file.

A **character constant** is a single character enclosed in single quotes, e.g. 'a', '5', 'R', '+'. The **value** of a character constant is the numeric value of the character in the machine's character set. This means that the value of a character constant can vary from one machine to the next, depending on the character set being used on the particular machine. For example, on an ASCII machine the value of 'A' is 65 and on an EBCDIC machine it is 193. Using the character constant 'A', say, rather than the value of the code, makes a program independent of the particular character set.

In C, the non-printable characters are represented by an *escape sequence* consisting of a backslash (\) followed by another character. For example, the NEWLINE character is represented by '\n', the NEWPAGE (FormFeed) character is represented by '\f', and the BACKSPACE character is represented by '\b'.

Since the single quote is used to delimit character constants, it is represented by '\'' (single quote, backslash, single quote, single quote). The backslash is represented by '\\'.

Another way of writing a character constant is to use '\ddd', where ddd can be 1, 2 or 3 octal digits or '\xhh' where hh is a sequence of hexadecimal digits. ddd is the octal equivalent of the numeric value of the character in the machine's character set. hh is the hexadecimal equivalent of the numeric value of the character in the machine's character set. (There is no limit on the number of hexadecimal digits, but the behaviour is undefined if the resulting character value exceeds that of the largest character). For example, on an ASCII machine, the value of 'A' is $65_{10} = 101_8$. Thus the character constant 'A' could also be specified on this machine by $'\backslash101'$. Similarly, since $65_{10} = 41_{16}$, it could also be specified by $'\backslash x41'$. As another example, the NEWPAGE (or Form Feed, FF) character has a numeric value of 12 in the ASCII character set. Since $12_{10} = 014_8$, the FF character could also be written as $'\backslash014'$ or $'\backslash x0C'$. The special case $'\backslash0'$ is used to denote the *null character*, the character whose numeric value is 0.

  The complete list of escape sequences is

| | | | |
|---|---|---|---|
| \a | alert (bell) character | \\ | backslash |
| \b | backspace | \? | question mark |
| \f | formfeed | \' | single quote |
| \n | newline | \" | double quote |
| \r | carriage return | \ddd | character with this octal value |
| \t | horizontal tab | \xhh | character with this hexadecimal value |
| \v | vertical tab | | |

## 4.2 getchar **and** putchar

A large number of programs revolve around the idea of reading and writing one character at a time. The function getchar returns the next character from the 'standard input file'. The standard input file is usually the keyboard but it could also be a disk file, say, in which data has been stored. The value returned by getchar is the numeric value of the character in the machine's character set. If getchar is called and there is no more input, it returns a value which cannot be confused with the value of a valid character. The value returned depends on the system; many systems return the value of –1 and some return 0. In a C program, the symbolic constant EOF is used to denote the end-of-file character. For a given system, the value of EOF is predefined to the value returned by that system. This definition is contained in the header file stdio.h.

  To illustrate how getchar may be used, let us write a program (P4.1) to determine the position of the first non-blank character on an input line. For simplicity, we assume that there is at least one non-blank character on the line.

- The do...while is performed as long as getchar() returns the blank character. For each character read, position is incremented. The value of position is the position of the character just read.
- It is permissible to compare an int with a char constant as in ch == $'$ $'$. In this case, the value of ch is compared with the value of $'$ $'$.

**Program P4.1**

```
#include <stdio.h>

main()        /* find position of first
                    non-blank character */
{
    int ch, position;

    position = 0;
    do {
        ch = getchar();
        position++;
    } while (ch == ' ');
    printf("\nFirst non-blank character is in "
           "position %2d\n", position);
}
```

Recall that the value of a character constant is simply the numeric value of the character in the machine's character set.

- Note the use of == for comparing two quantities. It would be wrong to write the while condition as while (ch = ' '). If this were done, the value of ' ' (which is 32 in ASCII, for example) would be assigned to ch. The value of the assignment expression would be 32. Since this is non-zero, it is interpreted as true. The while condition would always be true – an infinite loop. The program would halt abruptly when it ran out of input.

Suppose we wanted to cater for the possibility that the first line of input contained blanks only. Now every time a character is read, we will have to check if it is the newline character. If it is, it means that the end of the line has been reached and no non-blank character has been found. Program P4.2 shows the changes needed to cater for a 'blanks only' line. Now, exit from the while loop takes place if either a non-blank character or the newline character is read.

The function putchar outputs a character onto the 'standard output file'. The standard output file is usually the screen but it can, for instance, be a file on disk. The argument to putchar must be a value which can be interpreted as a character. It is usually an int or a char variable.

## Program P4.2

```
#include <stdio.h>

main()   /* find position of first non-blank
          character, if any */
{
    int ch, position;

    position = 0;
    do {
        ch = getchar();
        position++;
    } while (ch == ' ' && ch != '\n');
    if (ch == '\n')
        printf("\nLine contains blanks "
                "only\n");
    else
        printf("\nFirst non-blank character is "
                "in position %2d\n", position);
}
```

Suppose, in the above program, we wanted to print the first non-blank character found on the line. The following could be used:

```
printf("\nThe first non-blank character is ");
putchar(ch);
```

This is rather artificial, though, since it can be written more compactly as

```
printf("\nThe first non-blank character is %c", ch);
```

Here %c specifies that the argument ch is to be printed as a character. For example, if the first non-blank character was 'T', the following would be printed:

```
The first non-blank character is T
```

In comparison, if we had used %d instead of %c, the integer value of ch would be printed, producing (the ASCII value of 'T' is 84)

```
The first non-blank character is 84
```

To illustrate a more realistic use of putchar, let us write a program (P4.3) which reads the input and prints it, numbering the lines.

---

**Program P4.3**

```c
#include <stdio.h>

#define TRUE 1
#define FALSE 0

main()        /* echo input, numbering the
                 lines */
{
    int ch, line, writelinenum;

    line = 0;
    writelinenum = TRUE;
    while ((ch = getchar()) != EOF) {
        if (writelinenum) {
            printf("%4d. ", ++line);
            writelinenum = FALSE;
        }
        putchar(ch);
        if (ch == '\n') writelinenum = TRUE;
    }
}
```

---

- Without the two if statements, this program will simply echo the input to the output. In the while condition, getchar reads the next character and assigns it to ch. The value of the assignment (i.e., the value of ch) is then compared with EOF. If the end-of-file has been reached, the while loop terminates and so does the program. If not, the loop is entered and the character is sent to the output by putchar.

Normally, putchar(ch) places the character ch in the next position in the output stream. For example, if ch contains 'T' and the output is being displayed on a screen, then putchar(ch) will display T on the screen. But if ch contains the newline character ('\n'), say, then putchar(ch) does not display this character, but rather produces the **effect** of terminating the current line. Note, however, that if the output was being sent to a disk file, say, the newline character would be stored in the file.

- writelinenum is used to delay the writing of the line number until it is determined that there is indeed such a line. As a simple test, if there is no input, the program simply terminates without printing anything. This is as it should be. We do not want to print line number 1 only to find that there is no such line.
- The construct

```
(ch = getchar()) != EOF
```

is very commonly used. However, be careful to include the brackets around ch = getchar() since '!=' has higher precedence than '='. Without the brackets it would be interpreted as

```
ch = (getchar() != EOF)
```

The value of the right-hand-side is TRUE or FALSE. It is TRUE if the character read is not EOF and FALSE, otherwise. It is this value (1 or 0) which would be assigned to ch, certainly not what was intended.

If the newline character is encountered, then writelinenum is set to TRUE. Only if the loop is re-entered is the line number incremented and printed; writelinenum is then set to FALSE. It will be reset to TRUE only when the next newline character is read.

- Observe the use of ++line in printf(...). This increments line **before** its value is printed. Since line is initialized to 0, the lines are numbered starting from 1.
- The use of the symbolic constants TRUE and FALSE makes the program more readable.

### 4.3 Example – letter frequency count

The next program counts the frequency of each letter in the input. It does not distinguish between upper and lower case; for example, 'E' and 'e' increment the same counter.

We will need an integer array with 26 elements to hold the count for each letter of the alphabet. Arrays in C are subscripted from 0. For example, the array `lettercount[26]` (declared below) consists of elements `lettercount[0]`, `lettercount[1]`,..., `lettercount[25]` where

> `lettercount[0]`    holds the count for 'A' and 'a'.
> `lettercount[1]`    holds the count for 'B' and 'b'.
> `lettercount[2]`    holds the count for 'C' and 'c'.
>       etc.
> `lettercount[25]` holds the count for 'Z' and 'z'.

The program works only for those character sets for which the letters of the alphabet have consecutive numeric codes. For example, in ASCII, the uppercase letters 'A' to 'Z' have codes from 65 to 90 and the lowercase letters 'a' to 'z' have codes from 97 to 122. This property is used in calculating the subscript of the element of `lettercount` which must be incremented for a given letter. If the character read, `ch`, is an uppercase letter, the subscript is calculated by

```
ch - 'A'
```

For example, if `ch` contains 'A', the calculation (`'A' - 'A'`) gives 0, so that `lettercount[0]` is incremented. If `ch` contains 'E', the calculation (`'E' - 'A'`) gives 4, so that `lettercount[4]` is incremented. Similarly, if `ch` is lowercase, the calculation

```
ch - 'a'
```

gives the appropriate element of `lettercount` to increment. Whether the character is uppercase or lowercase is determined by the standard 'functions' `isupper(...)` and `islower(...)`. (Strictly speaking, these are what are called **macros**, but the distinction isn't too important for our purposes). Using them allows us to ignore the idiosyncracies of the underlying character set. However, in order to use them, our program must be preceded by

```
#include <ctype.h>
```

As an example, for the ASCII character set (Appendix C), `isupper` could be implemented by

```
int isupper(int ch)
{
    return (ch >= 'A') && (ch <= 'Z');
}
```

Be reminded, however, that this works only because the uppercase letters have consecutive numeric codes.

Program P4.4 puts it all together. Note that if ch does not contain a letter, no element of lettercount is incremented.

---

**Program P4.4**

```
#include <stdio.h>
#include <ctype.h>

#define ALPHABETSIZE 26
main ()
{
    int lettercount[ALPHABETSIZE];
    int ch, n;

    for (n = 0; n < ALPHABETSIZE; n++)
        /* initialize array to 0 */
            lettercount[n] = 0;

    while ((ch = getchar()) != EOF)
        if (isupper(ch))
            ++lettercount[ch - 'A'];
        else if (islower(ch))
            ++lettercount[ch - 'a'];
    /* endwhile */

    for (ch = 'a', n = 0; n < ALPHABETSIZE;
        ch++, n++)
        printf("\t%c %d\n", ch, lettercount[n]);

} /* end of main */
```

---

The last `for` loop illustrates some of the expressive power of the `for` in C. It also shows the use of the **comma operator**. A pair of expressions separated by a comma is evaluated from left to right, and the type and value of the result are the type and value of the right operand. When the `for` loop is entered, ch is set to 'a' and n is set to 0. At the end of each execution of the loop, both ch and n are incremented. ch is used for printing the letters of the alphabet and n is used for subscripting the array `lettercount`. The following is a sample of the start of the output:

```
a       23
b       10
c       12
   etc.
```

In order to make the main program less dependent on the underlying character set, the `while` loop can be written in terms of a function `subscript(ch)`. The function returns NONLETTER(−1) if ch is not a letter. If ch is a letter, it returns the subscript of the appropriate element of `lettercount` to be incremented. In this way, character-set dependencies can be isolated in `subscript`. The required modifications are illustrated in program P4.5.

Note the declaration of the function prototype

```
int subscript(int ch);
```

in `main`. The first `int` specifies the type of value returned by the function; `int ch` specifies that the function must be supplied with an integer argument. As a final comment, note that the last `for` loop still depends on the (lowercase) letters having consecutive codes.

## 4.4 Strings (arrays of characters)

In Section 2.5.1 we introduced our discussion of strings. Now we give a more detailed treatment. So far, we have used string constants in, for example, `printf(...)` statements and we have used character constants (e. g. 'A') and character variables. As a reminder, a string constant is a **set** of characters enclosed in double quotes (") and a character constant is a **single** character enclosed in single quotes ('). In addition, special

**Program P4.5**

```
#include <stdio.h>
#include <ctype.h>

#define NONLETTER -1
#define ALPHABETSIZE 26
main ()
{
    int lettercount[ALPHABETSIZE];
    int subscript(int ch);
    int ch, n;

    for (n = 0; n < ALPHABETSIZE; n++)
        /* initialize array to 0 */
            lettercount[n] = 0;

    while ((ch = getchar()) != EOF)
        if ((n = subscript(ch)) != NONLETTER)
            ++lettercount[n];
    /* endwhile */

    for (ch = 'a', n = 0; n < ALPHABETSIZE; ch++, n++)
        printf("\t%c     %d\n", ch, lettercount[n]);

} /* end of main */

int subscript(int ch)
/* returns NONLETTER if ch is not a letter,
   otherwise returns the appropriate subscript */
{
    if (isupper(ch)) return(ch - 'A');
    else if (islower(ch)) return(ch - 'a');
    else return NONLETTER;
}
```

character constants are denoted by a backslash followed by another character (e. g. `'\n'`).

In C, a string is stored in an **array of characters**. Each character in the string is stored in one position in the array. The null character `'\0'` (the 'character' whose numeric value is zero) is put after the last character. This is done so that programs can tell when the end of a string has been reached. For example, the string

"Enter a number:"

is stored as follows (◊ denotes a space):

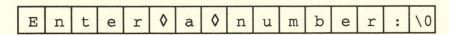

(Of course, inside the computer, each character is represented by its numeric code in the particular character set).

It is important to understand the distinction between, say, the character constant `'a'` and the string constant `"a"`. The character constant `'a'` has a numeric value (the value of its internal representation) associated with it; in the ASCII character set, this value is 97. On the other hand, `"a"` is a **string** which consists of one character. Internally, it is stored as the character `'a'` followed by the null character, thus:

Apart from using string constants in a program, it may be required, for instance, to read the input and pick out the words which appear. But where do we store the words? We will need to use an array of char; the size of the array will depend on the length of the longest word we wish to cater for. In addition, if we intend to use any of the standard string handling functions (for example, to compare two words) we must put the null character at the end of our words. This is necessary since these functions expect strings to be stored in this format. Thus our array must have enough room to hold the longest word as well as the null character.

Let us illustrate these ideas by writing a function getword which reads the input (one character at a time) and stores the next word found in a character array word. For our purposes, a word begins with a letter and consists of letters only; thus the next non-letter indicates the end of a word. The variable `maxwordsize` specifies how many characters will be stored. This **includes** the null character so that, in reality, the longest word which can be stored is of length `maxwordsize` − 1. The function returns the value of `INPUTEXHAUSTED` if EOF was encountered during the search for a word or `WORDFOUND` if a word has been stored in the array `word`. We assume that `INPUTEXHAUSTED` and `WORDFOUND` are global symbolic constants. Here is `getword`:

```
int getword(char word[], int maxwordsize)
    /* store the next word in word */
{
    int ch, next;

    do
        ch = getchar();
    while (!isalpha(ch) && ch != EOF);

    if (ch == EOF) return INPUTEXHAUSTED;

    /* The first letter of the word has been found */
    next = 0;
    word[next++] = ch;
    while (--maxwordsize > 0) {
        word[next++] = ch = getchar();
        if (!isalpha(ch)) break;
    }
    word[next - 1] = '\0';
    return WORDFOUND;
}
```

- In the declaration of the argument `word`, it is not necessary to specify the size of the array. Note, however, that if a size is specified, it **must** be a constant (numeric or symbolic).
- The `do...while` skips over non-letters until the first letter is read or the end of the input is reached. This construct could have been written using `while` thus:

```
while ((ch = getchar()) ! = EOF && !isalpha(ch))
    ;
```

The character returned by getchar() is assigned to ch and its value is then tested against EOF. The semicolon is put on a line by itself to make it clear that there is no 'statement' following the while condition. Or, to put it another way, the body of the while loop is the null statement.

• The while stores letters in word until either a non-letter is found or the array is filled up. Note the multiple assignment

```
word[next++] = ch = getchar();
```

This is done from right to left, and so is equivalent to

```
word[next++] = (ch = getchar());
```

On exit from the loop, the null character is stored after the last letter in the word.

The function works fine as long as the words do not exceed the maximum length catered for. But what happens if a word is too long? Suppose, for example, that maxwordsize is 5 (this means only 4 letters can be stored) and the next word in the input is 'Longevity'. The function would actually store the letters L, o, n, g, e in word[0] to word[4], respectively. On exit from the while loop, '\0' would be stored in word[4]. So what is actually returned in word is

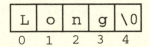

that is, the first four letters of the word properly terminated by \0. But now, on the next call to getword, the new word will start with the letter 'v', since 'e' has already been read.

One way to handle a word which exceeds the maximum length is to store what can be stored and ignore the rest of the word. The function must now read and discard extraneous letters. For the function getword, this can be accomplished by inserting the following just before 'return WORDFOUND':

```
while (isalpha(ch) && ch != EOF) ch = getchar();
```

isalpha(ch) is true the first time only if exit from the previous while was due to the array being filled up with letters.

In order to test the function `getword`, we could write a small main program which simply calls `getword` repeatedly, each time writing out the word returned. We could even count the number of words written. The following may be used.

```
#include <stdio.h>
#include <ctype.h>

#define INPUTEXHAUSTED 0
#define WORDFOUND 1
#define MAXLENGTH 20

main()
{
    char newWord[MAXLENGTH];
    int getword(char word[], int max);
    int wordcount = 0;

    while (getword(newWord, MAXLENGTH) == WORDFOUND) {
        printf("%s\n", newWord);
        wordcount++;
    }
    printf("\nNumber of words found = %d\n", wordcount);
}
```

- The declaration

```
    int getword(char word[], int max);
```

says that `getword` is a function which accepts a character array and an integer, and returns an integer value.
- The declaration

```
    int wordcount = 0;
```

allocates storage for `wordcount` **and** initializes it to 0. This form of declaration can be used to initialize variables, in general.
- In `printf(...)`, the conversion specification `%s` is used for printing

a string. printf(...) assumes that the string is properly terminated by \0.

The complete listing (with getword amended to truncate long words) is shown as program P4.6.

---

**Program P4.6**

```
#include <stdio.h>
#include <ctype.h>

#define INPUTEXHAUSTED 0
#define WORDFOUND 1
#define MAXLENGTH 20

main()
{
    char newWord[MAXLENGTH];
    int getword(char word[], int max);
    int wordcount = 0;

    while (getword(newWord, MAXLENGTH) == WORDFOUND) {
        printf("%s\n", newWord);
        wordcount++;
    }
    printf("\nNumber of words found = %d\n",
            wordcount);
}

int getword(char word[], int maxwordsize)
    /* store the next word in word */
{
    int ch, next;

    do
        ch = getchar();
    while (!isalpha(ch) && ch != EOF);

    if (ch == EOF) return INPUTEXHAUSTED;
```

```
/* The first letter of the word has been found */
next = 0;
word[next++] = ch;
while (--maxwordsize > 0) {
    word[next++] = ch = getchar();
    if (!isalpha(ch)) break;
}
word[next - 1] = '\0';
while (isalpha(ch) && ch != EOF) ch = getchar();
return WORDFOUND;
}
```

## 4.5  Example – word frequency count

Consider the following:

*Problem*:  Write a program to do a frequency count of the words in the input. Output must consist of an alphabetical listing of the words and the number of times each word appears in the input.

Ignoring, for the time being, how the words are arranged in alphabetical order, we can use the following outline for the frequency count:

> while there is input
>   get a word
>   search for word
>   if word is not in the table
>     insert word in table
>   endif
>   add 1 to frequency count
> endwhile

This is a typical 'search and insert' situation. We search for the word among the words stored so far. If the search fails, the word is put in the table. If the search succeeds, the word has been met before and we need only to increment its count. A major design decision here is how to search the table which, in turn, will depend on where and how a new word is inserted in the table. The following are two possibilities:

(1) A new word is inserted in the next (sequential) position in the table. This implies that a sequential search must be used to look for an incoming word. This method has the advantages of simplicity and easy insertion, but searching takes longer as more words are put in the table.

(2) A new word is inserted in the table in such a way that the words are always in order. This may entail moving words which have already been stored so that the new word may be slotted in the right place. However, since the table is in order, a binary search can be used to search for an incoming word. For this method, searching is faster but insertion is slower than in (1). Since, in general, searching is done more frequently than inserting, (2) might be preferable.

Another advantage of (2) is that, at the end, the words will already be in alphabetical order and no sorting will be required. If (1) is used, the words will need to be sorted to obtain the alphabetical order.

A third possibility is to use the method called **hashing**. This has the advantages of extremely fast search times and easy insertion. In order to explain the method, we will digress for a moment from the problem at hand.

### 4.5.1 Hashing

The classical statement of the 'search and insert' problem is:

*Problem*:   Given a `table` of keys (the table may be empty initially), search for a given `key` in the table. If the key is not found, insert it in the table.

Examples of keys are names and numbers (things like account number, employee number, student number, etc).

In order to keep the presentation simple, suppose that the keys are integers. To be more precise, suppose the keys are 2-digit integers, that is, numbers from 10 to 99. We will use an integer array to store the table. Suppose that the table is of size 12 and consists of elements `table[0]`, `table[1]`, ..., up to `table[11]`.

Suppose the next incoming key is 41. The problem is to search the (possibly empty) table for 41. The idea behind hashing is to convert the key 41 (somehow) into a table location k, say. If there is no key in `table[k]`, then 41 is stored in that location. If `table[k]` is occupied by another key, we say a **collision** has occurred, and we must find another location in which to attempt to insert 41. This is called **resolving the collision**.

The method used to convert a key to a table location is called the **hashing function**. **Any** calculation which produces a valid table location can be used, but, as we shall see, some functions give better results than others.

Suppose the following keys come in the order given:

$$41\ 74\ 33\ 92\ 27\ 53\ 20\ 60\ 39$$

and consider the function

$F(\text{key}) = \text{key mod } 12;$    the remainder when 'key' is divided by 12.

For any key, $F$ produces a value in the range 0 to 11, that is, a valid table location.

Since the method depends on knowing if a given table location is 'empty', each location will have to be initialized to some value which cannot be a possible key. In our example, we can use 0 to indicate an 'empty' location, since the keys range from 10 to 99.

For the first key, 41, the hash function $F$ produces a value 5. Since this is the first key, `table[5]` is empty (contains 0); 41 is stored in `table[5]`.

For the second key, 74, the hash function $F$ produces a value 2. Since `table[2]` is empty, 74 is stored in table[2].

The third key, 33, **hashes** to location 9 and is inserted in `table[9]`.

The next two keys, 92 and 27, hash to locations 8 and 3, respectively, and are inserted in those locations.

The next key, 53, hashes to location 5. But now `table[5]` is occupied by key 41. We say that 53 has collided with 41. We must now find a new location to attempt to insert 53; we must resolve the collision. There are many ways to resolve a collision, each with their own advantages and disadvantages. The simplest (and usually effective) method is to look at the **next** location. If that is empty, then the key is inserted there; if not, we look at the next location, and so on. For the purpose of determining the next location, we consider the table to be circular, that is, the location after `table[11]` is `table[0]`. In the case of 53, `table[6]` is available and so 53 is inserted there.

The next key, 20, hashes to location 8. This is occupied as well as location 9; `table[10]` is empty and so 20 is inserted there.

The next key, 60, hashes to location 0 and is inserted in `table[0]`. Finally, 39 hashes to location 3 and is inserted in `table[4]`. The diagram shows the table after all the keys have been inserted.

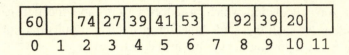

| 60 | | 74 | 27 | 39 | 41 | 53 | | 92 | 39 | 20 | |
| 0 | 1 | 2 | 3 | 4 | 5 | 6 | 7 | 8 | 9 | 10 | 11 |

Consider now the problem of searching for a key, 33, say. Using the same hash function which was used to insert the key, the initial hash location, 9, is determined. We immediately search location 9 and the key 33 is found.

If we were searching for 53, the initial hash location would be 5. `table[5]` is occupied but not by the key we are looking for. We must therefore search the next location, 6; the key is found.

But what if we were searching for 81? 81 hashes to location 9. This is occupied and not by 81, so we look at location 10. This is also occupied and also not by 81. We therefore look at location 11. This is empty so we can conclude that 81 is not in the table. If required, we can now insert 81 in this location.

The following algorithm searches for `key` among the entries `table[0]` to `table[max − 1]` using a hashing function, *F*.

(1) k = *F*(key)        /* get initial hash location */
(2) if `table[k]` is empty, insert key in `table[k]` and stop.
(3) if `table[k]` = key, search is successful; stop.
(4) k = k + 1; if k = max then k = 0; /* get next location */
(5) repeat from (2)

Thus we search until either the key is found or we encounter an empty location. There is the possibility that the table may be completely full, in which case, if the search key is not there, we will never find the key nor an empty location. The 'search and insert' algorithm could be modified to handle this situation but, in practice, we never allow the table to become completely full and so there is always at least one empty location. For example, if the table has 100 locations, we consider it to be full when 99 locations are occupied. The simplified algorithm more than makes up for the sacrifice of one location.

To illustrate the use of a different hash function, consider the same situation above, with the same keys:

41 74 33 92 27 53 20 60 39

and the hash function

$$H(key) = INT((key*12)/100)$$

where INT takes the 'whole number' part of its argument. For example, INT(5.6) = 5 and INT(8.0) = 8.

Since the keys range from 10 to 99, $H$ will produce values in the range 1 to 11. This is valid even though $H$ cannot generate location 0 from any key. For the above keys, $H$ will produce the hash locations shown in brackets:

41(4) 74(8) 33(3) 92(11) 27(3) 53(6) 20(2) 60(7) 39(4)

and the diagram shows the table after all the keys have been inserted.

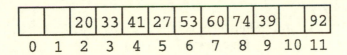

Note that, in general, different hash functions will place keys in different locations. The pattern of collisions could also be expected to be different. For example, with $F$, 39 was inserted after one collision but, with $H$, it was inserted after five collisions. On the other hand, with $F$, 20 was inserted after two collisions but, with $H$, it was inserted with no collisions.

All this seems to indicate that choosing a hash function can be tricky business. But by following a few simple guidelines, one can safeguard against a hash function performing really badly. A hash function should:

- be easy to calculate. Avoid lengthy and cumbersome computations. In many situations, the mod function works well.
- use as much of the key as possible. For example, if the key is a name, it would be unwise to use just the first letter to determine the hash location. Making use of the whole key gives a better chance of limiting the number of collisions.
- try to spread the keys uniformly over the table. Avoid a function which deliberately biases keys to a certain portion of the table.

The efficiency of the hashing technique depends mainly on the hashing function and the method of resolving collisions. The method described above is called the **linear** method and it gives good results provided that the table is no more than about 90% full. For example, for a table which is 90% full, the expected number of comparisons to find an item is 5.5. This value is independent of the size of the table. It depends only on the fraction of the table filled. When the table is more than 90% full, the expected number of comparisons for finding an item becomes unaccept-ably high for fast searching. For a table which is 95% full, the expected number of comparisons is 10.5 and when it is 99% full the expected number is 50.5.

### 4.5.2 Back to the problem

Going back to the problem of determining the frequency count of words in the input, we will use a hashing technique for the 'search and insert' part of the solution. The program will be developed based on the following outline:

```
while there is input
    get a word
    search for word
    if word is not in the table
        insert word in table
    endif
    add 1 to frequency count
endwhile
```

It seems fairly obvious that the table of words will be stored in an array. But what kind of array? It will be an array of 'words' but a word is itself stored in an array of characters. Thus the table is an array, each of whose elements is also an array. In C, a two-dimensional array is used to represent such a situation. Suppose we wished to cater for 100 words each of maximum length 20 (including a terminating \0), we could use a declaration such as

```
char wordtable[109][20];
```

(We use 109 so that when 100 words have been stored, the table will be approximately 90% full. The table will be considered full when 100 words have been stored. This will ensure that the performance of the hash technique does not deteriorate too much. The reason for 109 (rather than

110, say) is that a hash function based on 'modulus' performs better if the table size is a prime number). wordtable is considered to be a rectangular matrix with 109 rows and 20 columns, where each element of the matrix is a (single) character. Note that two sets of square brackets are used, as compared with wordtable[109, 20] of other languages. Each row of wordtable will be used for storing a word. In fact, even though wordtable is declared as a two-dimensional array (and normally requires two subscripts), we can use wordtable[k] (one subscript), say, to refer to a particular word; which word, of course, depends on the value of k. We could also use wordtable[k][j] to refer to the *j*th letter of the *k*th word.

We will use another array to store the frequency of the words. This could be declared as

```
int frequency[109];
```

and frequency[k] will be used to hold the number of times that the word in wordtable[k] appears in the input.

Since a hashing technique will be used for searching and inserting the words in the table, we will need a hashing function which, given a word, returns a valid table location. In our previous examples of hashing functions, the keys were numbers, and a simple calculation was used to generate a table location. Now a key is a word or, more precisely, an array of characters. Our problem, therefore, is to convert the letters of the word into a numeric value, v, say. We could then generate a table location from v by using v mod 109.

A simple solution is to add up the numeric values of the letters of the word. However, this has the disadvantage that words comprising the same letters will hash to the same location; for example, 'meat', 'team' and 'mate' all hash to the same location. A better approach is to 'weight' each letter depending on its position in the word. Any weighting can be used. As an example, the first letter could be multiplied by 1, the second by 3, the third by 5, etc. This method will be used in our sample program. In fact, we can write the hash function without regard to the rest of the program. To illustrate:

given word and maxtablesize, the following function returns a value from 0 to (maxtablesize − 1), that is, a valid table location. The function assumes that word is properly terminated by \0.

```
int gethashloc(char word[], int maxtablesize)
   /* returns the location to which word hashes */
{
    int j = 0;
    int weight = 1;
    int wordvalue = 0;

    while (word[j] != '\0') {
        wordvalue += word[j] * weight;
        weight += 2;
        j++;
    }
    return (wordvalue % maxtablesize);
}
```

We now write the search routine which, given a word and the table of words, determines whether or not the word is in the table. If the word is in the table, it returns the table location of the word. If the word is not in the table, it returns the location where the word must be inserted. Writing the search routine this way allows the caller the flexibility to decide what to do if the word is in the table or not. In our specific problem at hand, if the word is already present, then its count is incremented. In a different situation, something else may be needed to be done if a word is present. However, the same search routine could be used. Here we are following the general principle that a function should perform one specific task; this gives a function a better chance of being reused in a different situation. The search routine would be inflexible if it also performed the actions required when the result of the search is known. Here is the function searchword. It is written using the more general terms key and keytable. We also assume that the following declaration precedes main:

```
#define MAXWORDLENGTH 20
```

```
int searchword (char key[],
   char keytable[][MAXWORDLENGTH], int maxtablesize)
   /* if key is found, its location is returned;
      if key is not found, the location where it may
      be inserted is returned.*/
{
    int hashloc;
    int gethashloc(char key[], int max);
```

```
hashloc = gethashloc(key, maxtablesize);
while   (strcmp(keytable[hashloc], key) != 0 &&
         strcmp(keytable[hashloc], EMPTYSTRING) != 0)
   hashloc = (hashloc + 1) % maxtablesize;
/* endwhile */
return hashloc;
}
```

- Note the declaration of the parameters `key` and `keytable`. When a one-dimensional array (e.g. `key`) is a function argument, the size of the array need not be specified but the (square) brackets must be present. This is allowed because when the function is 'called', only the address of the first element of the array is passed. However, when a two-dimensional array (e.g. `keytable`) is a function argument, the first subscript need not be specified but the **second** subscript **must** be given. This is to enable the compiler to work out the starting address of each row, given the row subscript. The declarations could also have been written:

```
char key[20], char keytable[109][20]
```

but this is too restrictive and inflexible.
- In C, one cannot use the usual relational operators (e.g. `==`, `<`) for comparing strings. So, for instance, it would be wrong to write

```
if (key == keytable[hashloc]) ...
```

Strings can be compared using the standard string function `strcmp`. If `str1` and `str2` are two strings, then

```
strcmp(str1, str2)
```

returns a negative value if `str1` is less than `str2`, zero if `str1` is equal to `str2`, and a positive value if `str1` is greater than `str2`. Note that `strcmp` expects its arguments to be properly terminated by \0. In order to use `strcmp` (and other string functions), our program must be preceded by

```
#include <string.h>
```

- Since the hashing method of searching relies on the program finding an 'empty' location, all locations in the table are initialized to EMPTYSTRING. This will be declared as a global symbolic constant, thus:

```
#define EMPTYSTRING ""   /* two consecutive
                            double quotes */
```

The **null** string (a string with 0 characters) is written as two consecutive double quotes. Internally, it is stored as

We can now write (an incomplete) main in terms of the functions we have developed so far. Observe that it closely follows the outline given on page 98.

```
#include <stdio.h>
#include <ctype.h>
#include <string.h>

#define EMPTYSTRING ""
#define INPUTEXHAUSTED 0
#define WORDFOUND 1
#define MAXTABLESIZE 109
#define MAXWORDLENGTH 20
#define MAXWORDS 100

main()   /* this is incomplete */
{
    char wordtable[MAXTABLESIZE][MAXWORDLENGTH];
    int frequency[MAXTABLESIZE];
    char word[MAXWORDLENGTH];
    int loc, getword(char word[], int max);
    int searchword(char word[],
        char table[][MAXWORDLENGTH], int max);

    /* initialize the word table and set the
       frequency counts to 0 */
```

```
    for (loc = 0; loc < MAXTABLESIZE; loc++) {
        strcpy(wordtable[loc], EMPTYSTRING);
        frequency[loc] = 0;
    }


    while (getword(word, MAXWORDLENGTH) == WORDFOUND) {
        loc = searchword(word, wordtable, MAXTABLESIZE);
        if (strcmp(wordtable[loc], EMPTYSTRING) == 0)
                            /* word is not in the table */
            strcpy(wordtable[loc], word);
                            /* store word in table */
        /* endif */
        ++frequency[loc];

    }

}
```

- The `for` loop initializes each word in the table to the null string. It also sets the frequency counts to 0. In order to assign a string value to a string (array of character) variable, the standard function `strcpy` (string copy) must be used. In general, if `str1` and `str2` are strings,

  ```
  strcpy(str1, str2)
  ```

  copies `str2` to `str1` (in effect, `str1 = str2`). Observe that the second argument is copied into the first argument (similar to normal assignment).
- Since `searchword` simply returns a table location, `main` must check the contents of that location to determine the result of the search. If the location contains the null string, then the word is not in the table and it must be inserted in that location. The word is copied into the table using `strcpy`.

As written so far, `main` does not count the words as they are inserted in the table. Since we do not want to put more than MAXWORDS words in the table, we would need to increment a counter each time a new word is about to be stored. If the counter exceeds MAXWORDS, then the table is declared 'full'. What action should be taken in this situation? There are several possibilities.

(1) One could simply halt the program with a message that the table size is too small.
(2) One could print the word which caused the table to 'overflow', stop reading any more input and print the information in the table up to that point.
(3) One could continue reading the input, incrementing the count for words already stored and printing the (new) words which cannot be stored. At the end of the input, the information in the table could be printed.

Our sample program will be based on (3).

We will delegate the handling of a new word to the function newWord. Since this function does not return a value, its type is declared as void.

```
void newWord   (char word[],
                char wordtable[][MAXWORDLENGTH],
                int frequency[], int loc, int maxwords)
    /* inserts a new word in the table, provided
       there is room */
{
    static int wordcount = 0;

    if (wordcount == maxwords) /* no more words can
                                  be stored */
        printf("%-20s cannot be stored - table "
               "full\n", word);
    else {           /* wordcount < maxwords */
        wordcount++;
        strcpy(wordtable[loc], word);
        frequency[loc] = 1;
    }
}
```

When newWord is entered for the first time, storage is allocated to wordcount which is then initialized to 0. Because it is declared as static, it retains its value between calls to newWord. (Storage classes, including static, are discussed in Section 6.5). As long as wordcount is less than maxwords, the new word is inserted in the table. However, when wordcount reaches maxwords, no more words are put in the table. Each new word is simply printed with a message that it cannot be stored.

In the printf(...) statement, the specification %–20s means that the string is to be printed left justified ( – ) in a field width of 20. If the specification were %20s, then the string would be printed right justified in a field width of 20.

With the introduction of newWord, the while loop in main now becomes:

```
while (getword(word, MAXWORDLENGTH) == WORDFOUND) {
    loc = searchword(word, wordtable, MAXTABLESIZE);
    if (strcmp(wordtable[loc], EMPTYSTRING) == 0)
            /* word is not in the table */
        newWord(word, wordtable, frequency, loc, MAXWORDS);
    else        /* word is there; increase its count */
        ++frequency[loc];
}
```

Now, if the word is not in the table then newWord is called. If it is already there, then its count is simply incremented by 1.

We have now written all the code to get the words and count them. The above while loop will be performed until all the input has been read. When the while loop terminates, the words and their counts will be stored in the arrays wordtable and frequency, respectively. However, because of the way the hashing technique works, the words will be in arbitrary order. In addition, there will be locations in the table which are still 'empty'. As an illustration, a table with 8 locations and 5 words might look like Table 4.1:

**Table 4.1**

|   | wordtable | frequency |
|---|-----------|-----------|
| 0 | store | 2 |
| 1 | | 0 |
| 2 | program | 4 |
| 3 | computer | 1 |
| 4 | a | 7 |
| 5 | | 0 |
| 6 | disk | 3 |
| 7 | | 0 |

The words in the table must now be sorted. The sorting method can treat the empty locations as if they contained words. (In fact, they each contain the null string). Because of the way strings are compared, the null string will compare **less** than any non-null string. The end result is that the sorting process will move all the empty locations to the head of the table. We must be careful to ensure that the frequency count for a word remains with the word. So that if, for instance, 'disk' is being moved from location 6, then its frequency count 3 must also be moved. After sorting, Table 4.1 would be transformed into Table 4.2.

**Table 4.2**

|   | wordtable | frequency |
|---|-----------|-----------|
| 0 |           | 0         |
| 1 |           | 0         |
| 2 |           | 0         |
| 3 | a         | 7         |
| 4 | computer  | 1         |
| 5 | disk      | 3         |
| 6 | program   | 4         |
| 7 | store     | 2         |

The program can now skip over the null strings at the beginning of the table and print the table starting from the first word.

The only question which remains is how do we sort the words? There are several sorting methods from which to choose. Some of these methods go by the names bubble sort, selection sort, insertion sort, Shell (diminishing increment) sort, quicksort and heapsort. Our sample program will use an **insertion** sort to arrange the words in alphabetical order. We again digress for a moment to explain how the method works.

### 4.5.3 Insertion sort

The explanation of the method is easier to follow if we use an array of integers. Consider the array num with the following values:

num

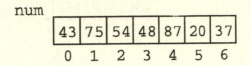

We wish to arrange the numbers in ascending order. An insertion sort proceeds by 'processing' the elements of the array, one at a time, starting from the second element (the one in location 1). If the second element is greater than or equal to the first, nothing is done and we go on to the third element. If the second is smaller than the first, the two elements are interchanged, putting them in ascending order. We then 'process' the third element; this involves placing the third element among the previous two, so that all three elements are in order. When we come to 'process' the fourth element, we assume that the previous three elements are sorted among themselves. The method then inserts the fourth element among the first three so that the four elements are now sorted among themselves. The method then goes on to process the fifth element. In general, when we come to process the $j$th element, we can assume that the previous $(j - 1)$ elements are sorted among themselves. The method then inserts the $j$th element among these sorted elements so that the $j$ elements are now sorted among themselves. Note that, since one element (by itself) can be considered to be sorted, when we start by processing the second element, our assumption that the previous element is sorted is true.

The method of insertion sort will sort num as follows:

(1) We start with the value in location 1, that is, 75, and compare it with num[0], that is, 43. Since 75 is greater than 43, these two values are already in order (with respect to each other), so there's nothing to be done and we go on to num[2], that is, 54.
(2) We attempt to place 54 in its correct position with respect to num[0] and num[1].
(3) Since 54 is less than 75, we move 75 to location 2, thus vacating location 1.
(4) We then compare 54 with 43. Since 54 is greater than 43, we have found the position where 54 must go. Thus 54 is placed in location 1,

giving

num

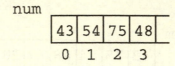

(5) Next we process num[3], 48. In processing 48, we can assume that the previous three numbers are sorted with respect to each other. All that is needed is to place 48 in its proper position with respect to these three. The following actions occur:

- 75 is moved to location 3;
- 54 is moved to location 2;
- 48 is inserted in location 2.

This gives:

num

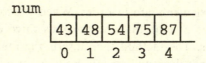

(6) Next we process num[4], 87. But since 87 is larger than all the previous elements, there is nothing to be done, so we go on to num[5], that is, 20.

(7) Again, you must remember that when we come to process num[5], we can assume that the elements in num[0] to num[4] are in order. The actions caused by processing 20 are:

- 87 is moved to location 5;
- 75 is moved to location 4;
- 54 is moved to location 3;
- 48 is moved to location 2;
- 43 is moved to location 1.

Since there is nothing left with which to compare 20, we can insert 20 in location 0, giving:

num

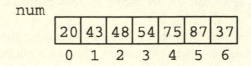

(8) Finally, the processing of 37 would cause

- 87 to be move to location 6;
- 75 to be move to location 5;
- 54 to be move to location 4;
- 48 to be move to location 3;
- 43 to be move to location 2;

Since 37 is greater than 20, 37 is inserted in location 1.

All the elements have now been processed so the array is sorted thus:

num

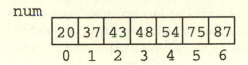

The following function will sort an integer array `table` of size `max` using an insertion sort. It is declared as `void` since it does not return a value.

```
void insertionsort(int table[], int max)
{
    int j, k, key;

    for (j = 1; j < max; j++) {
    /* process elements table[1] to table[max-1] */
        key = table[j];
        for (k = j - 1; k >= 0; k--)
            if (key < table[k])
                table[k + 1] = table[k];
            else
                break;
            /*endif*/
        /*endfor*/
        table[k + 1] = key;
    }
}
```

`key` is the current element being processed. If `key` is greater than or equal to any previous element in the array, a forced exit from the inner `for` loop occurs, since the place where `key` must be inserted has been found.

A normal exit (with k being −1) from the inner for loop occurs if key is smaller than all the previous keys; key is then placed in table[0].

### 4.5.4 Sorting the words

We will use the method of insertion sort as described above to sort the words. However, in our specific problem, the following adjustments will have to be made:

- Since the 'keys' to be sorted are now strings, we will need to use the standard function strcmp for comparing two words. Also, the function strcpy will be used to assign one string to another.
- Whenever a word is moved, its corresponding count must also be moved.

The following function uses insertion sort to arrange the words in the table in alphabetical order. It is called 'parallelsort' since the values in two separate arrays have to be moved together, or in parallel.

```
void parallelsort(char keytable[][MAXWORDLENGTH],
        int frequency[], int maxtablesize)
{
    int j, k, keycount;
    char key[MAXWORDLENGTH];

    for (j = 1; j < maxtablesize; j++) {
    /* process words, one at a time */
        strcpy(key, keytable[j]);
        keycount = frequency[j];

        /* insert the jth key in its proper position */
        for (k = j - 1; k >= 0; k--)
            if (strcmp(key, keytable[k]) < 0) {
                strcpy(keytable[k + 1], keytable[k]);
                frequency[k + 1] = frequency[k];
            }
            else
                break;
            /*endif*/
```

```
      /*endfor*/
      strcpy(keytable[k + 1], key);
      frequency[k + 1] = keycount;
   }
} /* end parallelsort */
```

### 4.5.5 Printing the table

Finally, the words (now arranged) in the table must be printed together with their frequencies. As mentioned before, the first few locations in the table will each contain the null string. These are skipped over before the printing of the actual words begins. The following function is one way of doing the job.

```
void printTable(char keytable[][MAXWORDLENGTH],
      int frequency[], int maxtablesize)
{
   int j = 0;

   while (j < maxtablesize &&
         strcmp(keytable[j], EMPTYSTRING) == 0) j++;

   if (j == maxtablesize)
      printf("\n\n***No words in table***\n");
   else {
      printf("\n\nWord%17cFrequency\n\n", ' ');
      for ( ; j < maxtablesize; j++)
      printf("%-20s %3d\n", keytable[j], frequency[j]);
   }
}
```

- The `while` loop skips over the null strings at the beginning of the table. It works even if there are no null strings or if all the locations contain null strings.
- In the `else` part, the first `printf(...)` prints a heading. Using `%17c` in conjunction with the blank character, `' '`, leaves 17 spaces between `Word` and `Frequency`. In effect, the meaning is print a space in a field width of 17.

• In the `for` loop, the initialization expression is omitted (but the semicolon must be present). On exit from the preceding `while` loop, the value of `j` is the location of the first word, if any. In effect, it is already initialized.

We now give the complete version of the program (P4.7). It comprises the finished version of `main` preceded by the required `#include` statements and the symbolic constants, as well as all the function declarations and definitions.

---

**Program P4.7**

```
#include <stdio.h>
#include <ctype.h>
#include <string.h>


#define EMPTYSTRING ""
#define INPUTEXHAUSTED 0
#define WORDFOUND 1
#define MAXTABLESIZE 109
#define MAXWORDLENGTH 20
#define MAXWORDS 100
main()    /* this is now complete */
{
    char wordtable[MAXTABLESIZE][MAXWORDLENGTH];
    int frequency[MAXTABLESIZE];
    char word[MAXWORDLENGTH];
    int loc, getword(char word[], int max);
    int searchword(char word[],
        char table[][MAXWORDLENGTH], int max);
    void newWord  (char word[],
                   char wordtable[][MAXWORDLENGTH],
                   int frequency[], int loc,
                   int maxwords);
    void parallelsort (char keytable[][MAXWORDLENGTH],
                   int frequency[], int maxtablesize);
    void printTable (char keytable[][MAXWORDLENGTH],
                   int frequency[], int maxtablesize);
```

```
    /* initialize the word table and set the
       frequency counts to 0 */
    for (loc = 0; loc < MAXTABLESIZE; loc++) {
        strcpy(wordtable[loc], EMPTYSTRING);
        frequency[loc] = 0;
    }

    while (getword(word, MAXWORDLENGTH) == WORDFOUND) {
        loc = searchword(word, wordtable, MAXTABLESIZE);
        if (strcmp(wordtable[loc], EMPTYSTRING) == 0)
                /* word is not in the table */
          newWord(word, wordtable, frequency, loc,
                  MAXWORDS);
        else    /* word is there; increase its count */
          ++frequency[loc];
    }

    parallelsort(wordtable, frequency, MAXTABLESIZE);
    printTable(wordtable, frequency, MAXTABLESIZE);
}

int getword(char word[], int maxwordsize)
    /* store the next word in word */
{
    int ch, next;

    do
        ch = getchar();
    while (!isalpha(ch) && ch != EOF);

    if (ch == EOF) return INPUTEXHAUSTED;

    /* The first letter of the word has been found */
    next = 0;
    word[next++] = ch;
    while (--maxwordsize > 0) {
        word[next++] = ch = getchar();
        if (!isalpha(ch)) break;
    }
```

```
        word[next - 1] = '\0';
        while (isalpha(ch) && ch != EOF) ch = getchar();
        return WORDFOUND;
}

int searchword(char key[],
        char keytable[][MAXWORDLENGTH], int maxtablesize)
        /* if key is found, its location is returned; if
           key is not found, the location where it may be
           inserted is returned. */
{
        int hashloc;
        int gethashloc(char key[], int max);

        hashloc = gethashloc(key, maxtablesize);
        while (strcmp(keytable[hashloc], key) != 0 &&
                strcmp(keytable[hashloc], EMPTYSTRING) != 0)
            hashloc = (hashloc + 1) % maxtablesize;
        /* endwhile */
        return hashloc;
}

int gethashloc(char word[], int maxtablesize)
        /* returns the location to which word hashes */
{
        int j = 0;
        int weight = 1;
        int wordvalue = 0;

        while (word[j] != '\0') {
            wordvalue += word[j] * weight;
            weight += 2;
            j++;
        }
        return(wordvalue % maxtablesize);
}

void newWord(char word[],
            char wordtable[][MAXWORDLENGTH],
            int frequency[], int loc, int maxwords)
```

```
    /* inserts a new word in the table, provided there
       is room */
{
    static int wordcount = 0;

    if (wordcount == maxwords) /* no more words
                                          can be stored */
        printf("%-20s cannot be stored - table "
               "full\n", word);
    else {        /* wordcount < maxwords */
        wordcount++;
        strcpy(wordtable[loc], word);
        frequency[loc] = 1;
    }
}


void parallelsort(char keytable[][MAXWORDLENGTH],
                    int frequency[], int maxtablesize)
{
    int j, k, keycount;
    char key[MAXWORDLENGTH];
    for (j = 1; j < maxtablesize; j++) {
    /* process words, one at a time */
        strcpy(key, keytable[j]);
        keycount = frequency[j];

        /* insert the jth key in its proper position */
        for (k = j - 1; k >= 0; k--)
            if (strcmp(key, keytable[k]) < 0) {
                    strcpy(keytable[k + 1], keytable[k]);
                    frequency[k + 1] = frequency[k];
            }
            else
                    break;
            /*endif*/
        /*endfor*/
        strcpy(keytable[k + 1], key);
        frequency[k + 1] = keycount;
    }
```

```
} /* end parallelsort */

void printTable(char keytable[][MAXWORDLENGTH],
                int frequency[], int maxtablesize)
{
    int j = 0;

    while (j < maxtablesize &&
           strcmp(keytable[j], EMPTYSTRING) == 0) j++;

    if (j == maxtablesize)
       printf("\n\n***No words in table***\n");
    else {
       printf("\n\nWord%17cFrequency\n\n", ' ');
       for ( ; j < maxtablesize; j++)
          printf("%-20s    %3d\n",
                 keytable[j], frequency[j]);
    }
}
```

When program P4.7 was supplied with the following input:

```
Where the mind is without fear and the head is held high;
Where knowledge is free;
   ...
Where the clear stream of reason has not lost its way
   into the dreary desert sand of dead habit;
   ...
Into that heaven of freedom, My Father,
Let my country awake.
            Rabindranath Tagore (from The Gitanjali)
```

it produced the output shown in Table 4.3.

Observe that the words which begin with uppercase letters come first in the table since, in the ASCII character set, uppercase letters come before lowercase letters.

**Table 4.3**

| Word | Frequency |
|------|-----------|
| Father | 1 |
| Gitanjali | 1 |
| Into | 1 |
| Let | 1 |
| My | 1 |
| Rabindranath | 1 |
| Tagore | 1 |
| The | 1 |
| Where | 3 |
| and | 1 |
| awake | 1 |
| clear | 1 |
| country | 1 |
| dead | 1 |
| desert | 1 |
| dreary | 1 |
| fear | 1 |
| free | 1 |
| freedom | 1 |
| from | 1 |
| habit | 1 |
| has | 1 |
| head | 1 |
| heaven | 1 |
| held | 1 |
| high | 1 |
| into | 1 |
| is | 3 |
| its | 1 |
| knowledge | 1 |
| lost | 1 |
| mind | 1 |
| my | 1 |
| not | 1 |
| of | 3 |
| reason | 1 |
| sand | 1 |
| stream | 1 |
| that | 1 |
| the | 4 |
| way | 1 |
| without | 1 |

## Exercises 4

(1)   Write a C program to read two names and print the names in alphabetical order.

(2)   Write a function which returns the next integer in the input, reading it character by character. Hint: if ch contains a digit, then ch – '0' gives the integer value of the digit.

(3)   Write a function which returns the next number in the input, reading it character by character. A number consists of an optional sign followed by a string of digits possibly including a decimal point.

(4)   Write a function length which, given a string, returns the length of the string (not counting \0).

(5)   Write a function strcmp which, given two string arguments (s1 and s2, say), returns a positive value if s1 > s2, returns 0 if s1 = s2 and returns a negative value if s1 < s2. The comparison is done character by character using the collating sequence of the underlying machine.

(6)   Write a function substr which, given two string arguments (pattern and source, say), searches source to find the first occurrence of the string in pattern. If pattern is found, the value returned is the position in source of the first character of pattern; otherwise, the value returned is 0.

(7)   Write a function delete which, given a string parameter source and two integer parameters (n and amount, say), deletes amount characters from source, starting at position n.

(8)   Write a function which gets the next input line (up to the next \n) and stores it in a character array.

(9)   Write a function which reads input lines and prints the longest.

(10)  Write a function strcpy which, given two string arguments, copies the second to the first.

(11)  Write a function which, given a string, converts all lowercase letters to uppercase, leaving the others unchanged.

(12)  Write a function which, given a string, converts all uppercase letters to lowercase, leaving the others unchanged.

(13)  Write a function which, given a string, returns TRUE if all the characters are distinct and FALSE if any character is repeated.

(14)  Write a function code which, given a string and an integer n, adds n to each character of the string.

(15)  Write a function which, given two strings, determines if one is an anagram of the other, that is, whether one string is a permutation of the characters in the other string, e.g. mate, team.

(16)  Write a function which, given a string containing roman numerals, returns the equivalent decimal integer. Return –1 if the string contains an invalid roman numeral.

(17)  Write a C program to input a syntactically correct C program and output the program followed by an alphabetic listing of all user identifiers and the number of times each identifier appears in the program.

      No reserved words (see Appendix A) or standard identifiers must be output.

Words within comments are not to be output.
Words within character strings are not to be output.
Character constants are not to be output.

(18) Each line of data consists of a student's name followed by marks (out of 100) made in three assignments. Data is terminated by the name END. Write a C program to read the data, and for each student, calculate the average mark obtained. Output your results under suitable headings. For each student, print the name, the three marks, the average and a message 'Pass' or 'Fail'. (A student passes if the average is greater than or equal to 50).

At the end, print the number of students processed, the number who passed, the number who failed and the name of the student obtaining the highest average. (Ignore the possibility of a tie).

Also determine the class average for each of the three assignments.

Modify the program to list the students in (a) alphabetical order (b) in descending order by average mark.

(19) Write a program to analyse the results of a multiple-choice examination. The examination consists of twenty questions; each question has five choices, labelled A, B, C, D and E. The first line of data contains the correct answers to the twenty questions; one or more spaces are used to separate the answers, for example

B E C D C B A A D E B A C B A E D D B E

The data on each subsequent line consists of a 4-digit candidate number followed by the twenty answers given by the candidate; the answers are separated by one or more spaces. An X is used if a candidate did not answer a particular question. The number of candidates is not known beforehand, but it is known to be less than 100. Data is terminated by a candidate number of 0.

(a) Determine the score for each candidate based on the following scoring system:

| | |
|---|---|
| correct answer | 4 points |
| wrong answer | −1 point |
| no answer | 0 points |

(b) Print a list of candidate numbers and scores in descending order by score.

# 5

# Functions and Pointers

In this chapter, we expand on our earlier discussion of functions. First, we take a closer look at how arguments are passed to C functions, in particular array arguments. We then introduce a new kind of variable – the pointer variable – and use it to explain how a C function can change the value of an argument passed to it. Put another way, we explain how 'call by reference' is achieved in C.

'A voting problem' (Section 5.3.1) is a detailed example illustrating many ideas involved in writing and using functions. Specifically, it highlights the differences between array arguments and simple variable arguments.

Following this example, several issues involving pointers are discussed. These include

- character pointers – a commonly used type of pointer;
- pointer arithmetic;
- pointers to functions.

The last section deals with recursive functions – functions which call themselves – in C. Examples discussed include Towers of Hanoi, conversion from decimal to binary and quicksort.

## 5.1 Parameter passing

Consider the program P5.1 (the 'comments' after `printf(...)` are for reference only):

---

**Program P5.1**

```
#include <stdio.h>

main()
{
    void test(int x);
    int n = 5;

    printf("%d\n", n);      /* printf1 */
    test(n);
    printf("%d\n", n);      /* printf2 */
    test(n);
}

void test(int n)
{
    n = n + 3;
    printf("%d\n", n);      /* printf3 */
{
```

---

When this program is run, it will print

```
5
8
5
8
```

Why? It is fairly obvious that printf1 prints 5. The function test is then called with n as its argument. Before control is handed over to test, the value of n (5) is stored in a temporary location, and it is this **copy of** n that is passed to test. In test, this **copy of** n is incremented by 3 and printf3 prints the value 8. (Note that n in main is unaffected). When test is finished and is about to return to main, the storage occupied by the **copy of** n is released. Back in main, printf2 prints the value of n, which is **still** 5. The call to test has had no effect on the value of n in main. The next call to test is simply a repeat of the first call. It is worth noting that the storage location allocated to the **copy of** n on the second call is not necessarily the same as that allocated on the first call.

All of this can be summarized by saying that, in C, arguments to functions are passed 'by value'. One implication of this is that a function cannot normally affect the value of an actual argument passed to it (but see Section 5.2).

It should be noted that it would make absolutely no difference (in terms of execution) if test were defined as follows:

```
void test(int a)
{
    a = a + 3;
    printf("%d\n", a);    /* printf3 */
}
```

Here we have replaced the 'formal parameter' n by a. Now when test is called, the copy of the actual argument will be known as a and execution is exactly the same as before. A formal parameter in the **definition** of a function is usually referred to as a 'dummy parameter' or 'dummy argument' since the **name** given to the argument is immaterial, as well as the fact that no storage is associated with it until the function is called.

The reason a function cannot normally affect the value of an actual argument is due to the fact that the **address** of the actual argument is **not** passed to the function. Rather, a temporary address (containing the **value** of the actual argument) is what is passed. The function can change the value in this temporary location but not the value in the original location.

Using the example above, suppose n in main is stored in memory location 375. When test is called, the value of n (5) is stored in a temporary location (2745, say), and location 2745 is passed to test. {Actually, the 'temporary location' is a location at the top of a stack, but the principle is the same.} In test, reference to the formal parameter a is to this location. The function test can do whatever it wants to location 2745 (i. e., a) but there is no way it can affect location 375 since it has no access to it. When test is finished, location 2745 is released and no longer exists (as far as test is concerned).

However, when the actual argument is an **array name**, something quite different occurs. To illustrate, consider the program P5.2.

**Program P5.2**

```
#include <stdio.h>

main()
{
    void test(int val[], int max);
    int j, num[5];

    for (j = 0; j < 5; j++) num[j] = j;
    test(num, 5);
    for (j = 0; j < 5; j++) printf("%d ", num[j]);
}


void test(int val[], int max)
/* add 25 to each of val[0] to val[max - 1] */
{
    int j;

    for (j = 0; j < max; j++) val[j] += 25;
}
```

In main, the first for loop sets the elements of num to 0, 1, 2, 3 and 4, respectively. test is then called, and the formal array argument val matches with the actual array argument num. In test, 25 is added to each element of val. On return from test, the values in the array num are printed, giving:

$$25 \quad 26 \quad 27 \quad 28 \quad 29$$

Clearly, the function test has managed to change the values in num. This happened because, in C, when an **array name** is used as an actual argument in a function call, the **address of its first element** is passed to the function. (In other words, the **value** of an **array name** is the **address** of its first element, and it is a **copy of** this value that is passed to the function.) Thus the function has access to the original array. In the example, when the call

```
test(num, 5);
```

is made, the **address** of num[0] is passed to the function to match with the formal parameter val. Herein also lies the reason why, in the function, it is not necessary to specify the size of val in its declaration; we simply use

```
int val[];   /* the square brackets indicate it's
                an array */
```

When the function is called, the address passed is taken to be the address of val[0]. The function is free to assume any size it wishes for val. Obviously, this can land us in trouble if we attempt to process array elements which do not exist. Hence the reason for the second argument which tells us how many elements to process. As a matter of interest, one may wonder if we could have used the declaration

```
int val[max];
```

in the function test. Unfortunately, the answer is **no**. In C, the size of an array dimension, if specified, must be a constant expression – something which can be evaluated at compile time. Constants (e.g. 25) or symbolic constants (e.g. MAXWORDS) are commonly used.

As another example, suppose the call in main had been:

```
test(num, 3);
```

As before, the **address** of num[0] is passed to the function and becomes the address of val[0]. However, now the function adds 25 to the elements val[0], val[1] and val[2] only, since max is now 3. On return to main, the following values will be printed:

```
25    26    27    3    4
```

The function has affected the values in the actual argument num. In programming terminology, we say that arrays in C are 'passed by reference'.

From the preceding discussion, one may conclude that a function can affect the value of an actual argument if the **address** of the actual argument (as opposed to its **value**) is passed to the function. C provides facilities for taking the address of a variable and manipulating it in various ways.

## 5.2 Pointer variables

A pointer variable is a variable whose value can be a storage address. Suppose n is an integer variable allocated storage starting at memory location 375. The unary operator & gives the **address** of its operand. Thus &n refers to the address of n, that is, 375. This value can be assigned to a pointer variable, ptr, say, as in:

```
ptr = &n;
```

This statement stores the **address of** n (whatever it may be) in ptr. We say that ptr 'points to' n.

But how do we declare ptr to be a pointer variable? First, we make the observation that, in C, a given pointer variable can 'point to' values of **one type** only (but see void pointers below). The declaration of the pointer variable specifies the type. For example,

```
int *ptr;
```

can be read 'integer pointer ptr' and declares ptr to be a pointer variable which can 'point to' integer values only. (Of course, since ptr can assume only one value at a time, it can point to only one integer at any given time). Suppose the **address** of n is 375 and the **value** of n is 17. The statement

```
ptr = &n;
```

assigns the value 375 to ptr and *ptr refers to 'the value pointed at by ptr' (in effect, the value of n), and can be used in any context that an integer can. For example, if m is integer, then

```
m = *ptr + 7;
```

assigns the value 24 $(17+7)$ to m.

It is sometimes helpful to think of * and & as cancelling out each other. For instance, if ptr = &n, then

```
*ptr ≡ *(&n) ≡ n
```

An interesting assignment is

```
n = *ptr + 1
```

This is exactly equivalent to

```
n = n + 1
```

It could even be written as

```
(*ptr)++
```

This says increment whatever `ptr` is pointing at. The brackets around `*ptr` are necessary since ++ has higher precedence than `*`. Without the brackets `*ptr++` means 'increment the value of `ptr`, then take the value now pointed to by `ptr`'. To increment n by a value other than 1 (5, say) one could write

```
(*ptr) += 5
```

`ptr` is just like any other variable and we can change its value if necessary. For example,

```
ptr = &m
```

assigns the **address** of m to `ptr`. Now `ptr` points to the value of m rather than n.

### Void *pointers*

ANSI C allows the declaration and use of 'void' (also called 'generic') pointers – pointers which may point to any type of object. For example,

```
void * pv;
```

declares `pv` as a void pointer, and

```
void *memory(unsigned int size);
```

declares `memory` as a function which returns a `void` pointer.

A void pointer can be assigned to any other type of pointer as in:

```
ptr = pv;                /* assume int *ptr */
```

The reverse is also valid, thus:

```
pv = ptr;
```

However, even though pv and ptr have the same pointer value after the above assignment, it is invalid to think of *pv as an integer. In other words, we should not attempt to de-reference a void pointer.

Void pointers are useful for writing general-purpose functions where you don't want to restrict a function to returning a specific type of pointer. Also, declaring a function parameter as a void pointer allows the **actual** argument to be any type of pointer.

We now illustrate how pointers can be used to implement 'call by reference' in C. Consider, again, the program (P5.1) discussed at the beginning of Section 5.1. Here it is again for easy reference (using formal parameter a in test).

---

**Program P5.1**

```
#include <stdio.h>

main()
{
    void test(int x);
    int n = 5;

    printf("%d\n", n);      /* printf1 */
    test(n);
    printf("%d\n", n);      /* printf2 */
    test(n);
}

void test(int a)
{
    a = a + 3;
    printf("%d\n", a);      /* printf3 */
}
```

---

As written, there is no way for test to change the value of n (declared in main). Suppose, though, we wanted test to increment the original actual argument, n, by 3. The only way this can happen is if the **address of** n is passed to test. This can be accomplished by calling test with

```
test(&n);
```

But now, since the actual argument is a pointer, we must change the definition of the formal parameter in test so that it is also a pointer. Program P5.3 incorporates all the changes.

---

**Program P5.3**

```
#include <stdio.h>

main()
{
    void test(int *x);
    int n = 5;

    printf("%d\n", n);      /* printf1 */
    test(&n);
    printf("%d\n", n);      /* printf2 */
    test(&n);
}

void test(int *a)
{
    *a = *a + 3;
    printf("%d\n", *a);     /* printf3 */
}
```

---

The formal parameter a is now declared as a 'pointer to integer'. (This means, of course, that the actual argument must also be a 'pointer to integer'). The integer value 'pointed at' is denoted by *a. Now when test is called, the **address** of n (375, say) is passed to it. test, therefore, has access to whatever value is stored at this address, and may change it if desired. When the above program is run, it will print:

```
5          (printf1)
8          (printf3)
8          (printf2)
11         (printf3)
```

It should now be clear why it is necessary to put the ampersand (&) in front of variables when we use the standard input function `scanf(...)` to read data. The only way `scanf(...)` can put a value into an actual argument is if its address is passed to it. For example, in the statement

```
scanf("%d", &n);
```

the address of n is passed to `scanf`; this enables the function to store the value read in the location occupied by n.

## 5.3 More on parameter passing

In Section 5.1 it was explained that when an array name is used as an actual argument, the address of its first element is passed to the function. Recalling our example (program P5.2):

```
#include <stdio.h>

main()
{
    void test(int val[], int max);
    int j, num[5];

    for (j = 0; j < 5; j++) num[j] = j;
    test(num, 5);
    for (j = 0; j < 5; j++) printf("%d ", num[j]);
}

void test(int val[], int max) /* add 25 to each of val[0]
                                  to val[max − 1] */
{
    int j;

    for (j = 0; j < max; j++) val[j] += 25;
}
```

it should be noted that the call:

```
test(num, 5);
```

could be replaced by

```
test(&num[0], 5);
```

since, in both cases, the address of the first element of num is passed to the function. In other words, an array name is a pointer – the address of the first element of the array. An interesting variation is the call

```
test(&num[2], 3);
```

Here, the address of element num[2] is passed to test. As far as it is concerned, test matches the address given with val[0]. The net effect is that

        val[0] matches with num[2];
        val[1] matches with num[3];
        val[2] matches with num[4];

These elements are incremented by 25 so that the program prints

    0    1    27    28    29

In case you are wondering, it would be invalid to attempt something like

```
test(&num[2], 5);
```

since this implies that, starting at num[2], there are at least five elements in the array, and, in our case, there are only three. What would happen is that, in the function, val[3] and val[4] would be associated with the locations in memory immediately following num[4]. The contents of these locations would be altered with unpredictable consequences.

### 5.3.1 A voting problem

This example will be used to illustrate several points concerning the passing of arguments to functions. It further highlights the differences between array arguments and simple variable arguments and illustrates how a function can change the value of an actual argument passed to it.

*Problem*: In a certain election, there are seven candidates. Each voter is allowed one vote for the candidate of his/her choice. The vote is recorded as a number from 1 to 7. The number of voters is unknown beforehand but the votes are terminated by a vote of 0. Any vote which is not a number from 1 to 7 is an invalid (spoilt) vote.

Write a C program to

(a) Read the names of the 7 candidates and store them in an array.
(b) Read the votes (one at a time) and evaluate the results of the election.

Your output should specify the total number of votes, the number of valid votes, the number of spoilt votes and the winner(s) of the election.

The solution is based on the following outline:

```
initialize
process the votes
print the results
```

A two-dimensional character array `candidate` will be used to hold the names of the seven candidates and an integer array `votecount` will be used to hold the number of votes obtained by each candidate. Integer variables `goodvotes` and `spoiltvotes` are used to count the number of valid and invalid votes, respectively. The above outline can be refined as follows:

```
initialize
    for each candidate,
        get the name
        set his score to 0
    endfor
```

process the votes
        get a vote
        while the vote is not 0
            if the vote is valid
                add 1 to goodvotes
                add 1 to the score of the appropriate candidate
            else
                add 1 to spoiltvotes
            endif
            get a vote
        endwhile
printresults
        print the number of voters, valid votes and spoilt votes
        print the score of each candidate
        determine and print the winner(s)

The following is the function `main`. We have illustrated the writing of function prototypes without using identifiers in the parameter list – only the type is specified. This is usually referred to as an 'abstract declarator'. For example, the prototype for `initialize` says that this function takes three arguments – the first is a two-dimensional array whose second dimension must be of size `NAMELENGTH`, the second is an array of integers and the third is an integer.

```
#include <stdio.h>

#define MAXCANDIDATES 7
#define NAMELENGTH 20

main()
{
    void initialize(char [][NAMELENGTH], int [], int);
    void processvotes(int [], int, int *, int *);
    void printresults(char [][NAMELENGTH], int [], int,
                      int, int);

    char candidate[MAXCANDIDATES][NAMELENGTH];
    int votecount[MAXCANDIDATES], goodvotes, spoiltvotes;
    goodvotes = spoiltvotes = 0;
```

```
initialize(candidate, votecount, MAXCANDIDATES);
processvotes(votecount, MAXCANDIDATES, &goodvotes,
             &spoiltvotes);
printresults(candidate, votecount, MAXCANDIDATES,
             goodvotes, spoiltvotes);
}
```

The program assumes that the data consists of the names of the seven candidates followed by the votes, terminated by 0, for example,

Victor Denise Gary Michael Debra Carol Kenneth
3 1 2 5 4 3 5 3 5 3 2 8 6 7 7 3 5 6 9 3 4 7 2 4 5 5 1 0

`initialize` will read the names and set the vote counters to 0. This means that `initialize` must put values in the array arguments passed to it. Since, in C, arrays are passed by reference, nothing special needs to be done for these arguments.

`processvotes` will read the votes, one at a time, until a vote of 0 is read. If the vote is valid, `goodvotes` is incremented by 1 and if the vote is invalid, `spoiltvotes` is incremented by 1. For each valid vote, the appropriate element of `votecount` is incremented by 1. Note that if the vote is v, then element `votecount[v - 1]` is incremented. Thus `processvotes` must also change the values of the arguments passed to it. In the case of the array argument `votecount`, this can be passed in the normal way since it is passed 'by reference'. (Arrays in C are **always** passed by reference). However, in the case of the 'simple' variables `goodvotes` and `spoiltvotes`, their addresses must be passed, hence the reason for `&goodvotes` and `&spoiltvotes`. Of course, in the definition of `processvotes`, the corresponding parameters must be declared as pointers.

`printresults` will print the results of the election, indicating the total number of voters, the number of valid and invalid votes, the individual score for each candidate and the winner(s) of the election. It will call the function `findlargest` to determine the location in `votecount` which contains the highest score.

We now write these functions starting with `initialize`.

```
void initialize(char name[][NAMELENGTH], int score[],
                int max)
{
    int n;

    for (n = 0; n < max; n++) {
        score[n] = 0;
        scanf("%s", name[n]);
    }
} /* end initialize */
```

Note that using `scanf` with the `%s` specification to read a name implies that the name may not contain a blank. This is because `scanf` will read characters up to the next white space character (blank, tab or newline) to construct the string. Even if a field width is specified (e.g. `%20s`), a blank still may not be included in the name since now `scanf` will read characters until the next white space character or until the field width is exhausted, **whichever comes first**. If it is required to read names containing blanks, you will have to write a function (`getname`, say) which gets characters until some agreed-upon character (indicating the end of the name) is read. For example, `getname` can assume that the newline character (\n) terminates a name. (The standard function `gets` – get a string, see Section 9.4.2 – may also be used).

Next comes `processvotes`. Note the declaration of the formal parameters `goodptr` and `spoiltptr`. The actual arguments corresponding to these will be addresses of integer variables. Therefore these are declared to be 'pointers to integers'.

```
void processvotes(int score[], int max, int *goodptr,
                  int *spoiltptr)
{
    int vote;

    if (scanf("%d", &vote) != 1) vote = 0;
    /* if scanf does not assign a value to vote,
       set it to 0 */
    while (vote != 0) {
        if (vote >= 1 && vote <= max) {
            (*goodptr)++;
            score[vote - 1]++;
        }
```

```
      else {
          printf(" invalid vote - %d\n", vote);
          (*spoiltptr)++;
      }
      if (scanf("%d", &vote) != 1) vote = 0;
   }
} /* end processvotes */
```

Next, we write `printresults`. The output specification `%-20s` in `printf` means to print a string left justified in a field width of 20. The '–' before the field width indicates left justification. The function `findlargest` returns the location of the largest element in the array passed to it. The value in this location is the highest score. In order to cater for a possible tie among two or more candidates, a pass is made through the array and each candidate with the highest score is declared as the joint winner.

```
void printresults(char name[][NAMELENGTH], int score[],
                  int max, int valid, int invalid)
{
    int n, win, highestscore;
    int findlargest(int score[], int max);

    printf("\nNumber of voters = %d\n", valid + invalid);
    printf("\nNumber of valid votes = %d\n", valid);
    printf("\nNumber of invalid votes = %d\n", invalid);

    printf("\nThe individual scores are: \n\n");
    for (n = 0; n < max; n++)
        printf("\t%-20s %d\n", name[n], score[n]);

    win = findlargest(score, max);
    highestscore = score[win];
    printf("\nThe winner(s): \n\n");
    for (n = 0; n < max; n++)
        if (score[n] == highestscore)
            printf("\t%s\n", name[n]);

    printf("\nEnd of election results\n");
} /* printresults */
```

Finally, here is `findlargest`. First, it assumes that element 0 contains the largest value (`bigloc = 0`). It then makes a pass through the rest of the array and if any element if bigger, it is kept as the largest one so far. At the end, `bigloc` contains the location of the largest element.

```c
int findlargest(int score[], int max)
{
    int n, bigloc;

    bigloc = 0;
    for (n = 1; n < max; n++)
        if (score[n] > score[bigloc]) bigloc = n;
    return bigloc;
{ /* end findlargest */
```

The complete listing is shown as program P5.4.

---

**Program P5.4**

```c
#include <stdio.h>

#define MAXCANDIDATES 7
#define NAMELENGTH 20

main()
{
    void initialize(char [][NAMELENGTH], int [], int);
    void processvotes(int [], int, int *, int *);
    void printresults(char [][NAMELENGTH],
                      int [], int, int, int);

    char candidate[MAXCANDIDATES][NAMELENGTH];
    int votecount[MAXCANDIDATES], goodvotes, spoiltvotes;

    goodvotes = spoiltvotes = 0;
    initialize(candidate, votecount, MAXCANDIDATES);
    processvotes(votecount, MAXCANDIDATES, &goodvotes,
                 &spoiltvotes);
```

```
    printresults(candidate, votecount, MAXCANDIDATES,
                goodvotes, spoiltvotes);
}


void initialize(char name[][NAMELENGTH],
                int score[], int max)
{
    int n;

    for (n = 0; n < max; n++) {
        score[n] = 0;
        scanf("%s", name[n]);
    }
{ /* end initialize */


void processvotes(int score[], int max,
                int *goodptr, int *spoiltptr)
{
    int vote;

    if (scanf("%d", &vote) != 1) vote = 0;
            /* if scanf does not assign a value to vote,
                set it to 0 */
    while (vote != 0) {
        if (vote >= 1 && vote <= max) {
            (*goodptr)++;
            score[vote - 1]++;
        }
        else {
            printf(" invalid vote - %d\n", vote);
            (*spoiltptr)++;
        }
        if (scanf("%d", &vote) != 1) vote = 0;
    }
} /* end processvotes */

int findlargest(int score[], int max)
{
    int n, bigloc;
```

```
        bigloc = 0;
        for (n = 1; n < max; n++)
            if (score[n] > score[bigloc]) bigloc = n;
        return bigloc;
    } /* end findlargest */

    void printresults(char name[][NAMELENGTH],
                      int score[], int max, int valid,
                      int invalid)
    {
        int n, win, highestscore;
        int findlargest(int score[], int max);

        printf("\nNumber of voters = %d\n", valid + invalid);
        printf("\nNumber of valid votes = %d\n", valid);
        printf("\nNumber of invalid votes = %d\n", invalid);

        printf("\nThe individual scores are: \n\n");
        for (n = 0; n < max; n++)
            printf("\t%-20s %d\n", name[n], score[n]);

        win = findlargest(score, max);
        highestscore = score[win];
        printf("\nThe winner(s): \n\n");
        for (n = 0; n < max; n++)
            if (score[n] == highestscore)
                printf("\t%s\n", name[n]);

        printf("\nEnd of election results\n");
    } /* printresults */
```

When the program is run and the following data is supplied:

    Victor Denise Gary Michael Debra Carol Kenneth
    3 1 2 5 4 3 5 3 5 3 2 8 6 7 7 3 5 6 9 3 4 7 2 4 5 5 1 0

the output produced is

```
    invalid vote - 8
    invalid vote - 9
```

```
Number of voters = 27

Number of valid votes = 25

Number of invalid votes = 2

The individual scores are:

          Victor        2
          Denise        3
          Gary          6
          Michael       3
          Debra         6
          Carol         2
          Kenneth       3

The winner(s):

          Gary
          Debra

End of election results
```

## 5.4 Character pointers

Suppose `word` is declared as an array of characters:

```
char word[20];
```

We have emphasized that the array name `word` is a synonym for the address of its first element, `word[0]`. Thus

```
word ≡ &word[0]
```

In effect, `word` 'points to' the first character of the array and is, in fact, a pointer – a character pointer, to be more precise. However, `word` is not a pointer variable but, rather, a pointer constant – we can't change its value, which is the address of `word[0]`.

Whenever a string constant appears in a program, the characters (terminated by \0) are stored somewhere in memory and the address of the first character is used in place of the string. For example, in

```
printf("Enter a number:");
```

what is actually passed to `printf` is a character pointer whose value is the address of the first character of the string

```
"Enter a number:"
```

stored somewhere in memory.

Consider the declaration:

```
char *errormessage;
```

It is permitted to write

```
errormessage = "Cannot divide by 0\n";
```

The effect is that the characters of the string (properly terminated by \0) are stored somewhere in memory and the address of the first character is assigned to `errormessage`. This can be used as in:

```
printf("%s", errormessage);
```

or, simply

```
printf(errormessage);
```

Note that **errormessage** is a pointer variable whose value can be changed, if desired. For example,

```
errormessage = "Negative argument to square root\n";
```

sets `errormessage` to point to the new string. Of course, the string previously pointed at by `errormessage` now becomes inaccessible. If we wanted to save the old value of `errormessage`, we could have done something like

```
oldmessage = errormessage;
```

assuming that oldmessage is also a character pointer. It is important to observe that this assignment simply stores the (pointer) value of errormessage in oldmessage. No characters are copied. For example, suppose

```
"Cannot divide by 0\n"
```

was stored starting at address location 500. After the assignment (above), the value of oldmessage is 500 and, hence, points to the string. There is nothing wrong or invalid in having several variables 'point to' the same location. It is exactly the same as, for instance, several integer variables having the same value.

### 5.5 Pointer arithmetic

We saw above that a pointer variable could be assigned to another pointer variable. C also permits us to increment and decrement pointer variables but these operations have special meanings when they relate to pointers.

Consider

```
verse = "The road is long";
```

where verse is declared as

```
char *verse;
```

The string "The road is long" is stored somewhere in memory and verse is assigned the address of the first character ('T'). In addition,

verse + 1   is the address of 'h';
verse + 2   is the address of 'e';
verse + 3   is the address of ' ';
etc.

If required, we could change the value of verse with constructions such as

```
    verse++;
or  verse += j;
```

As an example, the following will print the characters of the string pointed

*Functions and Pointers*

at by verse, one per line:

```
while (*verse != '\0')
    printf("%c\n", *verse++);
```

*verse refers to the character currently pointed at by verse. After this character has been printed, verse is incremented to point to the next character.

The above discussion relates to character pointers. But suppose ptr is a pointer to integers, say. What is the meaning of

ptr + 1 or ptr + k?

To illustrate the ideas involved, consider an integer array num declared as

```
int num[5];
```

We know by now that the name num refers to the address of num[0]. What is new is that

num + 1   is the address of num[1];
num + 2   is the address of num[2];
num + 3   is the address of num[3];
num + 4   is the address of num[4];

This holds regardless of how many storage locations are occupied by an integer. For example, suppose an integer occupies 4 bytes and the address of num[0] is 750. Thus the value of the array name num is 750, and the value of, say, num + 1 (pointer arithmetic) is the address of num[1], that is, 750 + 4 = 754. Similarly,

the value of num + 2 is 758;
the value of num + 3 is 762;
the value of num + 4 is 766;

In general, suppose a pointer, p, is declared to point at a type of value which occupies k locations of storage. Incrementing p by 1 has the effect of adding k to the current value of p so that p now points to the next item of the type that p is declared to point at. Thus, using pointer arithmetic, 'adding 1' means getting the address of the next item (no matter how

many locations away) and 'adding j' means getting the address of the jth
item beyond the current one. Thus p + j is the address of the jth element
beyond the one pointed to by p.

Since, for example,

num + 2 is the address of num[2], i.e., &num[2],

it follows that

*(num + 2) is equivalent to *(&num[2]), that is, num[2].

(Think of * and & as cancelling each other).

The following prints the values in the array num, one per line:

```
for (j = 0 ; j < 5; j++)
    printf("%d\n", *(num + j));
```

*(num + j) could be replaced by num[j] and the effect would be exactly
the same.

One might wonder, in this example, about the meaning of num + 5, say.
Theoretically, this is the address of element num[5], but this element
does not exist. However, it is not invalid to attempt to use num + 5. But
if, for instance, we attempt to print *(num + 5), we will print whatever
happens to be stored in memory at the address designated by num + 5,
or worse, get a memory access or address error. In either case, the moral
is that you must not attempt to refer to array elements you have not
declared.

We will illustrate the intimate relationship between arrays and pointers
by writing two versions of a function, length, which finds the length of
a string.

Suppose word is declared as

```
char word[MAXLENGTH];   /* MAXLENGTH is a symbolic
                            constant */
```

then in order to find the length of a string stored in word, one can use
the function call

```
length(word);
```

length assumes that word consists of characters terminated by \0. The value returned is the number of characters excluding \0. Since what is passed to the function is the address of the first character (i.e., &word[0]), the function can be written with the formal parameter declared either as an array or as a pointer. Which version is used has no effect on how the function is called. First we write the array version.

```
int length(char string[])
{
    int n = 0;

    while (string[n] != '\0')
        n++;
    return n;
}
```

Now we write the pointer version:

```
int length(char *strptr)   /* string pointer */
{
    int n = 0;

    while (*strptr != '\0') {
        n++;
        strptr++;
    }
    return n;
}
```

We could even increment strptr as part of the while test, giving:

```
int length(char *strptr)   /* string pointer */
{
    int n = 0;

    while (*strptr++ != '\0')
        n++;
    return n;
}
```

Which version is better? It depends on your point of view. Whereas the array version is more readable, the pointer version is more efficient. In the array version, it is clear that at each step we are looking at the nth element of the string. This is not so obvious in the pointer version. However, evaluating `string[n]` requires evaluation of the subscript n which is then converted into the address of element n. The pointer version deals with the address directly.

We have mentioned before that an array name is a constant and, hence, it's value can't be changed. There may appear to be a conflict in that the function, when passed the array name, increments it (`strptr++`) to move on to the next character. But remember that the formal parameter in the function definition **is** a variable. When the function is called with `length(word)`, say, the value of `word` (the address of the first character) is copied to a temporary location and this location is passed to the function, where it is known as `strptr`. The effect is that `strptr` is simply initialized to the value of `word`. Incrementing `strptr` in the function has no effect on the value of `word` in the calling function.

## 5.6 Pointers to functions

In the same way that an array name is the address of its first element, so too a function name is the address of the function. To put it another way, a function name is a **pointer** to the function in much the same way that an array name is a pointer to the array. In C, a pointer to a function can be manipulated in much the same way as other pointers; in particular, it can be passed to functions. This is especially handy for writing general-purpose routines.

As an example, consider the problem of producing two-column tables such as tables of squares, reciprocals, square roots, weight conversions, temperature conversions, etc. In each table, the first column consists of an ascending sequence of integers and the second has the associated values. We could write separate functions for each type of table we want to produce. But we could also write **one** function (called `maketable`, say) which produces the various tables. Which specific table is produced depends on which function is passed to `maketable`. How do we specify a function as a parameter? Consider the function definition:

```
void maketable(int first, int last, float (*f) (int))
   {
       int j;
       for (j = first; j <= last; j++)
           printf("%d %f\n", j, (*f)(j));
   }
```

The heading says that maketable takes three arguments – the first two are integers and the third, f, is a pointer to a function which takes an int argument and returns a float value. The brackets around *f in

```
float (*f)(int)
```

are necessary. If they are omitted,

```
float *f(int)
```

would mean that f is a function returning a pointer to a float, which is quite different from what is intended.

In the printf statement, the function call (*f)(j) is interpreted as follows:

- f is a pointer to a function; *f is the function.
- j is the actual argument to the function call; the brackets around j are the usual brackets around a function's argument(s).
- the value returned by the call should be a float which would match the %f specification.
- The brackets around *f are necessary since () has higher precedence than *. Without them, *f(j) would be equivalent to *(f(j)) which is meaningless in this context.

But how do we use this function to produce a table of reciprocals, say? Suppose we wanted to produce the table from 1 to 10. We would like to use a statement such as:

```
maketable(1, 10, reciprocal);
```

to get the required table, where reciprocal is a function which takes an integer and returns a float value – the reciprocal of the integer. It could be written as:

```
float reciprocal(int x)
   {
       return(1.0/x);
   }
```

Note that in the call

```
maketable(1, 10, reciprocal);
```

reciprocal is a pointer to a function, so it matches the third formal parameter of maketable. All the pieces are put together in one complete program P5.5.

---

**Program P5.5**

```
#include <stdio.h>

main()
{
    void maketable(int, int, float (*f) (int));
    float reciprocal(int);

    maketable(1, 10, reciprocal);
}

void maketable(int first, int last, float (*f) (int))
{
    int j;

    for (j = first; j <= last; j++)
        printf("%d %f\n", j, (*f)(j));
}

float reciprocal(int x)
{
    return(1.0/x);
}
```

---

To create a table of squares, all we need are

the function prototype:

```
float square(int);
```

the function call:

```
maketable(1, 10, square);
```

and the function definition:

```
float square(int x)
}
    return (x * x);
}
```

As another example, consider the problem of evaluating the definite integral

$$\int_a^b f(x)\,dx$$

using the Trapezoidal Rule with *n* strips. The rule states that an approximation to the above integral is given by

$$h\{(f(a)+f(b))/2+f(a+h)+f(a+2h)+\ldots+f(a+(n-1)h)\}$$

where $h=(b-a)/n$.

We would like to write a general function integral which, given a, b, n and a function, f, returns the value of the integral. To evaluate the integrals of different functions, we would need only to pass the appropriate function to integral. Consider the following version of integral:

```
float integral(float a, float b, int n, float (*f) (float))
{
    float h, sum;
    int j;

    h = (b - a)/n;
    sum = ((*f)(a) + (*f)(b))/2.0;
    for (j = 1; j < n ; j++)
        sum += (*f)(a + j * h);
    return (h*sum);
}
```

The declaration

```
float (*f) (float)
```

says that f is a pointer to a function which takes a float argument and returns a float value. *f denotes the function and (*f)(a) is a call to the function with argument a.

To illustrate how integral can be used, suppose we wanted to find an approximation to

$$\int_0^2 (x^2 + 5x + 3)\, dx$$

using 20 strips.

We would need to write a function such as **quadratic**, thus:

```
float quadratic(float x)
{
    return (x * x + 5.0 * x + 3.0);
}
```

and the call

```
integral(0, 2, 20, quadratic)
```

would return the value of the integral.

## 5.7 Near, far and huge pointers

Though not part of the ANSI C Standard, some compilers (such as those written for machines with an Intel 8086 or 80x86 processor) allow the use of the type modifiers near, far and huge with pointer variables, for example:

```
int near *p1;
char far *p2;
```

near forces a pointer variable to use 16 bits rather than 32 bits.
far forces a pointer variable to use 32 bits rather than 16 bits.

huge forces a pointer variable to use 32 bits rather than 16 bits. It also allows the object pointed at to be bigger than 64K.

For details, you need to consult your specific compiler manual.

## 5.8 Recursion

In C, it is possible for a function to call itself, either directly or indirectly. In the direct case, the body of a function f contains a call to f. In the indirect case, a function f may call g which may call h which, in turn, calls f. The classic example of a recursively defined function is *n* factorial (*n*!) which is defined as

$$0! = 1,$$
$$n! = n(n-1)!, \ n > 0$$

or, using programming notation,

```
fact(0) = 1,
fact(n) = n * fact(n - 1), n > 0
```

A recursive definition consists of two parts – the end or terminating case (also called the **anchor** or **base**) and the recursive (or general) case. The end case usually gives a value for a specific argument; this allows the recursion to terminate eventually. For example,

```
fact(3) = 3*fact(2) = 3*2*fact(1)
        = 3*2*1*fact(0) = 3*2*1*1 = 6
```

where the definition of fact(0) is used to terminate the recursion.

A non-mathematical example of a recursive definition is that of **ancestor**.

> *a* is an ancestor of *b* if
> (1) *a* is the parent of *b*, or
> (2) *a* is an ancestor of *c* and *c* is a parent of *b*.

The following is the recursive version of factorial. Observe that within the body of the function there is a call to factorial.

```
int factorial(int n)
{
    if (n < 0) return 0;
    if (n == 0) return 1;
    return (n * factorial(n - 1));
}
```

In Section 3.1 we wrote the iterative version of factorial. Comparing the two, we see that the recursive version seems more natural and straightforward. It is also more readable. However, the iterative version will execute faster and use less space. The reason is that, for each recursive call, the arguments and local variables of the current call must be saved (on a stack). So, for example, the call factorial(10) will generate 10 recursive calls to factorial. When a call is completed and the function is about to return, arguments and local variables must be unstacked to restore the state of the previous call. All this stacking and unstacking takes time and occupies storage. One usually has to make a choice between a simple, compact and natural recursive function and a non-recursive one which runs faster and uses less space, but which is less readable and more difficult to develop. Using recursion is also appropriate when the data structure to be manipulated is defined recursively. Such a structure is the versatile **binary tree** which is discussed in Section 8.1.

### 5.8.1 An example – Towers of Hanoi

Another classic from the world of recursion is the 'Towers of Hanoi' puzzle. Legend has it that, when the world was created, some high priests in the Temple of Bramah were given three golden pins. On one of the pins were placed 64 golden disks. The disks were all of different sizes with the largest at the bottom and the smallest on the top, and no disk was placed on top of a smaller one. They were required to move the 64 disks from the given pin to another one according to the following rules:

- move one disk at a time; only a disk on top of a pin can be moved, and it must be moved to the top of another pin.
- no disk must be placed on top of a smaller one.

When all 64 disks have been transferred, the world will come to an end.

This is an example of a problem which can be solved quite easily by recursion but for which a non-recursive solution is quite difficult. Let us denote the pins by *A*, *B* and *C* with the disks originally placed on *A* and the destination pin being *C*.

Suppose there is one disk. This can be move directly from *A* to *C*. Next suppose there are three disks on *A*. Suppose we can transfer the top two from *A* to *B* using *C*. We can then move the third disk from *A* to *C*. It remains only to transfer the two disks from *B* to *C* using *A*. We have thus reduced the problem to transferring two disks from one pin to another. This, in turn, can be reduced to moving one disk from one pin to another; this we know how to do. The recursive solution for *n* disks is:

- transfer $n-1$ disks from *A* to *B* using *C*;
- move *n*th disk from *A* to *C*;
- transfer *n*–1 disks from *B* to *C* using *A*.

Of course, we can use this same solution for transferring the $n-1$ disks.

The following function transfers n disks from `startpin` to `endpin` using `workpin`.

```
void transfer(int n, char startpin,
                char endpin, char workpin)
{
    if (n > 0) {
        transfer(n-1, startpin, workpin, endpin);
        printf("Move disk from %c to %c\n",
            startpin, endpin);
        transfer(n-1, workpin, endpin, startpin);
    }
}
```

When called with the statement:

```
transfer(3,'A','B','C');
/* transfer 3 disks from A to B using C */
```

the function prints:

```
Move disk from A to B
Move disk from A to C
Move disk from B to C
Move disk from A to B
Move disk from C to A
Move disk from C to B
Move disk from A to B
```

### 5.8.2 An example – decimal to binary

Consider the problem of finding the binary equivalent of a positive decimal integer. The usual way is to perform successive divisions by 2 and save the remainder each time. The remainders, **in reverse order**, give the binary equivalent. This problem can be solved by storing the remainders in an array and then printing the array in reverse order. It can also be solved by recursion, as follows:

To print the binary equivalent of $n$, print the binary equivalent of $n/2$ (integer division) and then print $n$ % 2 (remainder).

The C function to implement this is:

```c
void binary(int n)
{
    if (n > 0) {
        binary(n / 2);
        printf("%d", n % 2);
    }
}
```

### 5.8.3 An example – quicksort

Quicksort is a method which sorts an array of items using a recursive technique. To illustrate the method, consider the integer array num

| 53 | 12 | 98 | 63 | 18 | 72 | 80 | 46 | 32 | 21 |
|----|----|----|----|----|----|----|----|----|----|
| 0  | 1  | 2  | 3  | 4  | 5  | 6  | 7  | 8  | 9  |

We attempt to 'partition' the elements with respect to the first element, 53. (This element is usually referred to as the **pivot**). This means that we try to put 53 in such a position that all elements to its left are smaller and all elements to its right are greater. If this is done, it must be that 53 is in its final position in the sorted order. For example, one method of partitioning (the one described below) might produce:

| 21 | 12 | 32 | 46 | 18 | 53 | 80 | 72 | 63 | 98 |
|----|----|----|----|----|----|----|----|----|----|
| 0  | 1  | 2  | 3  | 4  | 5  | 6  | 7  | 8  | 9  |

If, now, we can sort the portions to the left and right of 53, we would have sorted the entire array. Sorting the original array has been reduced to sorting two smaller arrays. To sort num[0] to num[4], we can partition **this** portion with respect to the first element, 21. This puts 21 in its final sorted position, leaving us to sort two smaller subarrays. This is illustrated by:

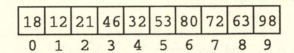

| 18 | 12 | 21 | 46 | 32 | 53 | 80 | 72 | 63 | 98 |
|----|----|----|----|----|----|----|----|----|----|
| 0  | 1  | 2  | 3  | 4  | 5  | 6  | 7  | 8  | 9  |

The portions which remain to be sorted are

```
num[0] to num[1];
num[3] to num[4];
num[6] to num[9].
```

This process is continued until all the little pieces have been sorted.

Observe that, as the sort progresses, we need to keep track of more and more smaller portions which remain to be sorted. It is exactly this information which will be kept automatically for each recursive call.

Consider the following function quicksort which, given two values left and right, sorts an array from elements left to right, inclusive. It calls a function partition; this will partition the elements with respect to some pivot and return a value dp (division point), say. quicksort can assume that all elements to the left of dp are smaller and all elements to the right are greater than the element in dp. It then calls itself to sort these two portions.

```c
void quicksort(int left, int right)
{
    int dp, partition(int, int);

    if (left < right) { /* only need to sort
                              >= 2 elements */
        dp = partition(left, right);
        quicksort(left, dp - 1);
        quicksort(dp + 1, right);
    }
}
```

In the above, quicksort makes no mention of the actual array to be sorted. Thus it can be used to sort **any** array. Of course, since partition will be doing all the work, it will need to know the name of the array. We assume that this array is declared 'external' (see Section 6.5.2) to partition. Another advantage of writing quicksort this way is that partition can choose any element it wishes for the pivot. This is usually the first element but sometimes it is advantageous to choose another. All that quicksort needs to know is that the element in dp divides the array as described above; where the pivot came from is totally immaterial. How do we write partition? In the following, we assume that the first element (the one in location left) is used as the pivot.

The gist of the algorithm is as follows:

(1) Assign to pivot the first element. Assume that this leaves a 'hole' in location lo, say. (lo will be the same as left, initially).
(2) Scan from the right for an element which is smaller than pivot. Suppose one is found in location hi, say. This is then moved to lo, leaving a 'hole' in location hi.
(3) We then scan from the left, starting at lo, for an element which is larger than pivot. This is then moved to hi, leaving a 'hole' in the location it came from.

Steps (2) and (3) are repeated until lo and hi meet. This will be the position where the pivot must go. Consider the array num from above:

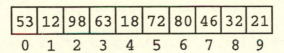

| 53 | 12 | 98 | 63 | 18 | 72 | 80 | 46 | 32 | 21 |
|----|----|----|----|----|----|----|----|----|----|
| 0  | 1  | 2  | 3  | 4  | 5  | 6  | 7  | 8  | 9  |

- pivot = 53, leaves a hole in location 0;
- scan from the right for a value smaller than 53. 21 is found. This is moved to num[0], leaving a hole in location 9.
- scan from the left for a value greater than 53. 98 is found. This is moved to num[9], leaving a hole in location 2.
- next, 32 is moved to num[2] and then 63 is moved to num[8].
- next, 46 is moved to num[3] and 72 is moved to num[7], leaving a hole in location 5.
- no more moves are possible, so the pivot, 53, is placed in num[5].

The above array is converted to:

| 21 | 12 | 32 | 46 | 18 | 53 | 80 | 72 | 63 | 98 |
|----|----|----|----|----|----|----|----|----|----|
| 0  | 1  | 2  | 3  | 4  | 5  | 6  | 7  | 8  | 9  |

The following implements the above algorithm:

```
int partition(int left, int right)
{
    int lo, hi, pivot;

    pivot = num[left];
    lo = left;
    hi = right + 1;

    do {
        do /* scan from right for a value smaller
                than pivot */
            hi = hi - 1;
        while (lo < hi && num[hi] >= pivot);
        if (lo < hi) {
            num[lo] = num[hi]; /* move value found to
                                    left side */
            do /* scan from left for a value greater
                    than pivot */
                lo = lo + 1;
            while (lo < hi && num[lo] <= pivot);
            if (lo < hi) num[hi] = num[lo];
            /* move value to right side */
        }
    } while (lo < hi); /* repeat if lo and hi
                            have not met */

    num[lo] = pivot; /* put the pivot in its
                            final position */
    return lo; /* the division point */
}
```

A quick test of quicksort is provided by the following:

```
#include <stdio.h>

int num[10] = {53, 12, 98, 63, 18, 72, 80, 46, 32, 21};
/* initialize num to these values - see Sections 6.5.2
    and 6.6.2 */
```

```
main()
{
    void quicksort(int left, int right);
    int j;

    quicksort(0, 9);
    for (j = 0; j < 10; j++) printf("%3d", num[j]);
}
```

Points to note:

- In general, the type of pivot must be the same as the type of elements being sorted.
- partition is called from quicksort only if left < right, so partition does not have to check for this.
- If the pivot happens to be the smallest or the largest element, the partitioning process reduces the size of the portion which is being sorted by 1 only! To avoid this potential problem, the pivot can be chosen to be the median of num[left], num[right] and num[(left + right)/2].
- For sorting small portions of the array, several recursive calls may be necessary. The overheads of these calls may take more time than if a simple method were used for sorting. We could modify quicksort so that if a portion to be sorted is less than some size n, say, then some simple method (insertion sort, say) is called to do the job.
- If the original array is already sorted, quicksort performs at its worst since, as indicated above, the partitioning operation will be almost useless.
- For data in random order, quicksort is one of the fastest methods available.

## Exercises 5

(1) What is meant by 'an argument is passed by value'?
(2) Which type of argument in C is not passed by value? How is it passed?
(3) How is it possible for a function to change the value of an actual argument?
(4) Write a function which interchanges the values of two integer arguments passed to it.
(5) Write a function sum such that the call

```
sum(a, b, c);
```

will store the sum of a and b in c.

(6)  Write a program to find out, for a class of students, the number of families with 1, 2, 3, ... up to 7 or more children. Data consists of the number of children in each pupil's family and is terminated by 0. Print the results under an appropriate heading.

(7)  Write a program which drills a user in English-French vocabulary. Two arrays, english and french, are used to hold the words such that french[j] contains the French equivalent of the word in english[j]. The program must display an English word and the user is requested to type the French for it. Incorporate a suitable scoring scheme, and give the user the opportunity to 'give up'.

Modify the program so that the user chooses whether to be given English words or French words.

(8)  A survey of 10 pop records is made. Each person votes by specifying three values (each from 1 to 10), in order, representing their choice of first, second and third. First choice scores 4 points, second choice scores 2 points and third choice scores 1 point. Data consists of the names of the 10 records followed by the voters' choices. Write a program to read the data, process the votes and print the most popular record. Appropriate validation should be done, for example, that a person does not vote for the same record more than once.

(9)  Explain the differences between a character pointer and an array of characters.

(10)  The character pointer msgptr is pointing to a string of characters. What happens when msgptr is assigned to another character pointer oldptr?

(11)  Many of the functions of Exercises 3 contain string parameters. Rewrite those functions using character pointers instead.

(12)  How does pointer arithmetic differ from ordinary integer arithmetic?

(13)  Write a function to calculate the definite integral

$$\int_a^b f(x)\, dx$$

using Simpson's rule (below) with $n$ strips. $n$ must be even. An approximation to the integral is given by

$$h/3\{(f(a)+4f(a+h)+2f(a+2h)+ \ldots +2f(a+(n-2)h)+4f(a+(n-1)h)+f(b)\}$$

where $h=(b-a)/n$. Test your function on some simple integrals.

What happens if the number of strips is increased for a given integral?

(14)  If a function $f$ is continuous in the interval $[a, b]$ and $f(a)f(b)<0$ then, since $f$ changes sign, there must exist some $c$ in $[a, b]$ for which $f(c)=0$. Assume there is one such $c$. It can be found as follows:

• bisect the interval $[a, b]$;
• determine in which half $f$ changes sign;

This is repeated giving a sequence of intervals, each smaller than the last and each containing $c$. The procedure can be terminated when the interval is arbitrarily small or $f$ is 0 at one of the endpoints.

Write a function which, given $f$ and $[a, b]$, returns an approximation to $c$. Test your function using the following:

$$5x^2 + 3x - 14$$

with a solution in the interval $[2, 3]$.

(15)  Write a recursive function which, given a real value $x$ and a positive integer $n$, returns the value of $x^n$.

(16)  Write a recursive function which, given an integer $n$, prints it with its digits reversed. For example, given 4735, it prints 5374.

(17)  Write a recursive function which, given an integer $n$, prints it with one blank after each digit.

(18)  The sequence of numbers 1, 1, 2, 3, 5, 8, 13, etc. are called Fibonacci numbers; each is the sum of the preceding two. Write a recursive function which, given $n$, returns the $n$th Fibonacci number.

(19)  Write a recursive function to return the greatest common divisor (gcd) of two integers $m$ and $n$, given that, in general,

$$\gcd(m, n) = \gcd(n, m \bmod n)$$

(20)  Write a recursive function which reads a line of data and prints it with the characters reversed.

(21)  Write a recursive function to sort a list of items based on the following:

> sort the first half of the list
> sort the second half of the list
> merge the two halves

# 6

# Data Types, Operators and Storage Classes

In this chapter, we formalize and expand on a number of issues mentioned in passing in previous chapters. These include a more detailed discussion of:

- data types, conversion rules in expressions, and operators;
- storage classes of variables in C;
- initialization of variables in C.

We also introduce some new features of the C language, including bit operators and conditional expressions.

## 6.1 Data types

In Section 1.3, we discussed the basic data types – `int`, `char`, `float` and `double`.

The type modifiers `short`, `long`, `signed` and `unsigned` may be applied to `int`. They may be combined as in `short unsigned int`.

`signed` and `unsigned` may be applied to `char`. Assuming that a character is stored in an 8-bit byte, the value stored in an `unsigned char` variable is interpreted as a positive 8-bit integer. For example, if the byte contains 11101101, then the value is the decimal equivalent, 237. On the other hand, a value stored in a `signed char` variable is interpreted as a signed integer, with the leading bit determining the sign (0 for positive, 1 for negative). In this case, if the byte contains 11101101, then the value is −19, assuming that negative numbers are stored using two's complement. (In two's complement, a negative number is stored by subtracting its positive binary equivalent from a string of 1's, then adding 1. For example, to store −19, we first find the binary equivalent of +19; this is 10011. Next, we subtract 10011 from a string of eight 1's, since we

Table 6.1. *Data types in C*

| Type | Size | Range/precision |
|------|------|-----------------|
| int | 16 | −32,768 to 32,767 |
| signed int | 16 | −32,768 to 32,767 |
| unsigned int | 16 | 0 to 65,535 |
| short int | 8 | −128 to 127 |
| signed short int | 8 | −128 to 127 |
| unsigned short int | 8 | 0 to 255 |
| long int | 32 | −2,147,483,648 to 2,147,483,647 |
| signed long int | 32 | −2,147,483,648 to 2,147,483,647 |
| unsigned long int | 32 | 0 to 4,294,967,295 |
| char | 8 | ASCII characters |
| signed char | 8 | −128 to 127 |
| unsigned char | 8 | 0 to 255 |
| float | 32 | approx. 6 significant digits |
| double | 64 | approx. 12 significant digits |
| long double | 128 | approx. 24 significant digits |

are using eight bits for our integers; this gives 11111111 − 10011 = 11101100. Adding 1 gives 11101101.)

`long` may be applied to `double` to get greater precision.

The range of values for the various types (modified and unmodified) varies from one machine to the next. Table 6.1 shows some typical values. It assumes a 16-bit word. Note that `signed`, when applied to integers, makes no difference to the range of values that can be stored. Also, there is no implication that `signed char` is necessarily the same as `short int`.

We have mentioned before that if different types of values appear in an expression, C does conversions that seem the most natural, and all operands are converted to the type of the largest operand. For any given expression, the following rules are applied, in order:

(1) `char` and `short int` are converted to `int`. Then
(2) If

any operand in an operand pair is `long double`, the other operand is converted to `long double`, and the result is `long double`.
else if
any operand in an operand pair is `double`, the other operand is converted to `double`, and the result is `double`.

else if

> any operand in an operand pair is float, the other operand is converted to float, and the result is float.

else if

> any operand in an operand pair is unsigned long int, the other operand is converted to unsigned long int, and the result is unsigned long int.

else if

> any operand in an operand pair is long int and the other operand is unsigned int, what happens depends on whether a long int can hold all the values of an unsigned int. If it can, the unsigned int operand is converted to long int and the result is long int; if not, both operands are converted to unsigned long int and the result is unsigned long int.

else if

> any operand in an operand pair is long int, the other operand is converted to long int, and the result is long int.

else if

> any operand in an operand pair is unsigned int, the other operand is converted to unsigned int, and the result is unsigned int.

else the operands must be int, and the result is int.

As an example, consider the expression:

```
(x + a * n) / ch
```

where x is double, a is float, n is int and ch is char. It is evaluated as follows:

- ch is converted to int.
- Since a is float, n is also converted to float, and the result of a*n (t1, say) is float.
- since x is double, t1 is converted to double and the result of the addition (t2, say) is double.
- since t2 is double, ch (now int) is converted to double, and the result of the division is double.

One must be careful with expressions like

```
a + m / n
```

where a is float and m, n are integers. Since m and n are of type int, an integer division (giving t, say) is performed. a and t are then converted to float and the result is float. For example, if a = 7, m = 14, n = 5, the result obtained is 9.0, not 9.8. If we wanted a floating-point division to be performed, we would need to use a cast, as in:

```
a + (float) m / n
```

This forces m to be float, in turn causing n to be promoted to float, so that a floating-point division is performed. Observe, however, that

```
a + (float) (m / n)      /* would not work */
```

would not work, since an integer division would first be performed and **this** result would then be converted to float. The effect would be exactly the same as a + m / n.

Conversions also take place in assignment statements where the type of the right hand side is different from the type of the variable on the left hand side. The value of the right hand side is converted to the type of the left hand side, which is the type of the result. Using the expression above and assuming that y is float, in the statement

```
y = (x + a * n) / ch;
```

the value of the right hand side is double; this is converted to float for assignment to y. Whether the value is rounded or truncated is implementation-dependent. However, if the value is too big to be stored in a float variable, the result is undefined.

Floating-point values are converted to integer values by discarding the fractional part. However, if the resulting value is outside the range capable of being stored in the integer variable, the result is undefined.

Longer ints are converted to shorter ones by dropping the excess high-order bits. For example, if long int is 32 bits and int is 16 bits, assigning a long int to an int uses the rightmost 16 bits of the long int.

When a function is called with actual arguments, conversions can also take place if the type of an actual argument is different from the type of the corresponding formal parameter. In the absence of a function prototype, char and short int are converted to int and float is converted to double. This may or may not be what the programmer intends – yet another reason why function prototypes are strongly recommended.

*Data type* void

In our discussions on functions, we encountered a fifth data type void. There are three ways in which void can be used:

(1) to indicate that a function does not return a value, as in:

```
void printmessage(char *msgptr)
```

(2) to indicate that a function does not take any arguments, as in:

```
int fun(void)
```

Here, fun is a function which takes no arguments and returns an int.

(3) to declare 'generic' pointers. Recall that, in C, a pointer must be declared to 'point to' one specific type of object and a pointer to one type may not be assigned to or compared with a pointer to another type. A void pointer can assume any pointer value and can be assigned to and from pointers to other types. A void pointer can also be compared with pointers to other types. A void pointer, p, say, can be declared using:

```
void *p;
```

Suppose p holds the address of a float value. If fp is a float pointer, we could write:

```
fp = p;
```

or

```
if (fp == p) . . .
```

Other examples of void pointers are discussed in Section 7.3.1.

### 6.2 Operators

Much of the expressive power in C is due to the rich set of built-in operators provided. In addition to the usual operators found in other

Table 6.2. *Operators, precedence and associativity*

|  | Operator | Associativity |
|---|---|---|
| Highest | () [] -> | left to right |
|  | ! ~ ++ − + − *(type) & sizeof | right to left |
|  | * / % | left to right |
|  | + − | left to right |
|  | << >> | left to right |
|  | < <= > >= | left to right |
|  | == != | left to right |
|  | & | left to right |
|  | ^ | left to right |
|  | \| | left to right |
|  | && | left to right |
|  | \|\| | left to right |
|  | ?: | right to left |
|  | = += −= *= /= %= >>= <<= &= ^= \|= | right to left |
| Lowest | , | left to right |

languages, C provides others which are distinctly C. We have met and used many of these operators in the previous chapters. A complete list is given in Table 6.2 which lists the operators in decreasing order of precedence (highest to lowest). Operators in the same row have the same precedence. The 'associativity' column indicates the order in which operators of the same precedence are evaluated, in the absence of parentheses. For example,

```
a * b % c
```

groups 'left to right' and, hence, is evaluated as

```
(a * b) % c
```

whereas

```
a += b = c
```

groups 'right to left' and is evaluated as

```
a += (b = c)
```

### Comments on Table 6.2

- Parentheses (round brackets), ( ), are operators that increase the precedence of the operations within them.
- Square brackets, [ ], are used to denote an array subscript.
- The operators —> (a 'minus' followed by a 'greater than' sign) and . (period) are used with structures and will be discussed in Chapter 7.
- The second row of the table contains the unary operators. (type) denotes the **cast** operator. The compile time operator sizeof is discussed in Chapter 7. It returns the amount of storage (in bytes) needed for storing its argument. For example,

```
sizeof(double)
```

returns the number of bytes needed for storing a double variable on the particular machine.
- C provides a number of operators for manipulating the bits of variables declared as char or int (modified or unmodified). In decreasing order of precedence, these are:

| | | |
|---|---|---|
| ~ | | the one's complement (NOT) |
| << | >> | shift left and shift right, respectively |
| & | | AND |
| ^ | | eXclusive OR |
| \| | | OR |

These operators are explained in detail in Section 6.3.
- The operator pair ? : is used for writing conditional expressions, and is discussed in Section 6.4.
- The relational operators (<, >, etc.) have higher precedence than the logical connectives && and | |. Hence expressions like

```
a < b && b > c
```

do not need extra brackets to be evaluated properly.
- In expressions involving && and | |, evaluation ceases as soon as the truth value of the expression is known. For example, in

```
j < 10 && num[j] == key
```

when $j = 10$, '$j < 10$' is false (making the entire expression false) so that no attempt is then made to compare key with num[10].

- For commutative and associative operators like + and *, C does not specify the order in which the operands are evaluated, even when brackets are present. For example, suppose e1, e2 and e3 are expressions and consider:

```
e1 + (e2 + e3)
```

There is no guarantee that e2 or e3 will be evaluated first. C might decide to evaluate e1 first, then e2, then (e1 + e2), then e3 and finally (e1 + e2) + e3. Usually this makes no difference to the final value, but if a particular sequence of evaluation is required, temporary variables can be used, as in:

```
t1 = e2 + e3;
t2 = e1 + t1;
```

Note that even this does not specify which of e2 or e3 will be evaluated first.

### 6.3 Bit operators

These operators allow the programmer to fiddle with bits, usually of an integer. In the examples below, assume that a, b and c are ints. The operators are:

(1) << – shift left

example: b = a << 3;

The bits of a are shifted left by three places. The vacated rightmost three bits are set to 0. The resulting bit pattern is stored in b. The second operand of << must be a positive integer.

(2) >> – shift right

example: b = a >> 3;

The bits of a are shifted right by three places. What is stored in the vacated leftmost three bits depends on the machine and the type of

a. If a is unsigned, the vacated bits are set to 0. If a is signed, the usual policy is to fill the vacated bits with the sign bit (called sign propagation), but, on some machines, 0's are used. The resulting bit pattern is stored in b. The second operand of >> must be a positive integer.

(3) &  —  bit-wise logical AND

example:    c = a & b;

Each bit of a is compared with the corresponding bit of b. If they are both 1, the corresponding bit in c is set to 1; otherwise, the corresponding bit in c is set to 0.

Suppose an int occupies 16 bits and we want to shift a right by 8 places, but we want to ensure that the vacated bits are set to 0. (They could be set to 1 if sign propagation is used on the machine). This could be accomplished by

```
a = (a >> 8) & 0377;     /* 377₈ = 0000000011111111₂ */
```

After a is shifted, & will set the leftmost eight bits to 0 while leaving the rightmost eight bits unchanged.

(4) |  —  bit-wise logical (inclusive) OR

example:    c = a | b;

Each bit of a is compared with the corresponding bit of b. If they are both 0, the corresponding bit in c is set to 0; otherwise, the corresponding bit in c is set to 1.

Suppose an int occupies 16 bits and we want to shift a right by 8 places, but we want to ensure that the vacated bits are set to 1. This could be accomplished by

```
a = (a >> 8) | 0177400;   /* 177400₈ = 1111111100000000₂ */
```

After a is shifted, | will set the leftmost eight bits to 1 while leaving the rightmost eight bits unchanged.

(5) ^  –  bit-wise exclusive-OR

    example:    `c = a ^ b;`

Each bit of a is compared with the corresponding bit of b. If they are both 0 or both 1, the corresponding bit in c is set to 0; otherwise, the corresponding bit in c is set to 1.

All of the above operators can be used in conjunction with = to form 'compound assignment' operators, thus:

```
<<=   >>=   &=   |=   ^=
```

examples:    `a <<= b;`    `/* a = a << b; */`
                `a &= 0377;`    `/* a = a & 0377 */`

(6) ~  –  one's complement

This is a unary operator which inverts the bits of its operand, that is, 1's become 0's and 0's become 1's. As an example, suppose we wanted to set the rightmost eight bits of an integer a to 0 while leaving the others unchanged. If we knew how many bits (16, say) an integer occupied on the given machine, we could write

```
a &= 0177400;   /* 177400₈ = 11111111000000002  */
```
$a \mathrel{\&=} 0177400; \quad /* \ 177400_8 = 1111111100000000_2 \ */$

But if we wanted our code to be machine-independent, we could use

```
a &= (~0377);
```

The brackets are not required for proper evaluation since ~ has higher precedence than &.

Bitwise operations are most commonly used in 'systems' programs, things like printer drivers, disk and tape utility programs, and communications programs.

As an example, consider the problem of writing a function, wordsize, which returns the number of bits required for storing an int on a given machine. To be useful, wordsize should work on any machine. One solution is obtained by setting the bits of an unsigned int variable (n, say) to all 1's, and counting the number of 1's by right-shifting them out, one at a time. Declaring n as unsigned ensures that vacated bits are set to 0 (rather than the sign bit) so that the value of n eventually becomes 0. The following function does the job:

```
int wordsize(void)
{
    unsigned int n, size;

    n = ~0;   /* set n to all 1's */
    for (size = 0; n != 0; n >>= 1)
        size++;
    return size;
}
```

### 6.4 Conditional expressions

A conditional expression consists of three expressions linked by the conditional operator '? :'. The general form is

```
expr1 ? expr2 : expr3
```

expr1 is evaluated. If it is true (non-zero), expr2 is evaluated and the value of the entire expression is the value of expr2. If expr1 is false (zero), expr3 is evaluated and the value of the entire expression is the value of expr3. For a given evaluation of expr1, only one of expr2 or expr3 is evaluated. As an example, consider

```
a = (a < 0) ? -a : a;
```

If a is negative, −a is assigned to a; otherwise, its value remains unchanged. The net effect is that a is set to its absolute value.

A classic example is

```
c = (a > b) ? a : b;
```

which sets c to the larger of a and b. One can even define a macro (see Section 11.1.1 for details) with

```
#define max(a, b) ((a) > (b) ? (a) : (b))
```

and then use it in expressions such as

```
c = 2 * max(x, y);
```

This is expanded by the C Preprocessor (Section 11.1) into:

```
c = 2 * ((x) > (y) ? (x) : (y))
```

A convenient use of a conditional expression is to provide the first argument
to printf. Suppose we wanted to print numbers, two per line. Assume
that num is the next number to be printed and count is the amount of
numbers already printed. Consider

```
printf((++count % 2 == 0) ? "%d\n" : "%d\t", num); /* % = mod */
```

Suppose count is 1, meaning that one number has been printed. The
present num is the second number to be printed. When printf is
encountered, count is incremented (making it 2). The remainder on
division by 2 is 0. The value of the conditional expression is therefore the
first string. In effect, the statement becomes:

```
printf("%d\n", num);
```

This prints the number followed by a newline. The next time count will
be incremented to 3. The remainder on division by 2 will be 1, so that
the value of the conditional expression is the second string. In effect, the
statement becomes:

```
printf("%d\t", num);
```

This prints the number followed by a tab.


## 6.5 Storage classes in C

In the most general case, a C program consists of a set of one or more
functions spread over one or more files. Good programming practice
dictates that a function should be as self-contained as possible. It should
perform one well-defined task. As far as possible, the data required by a
function should be passed via the parameter list, and variables used by

the function should not be accessible (except, perhaps, in a controlled way) to other functions. The latter is achieved by declaring the variables inside the function – they are then known as **local** (or **automatic**) variables.

In some cases, several functions may need to use the same item of data. Sometimes, it may be more convenient or efficient if that data were in a commonly accessible place. If this is done, the variable holding the data is said to be **global**.

When a large program is being developed, it is possible that portions of it may be in different files, since, for instance, many people may be working on it. When a C program is spread over several files, certain requirements arise. We may want to declare variables which are known in one file, but not in any other, and we may want to declare variables which are known only in certain selected files.

C provides the facilities which allow us to declare variables with the above properties.

In C, a variable can be one of

(1) automatic
(2) external
(3) static
(4) register

We will use the term **scope** (of a variable) to mean that portion of the program where the variable is 'known' (accessible).

### 6.5.1 *automatic*

Unless specified otherwise, a variable declared in a function is of type `auto` (an automatic variable). For example,

```
int linecount;
```

The word `auto` may be used to declare a variable as automatic, as in

```
auto int linecount;
```

but it is almost never used.

Storage is allocated to the variable each time the function is called and is released when the function returns. (A function 'returns' either when a `return` statement is encountered or the closing right brace } of the function is reached). There is **no** connection between the value left by a previous call and the initial value of the next call. Every time a function is called, an automatic variable is treated as brand new.

If initialization is specified, as in

```
int linecount = 0;
```

then the initialization is performed each time the function is called. Unless given a value explicitly, no assumption may be made about the initial value of an automatic variable (except, of course, you can assume that it contains garbage).

The scope of an automatic variable is the function in which it is declared. Another function may use a variable of the same name without conflict.

The formal parameters appearing in the definition of a function are treated as automatic variables. For example, in the following

```
int fun(int n, char ch)
{   .

    .
}
```

n and ch are considered to be automatic variables. They come into being when the function is called and cease to exist when the function returns. When the function is called, the values of the actual arguments supplied are stored in n and ch. Thus n and ch can be thought of as automatic variables initialized to the corresponding values supplied when the function is called. For example, the call

```
fun(20, 'a');
```

sets n to 20 and ch to 'a' before the function begins execution. The function may change these values, if desired. On exit from the function, n and ch no longer exist.

### 6.5.2 *external*

A variable declared outside of any function is considered to be **external**. We use the term **definition** (of a variable) to refer to a declaration which causes storage to be allocated to the variable, in addition to stating the properties of the variable. There can be only one definition of an external variable in a C program. (This holds true whether the program occupies one file or several files). Other functions may contain extern declarations to access the variable. Consider the following program structure and assume that the entire program is in one file.

```
int ch;

main ()
{   .
    .
}

int count;

fun1()
{
    extern int number;
    .
}

fun2()
{
    extern int ch;
    .
}

int number;

fun3()
{
    .
}
```

The declarations

```
int ch;       /* before main */
int count;    /* before fun1 */
int number;   /* before fun3 */
```

all define these as external variables since they appear outside of all functions. (In passing, it should be noted that each of these declarations may be optionally preceded by the word extern). However, the scope of each one is different.

The scope of ch is the entire program. In general, the scope of an external variable automatically includes all functions which come after it in the same file, provided it is not redeclared in some function. This means that main, fun1, fun2 and fun3 can all use ch without any further declarations being necessary. There exists just one instance of the variable which all functions may access. In fun2, the declaration

```
extern int ch;
```

is not necessary, but if a function is going to use an external variable, it is good programming practice to include an extern declaration for it. In effect, the declaration states that this function intends to use an int variable ch but it is defined somewhere else.

What if the word extern is omitted from the declaration, so it becomes simply

```
int ch;
```

In this case, we have a situation where an automatic variable ch is being declared in fun2. Now fun2 will have no access to the external variable ch. Using ch in fun2 is a reference to the local variable. As a matter of fact, ch can be redeclared to have a different type, for example:

```
fun2()
{
    float ch;
    .
}
```

Inside fun2, ch refers to the float variable rather than the external int variable.

In the absence of other declarations, the scope of count consists of fun1, fun2 and fun3. If fun3, for instance, intends to use count, it is recommended (though not necessary) that the declaration

```
extern int count;
```

be included in fun3. However, if main wants to use count, then it is

**mandatory** that the declaration

```
extern int count;
```

be included in main.

The scope of number is fun3. No declaration is necessary in fun3 in order to use number. However, the extern declaration in fun1 is absolutely necessary if that function wants access to number. The same holds for main and fun2.

The above discussion assumed that the entire program was in one file. If an external variable is defined in one file and a function in another file (but part of the same program) wants to use it, then the extern declaration is **required** in the other file.

If one needs to specify initialization for an external variable, then this can be done only at the place where it is being defined, as in

```
int wordcount = 0;
```

An extern declaration referring to this variable must not contain any initialization. It should simply be

```
extern int wordcount;
```

If no initialization is specified in the definition of an external numeric variable, then C **guarantees** that it will be initialized to 0. However, in general, if initialization is required, it is good programming practice to do so explicitly.

If an array is to be used as an external variable, then its size must be specified when it is being defined, for example,

```
char word[20];
```

An extern declaration referring to this variable need not specify the size, but the brackets must be present, as in

```
extern char word[];
```

To summarize:

- A variable is **global** if it is **defined** outside of any function. The variable can be used in any function which comes **after** the definition and is in the same file, without any further declaration being necessary. However, it is good programming practice to include an `extern` declaration in those functions which use the variable.

- The `extern` declaration is mandatory if a function wishes to use a global variable but appears **before** the definition of the variable.
- The `extern` declaration is mandatory if a function wishes to use a global variable but appears in a **different** file from the definition of the variable.
- If a variable, declared as global, is redeclared in a function, then the local definition is used within that function. In this case, the function has no access to the global variable.

### 6.5.3  static

A variable is declared to be **static** by prefixing its normal declaration with the word `static`, as in

```
static int linecount;
```

We could also use

```
int static linecount;
```

since the properties of a variable may be stated in any order. Initialization may be specified, as in

```
static int linecount = 0;
```

In the absence of explicit initialization, C guarantees that `static` variables will be initialized to 0.

A `static` variable can be either (a) internal or (b) external.

*(a) internal static*

If the declaration appears inside a function, as in

```
fun()
{
    static int linecount = 0;
    .
}
```

then the variable is known only inside the function, i.e. it is **local** to the function. Variables of the same name in other parts of the program will cause no conflict. Storage is allocated to an **internal static** variable once. (If specified, initialization is done at this time. In the absence of explicit initialization, C guarantees that `static` variables will be initialized to 0). This storage (and the value it contains) is retained between calls to the function. Thus if the value of `linecount` is 5 when the function returns the first time, the second call of the function can assume that the value of `linecount` is 5. In this example, `linecount` can be used to count the total number of lines printed by all the calls to this function.

*(b) external static*

If the declaration appears outside of any function, as in

```
static int linecount = 0;
fun()
{
    .
}
```

then the variable is known in the remainder of the file containing the declaration. In this example, `linecount` can be incremented, for example, by any function following the declaration, provided it is in the same file. Thus it can be used to count the total number of lines printed by all the functions which use it.

The difference between an **external** variable and an **external static** variable is that the latter is **unknown** outside of the **file** in which it is declared. Thus the scope of an **external static** variable is limited to one file only. The same variable name may be used in other files without conflict.

Normally, a function name is external, that is, it is known throughout the program. If we wish to restrict the scope of a function to a particular file, we can precede its normal declaration with the word `static`, as in:

```
static int fun(...)
```

Here, `fun` will be unknown outside the file in which this declaration appears.

The term `static` denotes permanence. Whether internal or external, a `static` variable is allocated storage only once, which is retained for the duration of the program. A `static` variable also affords a degree of 'privacy'. If it is internal, it is known only in the function in which it is declared. If it is external, it is known only in the file in which it is declared.

### 6.5.4 register

This storage class is usually applied to a variable which will be heavily used in the program. In any case, only `int`, `char` and pointer variables may be declared as `register` variables. Furthermore, `register` may be applied only to automatic variables and to the formal parameters of functions. Examples of `register` declarations are:

```
void fun(register int n, register char ch)
{
    register void *p;
    .
    .
}
```

Where possible, a `register` variable is assigned to a machine register, rather than a normal memory location. Presumably, this will result in a smaller, faster object program since a register access is much faster than a memory access. If there are more `register` declarations than available machine registers, then the word `register` is ignored for the excess declarations.

It is not allowed to take the address (using &) of a `register` variable since & returns a memory address and, theoretically at least, a `register` variable is not stored in memory.

### 6.5.5 Other scope rules

It is normal for automatic variables to be declared immediately following the opening left brace ( { ) of a function. But C allows automatic variables to be declared after the left brace that begins **any** compound statement. For example, the following is legal in C:

```
while (a != 0)
{
    int ch;
    .
    .
}
```

The variable ch comes into being when the body of the while is about to be executed, and ceases to exist when the terminating right brace is reached. If required, initialization may be specified in the declaration.

Previously, we stated that an external variable is known in all functions which come after it in the same file, provided it is not redeclared in some function. In the latter case, the new declaration takes precedence inside the function. Since the formal parameters of functions are considered as automatic variables, a similar rule applies. Consider the following:

```
int ch;
 .

 .
int fun(float ch)
{
     .
}
```

Inside fun, ch refers to the float variable rather than the extern int variable.

## 6.6 Initialization

We now summarize the rules which govern the initialization of the various classes of variables in C. The discussion refers to initialization at the time a variable is being defined, not assigning an initial value by means of an assignment statement, say.

Unless specified otherwise, **external** and **static** variables are guaranteed to be initialized to 0. In the absence of explicit initialization, **automatic** and **register** variables are undefined (i.e. contain 'garbage' values).

### 6.6.1 *Simple variables*

Simple (as opposed to array or struct (see Chapter 7)) variables of any storage class may be initialized by following the name with an equals sign (=) and a 'value'. In the case of **external** and **static** variables, the 'value' must be a constant, i.e., must be determinable at compile time, the time when the initialization is done. In the case of **automatic** or **register** variables, 'value' can be any valid expression which may include previously defined values such as global (external) variables or arguments to functions. The initialization is performed **each time** the function (or block) is entered.

Consider the following:

```
char blank = ' ';
int linecount = HEADLINES+1;/* HEADLINES is a
                                symbolic constant */
     .

     .

void fun(char word[], int size)
{
    static int maxlines = 55;
    int top = size - 1;
    int amtlines = linecount;

     .

     .

}
```

The **external** variables blank and linecount **must** be initialized to constants or constant expressions. The **static** variable maxlines must also be initialized to a constant or constant expression. However, this rule does not apply to automatic or register variables. For such variables, the initializer can be any valid expression involving previously defined values. In the example, each time fun is called, top is initialized using the value of size supplied to the function; amtlines is initialized to the current value of linecount.

### 6.6.2 Array variables

Any **external** or **static** array may be initialized on the same line in which it is being defined. **Automatic** arrays may **not** be initialized in this way. Where initialization is allowed, there are several possibilities, depending on the type of array.

Consider a one-dimensional integer array daysinmonth:

```
int daysinmonth[12] = {31,28,31,30,31,30,31,31,30,31,30,31}
```

Here, the 12 values supplied are stored in the 12 elements of the array daysinmonth, in the order written. Thus daysinmonth[0] = 31, daysinmonth[1] = 28, etc., up to daysinmonth[11] = 31. The initial values are enclosed in braces and separated by commas. No comma is necessary after the last value, but it is not an error to have one. If fewer than 12 values were supplied, then 0's would be used to fill out the array. If more than 12 values were supplied, then an error would result. The above declaration could also have been written:

```
int daysinmonth[] = {31,28,31,30,31,30,31,31,30,31,30,31}
```

where the size of the array is not specified. In this case, the compiler will count the number of initial values and determine the size of the array.

Next, consider a one-dimensional character array message:

```
char message[] = {'w','h','e','r','e',' ','t','o',
               ' ','f','l','y','\0'};
```

In effect, this declares message to be a character array of size 13, initialized to the characters within the braces. Since this kind of initialization occurs often, a shorthand is provided, thus:

```
char message[] = "where to fly";
```

In the latter case, the compiler adds the null character $(\0)$ at the end of the string, and works out the size of the array by adding 1 to the number of characters between the quotes. It is worth noting the difference between the above declaration and the following:

```
char *word = "where to fly";
```

Here, the string is stored somewhere and the **address** of the string is stored in word. For most practical purposes, the value in word is a constant. If we change it, we lose access to the string. In the first declaration, the contents of message may be changed by assigning a different string to it.

In the above example, word is a character pointer. Our next example concerns the initialization of an **array** of character pointers. Suppose we wanted to store the names of the seven days of the week in an array. One way to do it is as follows:

```
char *daysofweek[] = { "Sunday",
                       "Monday",
                       "Tuesday",
                       "Wednesday",
                       "Thursday",
                       "Friday",
                       "Saturday"
                   };
```

The compiler will store the seven strings somewhere, each properly terminated by '\0'. The amount of storage used for each string will be the length of the string + 1. The address of each string is then stored in the corresponding element of the array `daysofweek`. Thus `daysofweek[0]` will point to "Sunday", `daysofweek[1]` will point to "Monday", etc. The compiler will count the number of strings supplied to determine the size of the array. If we wanted, we could have specified the size of the array, as in

```
char *daysofweek[7] = { . . . };
```

Another approach would be to use a two-dimensional array of characters. But now, we would need to know the length of the longest string we wish to store, in order to declare the array size. Since "Wednesday" is the longest string (length 9), the 'column' subscript must be 10 (to cater for '\0'). The declaration could be:

```
char daysofweek[7][10] = { "Sunday",
                           "Monday",
                           "Tuesday",
                           "Wednesday",
                           "Thursday",
                           "Friday",
                           "Saturday"
                       };
```

The size of the first dimension (7) may be omitted. The compiler will determine the size from the number of strings supplied. The size of the second dimension **must** be supplied. In this example, 10 characters are reserved for storing each string. For all strings except "Wednesday", not all 10 characters will be used. We note, in passing, that the character pointer version should be used if the strings are not to be altered. If the strings need to be changed, the character array version should be used.

### 6.6.3 Two-dimensional arrays

In the case of a two-dimensional array (of integers, say), the initializers for each row must be enclosed in braces, as in the following example:

```
int num[4][3] = {
     {13, 15, 17},
     {21, 23, 25},
     {33, 35, 37},
     {41, 43, 45}
};
```

The outermost pair of braces encloses four data items separated by commas. Each data item (itself enclosed in braces) is the initializer for one row. Thus num[0][0] = 13, num[0][1] = 15, num[0][2] = 17, and so on, up to num[3][1] = 43 and num[3][2] = 45. In this example, all elements of the array are given specific values, and it would be an error to supply more initial values than there are elements. When all values are supplied, C permits an abbreviation, thus:

```
int num[4][3] = {13,15,17,21,23,25,33,35,37,41,43,45};
```

If fewer values are supplied, C fills in the first row, then the second row, etc. and puts zero in the remaining elements. For example, the declaration:

```
int num[4][3] = {13,15,17,21,23,25,33,35};
```

would cause num to be initialized as:

```
13    15    17
21    23    25
33    35     0
 0     0     0
```

To give an example of what is possible, suppose we wanted to initialize only the first two rows and first two columns of num, as follows:

```
13    15    0
21    23    0
 0     0    0
 0     0    0
```

then this could be accomplished by:

```
int num[4][3] = {
     {13, 15},
     {21, 23}
};
```

The first initializer is for the row num[0]; since only two values are supplied, they are stored in num[0][0] and num[0][1]; num[0][2] is set to 0, since no value is supplied for it. Similarly, the next initializer sets num[1] (the second row) to 21 23 0. Since no more initializers are supplied, the remaining rows are set to 0.

The initialization of an 'array of structures' is discussed in Section 8.3.

## Exercises 6

(1) Write a function which, given an integer, returns the number of 1-bits in its representation.

(2) Write the function whose prototype is:

```
unsigned int extractbits(unsigned num, unsigned pos,
               unsigned n);
```

Assume that the bits of num are numbered from the left, starting from 1. This function returns the value of the n-bit field starting at position pos.

(3) In the ASCII character set, 7 bits are used for storing a character. When such a character is stored in an 8-bit byte, the eighth (high-order) bit is used as a parity bit. In an even-parity scheme, the parity bit is set so that the number of 1-bits in the byte is even. Write a function which accepts a char and sets the parity bit for even parity.

(4) Using a conditional expression, write a function toupper which converts its char argument, ch, to uppercase if ch is lowercase and leaves it unchanged, otherwise.

(5)  Using a conditional expression, write a function `tolower` which converts its `char` argument, `ch`, to lowercase if `ch` is uppercase and leaves it unchanged, otherwise.

(6)  Name two ways by which a variable may be 'automatic'.

(7)  Explain the difference between the **definition** and a **declaration** of a variable.

(8)  An external variable is known to all functions which come after it in the same file; true or false?

(9)  An external variable defined in one file is known in all other files comprising the same program without any additional declarations being required; true or false?

(10)  A `static` variable can be internal or external; true or false?

(11)  A `static` variable is known only in the file in which it is declared; true or false?

(12)  A register variable is always stored in a machine register; true or false?

(13)  In its definition, a `static` variable can be initialized to the value of a formal parameter; true or false?

(14)  In its definition, an automatic variable can be initialized to the value of a formal parameter; true or false?

(15)  What values are stored in num by the following?

```
static int num[8] = {43,26,34}
```

(16)  Carefully explain the difference between the following declarations:

```
char phrase[] = "tempus fugit";
char *time = "tempus fugit";
char phrase[10] = "tempus fugit";
char phrase[13] = {'t','e','m','p','u','s',' ',
                   'f','u','g','i','t','\0'};
```

(17)  Write declarations (in two different ways) to store the names of the twelve horoscope signs in an array.

(18)  Initialize an array to the following values in three different ways:

| | | | | |
|---|---|---|---|---|
| 12 | 43 | 37 | 0 | 0 |
| 31 | 0 | 57 | 0 | 0 |
| 0 | 29 | 16 | 0 | 0 |
| 30 | 52 | 13 | 0 | 0 |
| 0 | 0 | 0 | 0 | 0 |
| 0 | 0 | 0 | 0 | 0 |

# 7

# Basic Structures and Linked Lists

In C, a structure is a collection of one or more variables, possibly of different types, grouped together under a single name for convenient handling.

There are many situations in which we wish to process data about a certain entity but the data itself consists of items of various types. For example, the data for a student (the student **record**) may consist of several **fields** such as a name, address and telephone number (all of type string), number of courses taken (of type integer), fees payable (of type float), names of courses (of type string), scores obtained (of type float), etc. Suppose there are 100 students. How can we store the data for these students in a program? One approach is to have a separate array for each field and the logic of the program will treat them as parallel arrays. Thus `name[j]`, `address[j]`, `fees[j]`, etc. refer to the data for the *j*th student. The problem with this approach is that if there are many fields, the handling of several parallel arrays becomes clumsy and unwieldy. For example, suppose we wanted to pass a student's data to a function via the parameter list. This will involve the passing of several arrays. Also, if we are sorting the students by name, say, each time two names are interchanged, we have to write statements to interchange the data in the other arrays as well. In such situations, C structures are convenient to use.

## 7.1 The voting problem revisited

Consider, again, the voting problem discussed in Section 5.3.1. The data for a candidate consisted of a name and the number of votes obtained. In our sample solution, we used two arrays `candidate` and `votecount` to store this data. The logic of the program assumed that `votecount[j]` contained the votes obtained by `candidate[j]`. We now explain how a C structure can be used to solve the same problem. Consider the declaration

```
struct persondata {
      char name[NAMELENGTH]; /* NAMELENGTH is a
                                        symbolic constant */
      int totalvote;
};
```

This declares a structure called persondata which consists of two fields (or members) – name (of type string) and totalvote (of type int). As written, this declaration does not allocate any storage but only specifies the format of the fields of the structure. In effect, this declares a new **type** called struct persondata. (struct is similar to the record type in Pascal). We can now declare variables of this type, if we wish. For example, the declaration

```
struct persondata person;
```

declares person to be a variable with two components of the form specified in the structure declaration of persondata. In addition, storage is allocated for all the fields of the variable person. Note that person refers to the entire structure (the two components, in this case). How do we refer to an individual field? This is done using the 'structure member' operator '.' (period or dot). For instance,

person.name refers to the first field, and
person.totalvote refers to the second field.

Note that person.name is a variable of type string (character array) and person.totalvote is a variable of type int and can be used in the same way that such variables can. For instance, we can write

```
scanf("%s", person.name);
```

or

```
person.totalvote = 0;
```

Suppose that human was also declared as

```
struct persondata human;
```

then we could assign all the fields of person to the corresponding fields of human with the statement

```
human = person;
```

This is exactly equivalent to the statements

```
strcpy(human.name, person.name);
human.totalvote = person.totalvote;
```

but, of course, is much shorter and, possibly, clearer.

Coming back to our voting problem, we need an array of items, each of which has the structure of persondata. The declaration

```
struct persondata candidate[MAXCANDIDATES];
```

declares candidate to be such an array. Now candidate[j] is not just a single data item but a structure consisting of two components. These components can be referred to as

```
candidate[j].name and candidate[j].totalvote
```

If it were required, we could use the single statement

```
candidate[j + 1] = candidate[j];
```

to assign both fields of candidate[j] to candidate[j + 1].

Before pursuing this example, we digress to introduce the typedef facility in C and discuss how structures are passed to functions.

### *7.1.1* typedef

**typedef** allows us to give a name to some existing type, and this name can then be used to declare variables of that type. typedef can be used to construct shorter or more meaningful names for predefined C types or for user-declared types, such as structures. As an example, the statement

```
typedef int Whole;
```

declares a new type name Whole which is synonymous with the predefined type int. (Note that Whole appears in the same position as a variable would, not right after the word typedef.) We can then declare variables of type Whole, as in

```
Whole amount, numcopies;
```

This is exactly equivalent to

```
int amount, numcopies;
```

For those accustomed to the term real of languages like Pascal or FORTRAN, the statement:

```
typedef float Real;
```

allows them to declare variables of type Real. In this book, we use at least one uppercase letter to distinguish type names declared using typedef.

For the example above, we could use:

```
typedef struct persondata {
    char name[NAMELENGTH]; /* NAMELENGTH is a
                                    symbolic constant */
    int totalvote;
} PersonType;
```

Then we could write declarations such as:

```
PersonType person, human, candidate[MAXCANDIDATES];
```

This is exactly equivalent to the more cumbersome:

```
struct persondata person, human, candidate[MAXCANDIDATES];
```

Since C distinguishes between upper and lower case, we could even use a declaration like:

```
typedef struct persondata {
    char name[NAMELENGTH]; /* NAMELENGTH is a
                              symbolic constant */
    int totalvote;
} PersonData;
```

or, even (omitting `persondata`)

```
typedef struct {
    char name[NAMELENGTH]; /* NAMELENGTH is a
                              symbolic constant */
    int totalvote;
} PersonData;
```

and then declare variables of type `PersonData`.

If we wished, we could declare pointers to the above `struct`, as in

```
PersonData *personPtr;
/* same as 'struct persondata *personPtr' */
```

We could even use our new type name `PersonData` in another `typedef`, as in

```
typedef PersonData *PersonPtr;
```

Subsequently, we could define variables of type `PersonPtr`. This could also have been achieved in one step in the original declaration, thus:

```
typedef struct persondata {
    char name[NAMELENGTH]; /* NAMELENGTH is a
                              symbolic constant */
    int totalvote;
} PersonData, *PersonPtr;
```

This declares two new type names – `PersonData` (equivalent to `struct persondata`) and `PersonPtr` (equivalent to `struct persondata *`).

### 7.1.2 Passing structures to functions

Consider a structure in which each field is a simple variable or a character array (string), for example,

```
struct child {
    char name[20];
    int age;
    char sex;
    float allowance;
};
struct child susan;
```

We could pass individual fields to functions in the usual way; for a simple variable, its value is passed but, for an array variable, its address is passed. Thus,

```
fun1(susan.age);    /* value of susan.age is passed */
fun2(susan.sex);    /* value of susan.sex is passed */
fun3(susan.allowance);   /* value of susan.allowance is
                             passed */
```

but,

```
fun4(susan.name);    /* address of susan.name is passed */
```

We could even pass the first letter of the name, as in:

```
fun5(susan.name[0]);    /* value of first letter is passed */
```

To pass the entire structure, we use:

```
fun6(susan);
```

Here the fields of susan are copied to a temporary place (on a stack) and the copy is passed to fun6, that is, the structure is passed 'by value'. If a structure is complicated or contains arrays, the copying operation could be time-consuming. In addition, when the function returns, the values of the structure elements must be popped from the stack; this adds to the overhead – the extra processing required to perform a function call. To avoid this overhead, the `address` of the structure could be passed, as in:

```
fun7(&susan);
```

Of course, in `fun7`, the corresponding formal parameter must be declared appropriately, such as:

```
void fun7(struct child *p)
```

Now the function has access to the original actual argument and can change it, if desired. Pointers to structures are discussed in detail in Section 7.2.

It is also possible to pass the address of an individual field. For array fields, of course, this happens automatically, as in:

```
fun4(susan.name);     /* address of susan.name is passed */
```

For simple variables, the structure name (not the field name) must be preceded by &, as in:

```
fun1(&susan.age);     /* address of susan.age is passed */
```

or

```
fun3(&susan.allowance); /* address of
                              susan.allowance is passed */
```

For example, we could read values for `age` and `allowance` with:

```
scanf("%d %f", &susan.age, &susan.allowance);
```

The following gives a summary of valid operations on structures:

(1) A field can be accessed using the 'structure member' (.) operator, as in `susan.name`.
(2) A structure variable can be assigned the value of another structure variable of the same type.

(3) The address-of operator & can be applied to a structure name to give the address of the structure, e.g. &susan. & can also be applied to an element of a structure; however, & must precede the structure name, not the field name, e.g., &susan.allowance is valid but susan.&allowance or &allowance is not.

(4) If p is a pointer to a structure, then *p refers to the structure. For example, if p contains the address of the structure susan, then

```
(*p).allowance /* brackets required since '.' has higher
                precedence than '*' */
```

refers to the allowance field. However, the 'structure pointer' (arrow) operator –> (a minus sign immediately followed by >) is more commonly used to refer to a field, as in:

```
p –> allowance
```

Pointers to structures are discussed in detail in Section 7.2.

### The voting problem (continued)

Let us rewrite the function initialize (Section 5.3.1) using our structure declaration. In the function, person is used as an array of structures; person[n] refers to the *n*th structure and the individual fields are referred to by person[n].name and person[n].totalvote. Henceforth, we will use the type name PersonData declared in Section 7.1.1.

```
void initialize(PersonData person[], int max)
{
    int n;

    for (n = 0; n < max; n++) {
        person[n].totalvote = 0;
        scanf("%s", person[n].name);
    }
} /* end initialize */
```

Previously, we needed to pass two separate arrays holding the names and vote counts. Now we need to pass only a single array – an array of structures.

The following discusses the changes required by the other functions. First, here is main.

```c
#include <stdio.h>

#define MAXCANDIDATES 7
#define NAMELENGTH 20


typedef struct persondata {
    char name[NAMELENGTH];
    int totalvote;
} PersonData;


main()
{
    PersonData candidate[MAXCANDIDATES];
    int goodvotes, spoiltvotes;
    void initialize(PersonData [], int);
    void processvotes(PersonData [], int, int *, int *);
    void printresults(PersonData [], int, int, int);

    goodvotes = spoiltvotes = 0;
    initialize(candidate, MAXCANDIDATES);
    processvotes(candidate, MAXCANDIDATES, &goodvotes,
                &spoiltvotes);
    printresults(candidate, MAXCANDIDATES, goodvotes,
                spoiltvotes);
}
```

The declaration of the structure persondata comes before main. This is done so that other functions (e.g. initialize) can refer to it, and not have to repeat the entire declaration. If it were declared in main, then the names persondata and PersonData would be known only in main and other functions would have no access to them. Notice the changes (from the previous versions, Section 5.3.1) in the argument list of the functions initialize, processvotes and printresults.

The function processvotes deals only with the vote counts and not with the names of the candidates. But since the vote counts are embedded as part of the structure persondata, the structure array candidate is passed to the function. The function is written using the formal parameter person. The variable v is used to hold each incoming vote.

```
void processvotes(PersonData person[], int max,
                  int *goodptr, int *spoiltptr)
{
    int v;

    if (scanf("%d", &v) != 1) v = 0; /* if scanf does not
                                         assign a value to
                                         v, set it to 0 */
    while (v != 0) {
        if (v >= 1 && v <= max) {
            (*goodptr)++;
            ++person[v - 1].totalvote; }
        else {
            printf("  invalid vote - %d\n", v);
            (*spoiltptr)++;
        }
        if (scanf("%d", &v) != 1) v = 0;
    }
} /* end processvotes */
```

The statement

```
++person[v - 1].totalvote;
```

adds 1 to the totalvote field of the array element person[v - 1]. It could also have been written

```
person[v - 1].totalvote++;
```

The operator '.' has higher precedence than '++' so this statement is equivalent to

```
(person[v - 1].totalvote)++;
```

The functions `printresults` and `findlargest` are similar to the previous versions except that the structure array `person` replaces the separate arrays `name` and `score`.

Program P7.1 gives the complete listing of the solution to the 'voting problem' using an array of structures.

---

**Program P7.1**

```c
#include <stdio.h>

#define MAXCANDIDATES 7
#define NAMELENGTH 20

typedef struct persondata {
    char name[NAMELENGTH];
    int totalvote;
} PersonData;

main()
{
    PersonData candidate[MAXCANDIDATES];
    int goodvotes, spoiltvotes;
    void initialize(PersonData [], int);
    void processvotes(PersonData [], int, int *, int *);
    void printresults(PersonData [], int, int, int);

    goodvotes = spoiltvotes = 0;
    initialize(candidate, MAXCANDIDATES);
    processvotes(candidate, MAXCANDIDATES, &goodvotes,
                &spoiltvotes);
    printresults(candidate, MAXCANDIDATES, goodvotes,
                spoiltvotes);
}
```

```
void initialize(PersonData person[], int max)
{
   int n;

   for (n = 0; n < max; n++) {
      person[n].totalvote = 0;
      scanf("%s", person[n].name);
   }
} /* end initialize */

void processvotes(PersonData person[], int max,
                  int *goodptr, int *spoiltptr)
{
   int v;

   if (scanf("%d", &v) != 1) v = 0;
   /* if scanf does not assign a value to v,
      set it to 0 */
   while (v != 0) {
      if (v >= 1 && v <= max) {
         (*goodptr)++;
         ++person[v - 1].totalvote; }
      else {
         printf(" invalid vote - %d\n", v);
         (*spoiltptr)++;
      }
      if (scanf("%d", &v) != 1) v = 0; ;
   }
} /* end processvotes */

int findlargest(PersonData person[], int max)
/* returns the index of the highest vote from person[0]
   to person[max - 1] */
{
   int n, bigloc;

   bigloc = 0;
   for (n = 1; n < max; n++)
      if (person[n].totalvote >
          person[bigloc].totalvote) bigloc = n;
   return bigloc;
} /* end findlargest */
```

```
void printresults(PersonData person[], int max,
                     int valid, int invalid)
{
    int n, win, highestscore;
    int findlargest(PersonData [], int);

    printf("\nNumber of voters = %d\n", valid + invalid);
    printf("\nNumber of valid votes = %d\n", valid);
    printf("\nNumber of invalid votes = %d\n", invalid);

    printf("\nThe individual scores are: \n\n");
    for (n = 0; n < max; n++)
        printf("\t%-20s %d\n", person[n].name,
                person[n].totalvote);

    win = findlargest(person, max);
    highestscore = person[win].totalvote;
    printf("\nThe winner(s): \n\n");
    for (n = 0; n < max; n++)
        if (person[n].totalvote == highestscore)
                        printf("\t%s\n", person[n].name);

    printf("\nEnd of election results\n");
} /* printresults */
```

Suppose it were required to print the names of the candidates in descending order by totalvote. To do this, the structure array candidate must be sorted in descending order using the totalvote field to control the sorting. This could be done by the function call

```
sortbyvote(candidate, MAXCANDIDATES);
```

where sortbyvote (shown below) uses an insertion sort (Section 4.5.3) and is written using the formal parameter person.

```
void sortbyvote(PersonData person[], int max)

    int j, k;
    PersonData key;
```

```
     for (j = 1; j < max; j++) {/* process person[1]
                                  to person[max-1] */
         key = person[j];

         /* insert the jth person in its proper
            position among the previous j - 1 */
         for (k = j - 1; k >= 0; k--)
             if (key.totalvote > person[k].totalvote)
                 person[k + 1] = person[k];
             else
                 break;
             /*endif*/
         /*endfor*/
         person[k + 1] = key;

     }

}
```

Observe that the structure of the function is pretty much the same as if
we were sorting a simple integer array. The major difference is in the `if`
statement where we must specify which field is used to determine the
sorting order. (In this example, we also use '>' (rather than '<') since we
are sorting in descending order). When we are about to process
`person[j]`, it is copied to the temporary structure `key`. When we need
to shift an array element to the right, the simple assignment

```
person[k + 1] = person[k];
```

is used to move the entire structure (two fields, in this example).

If we needed to sort the candidates in alphabetical order, we could use
the following function `sortbyname`:

```
void sortbyname(PersonData person[], int max)
{
    int j, k;
    PersonData key;

    for (j = 1; j < max; j++) { /* process person[1] to
                                  person[max - 1] */
        key = person[j];
```

```
    /* insert the jth person in its proper position
       among the previous j - 1 */
    for (k = j - 1; k >= 0; k--)
        if (strcmp(key.name, person[k].name) < 0)
            person[k + 1] = person[k];
        else
            break;
        /*endif*/
    /*endfor*/
    person[k + 1] = key;
}
}
```

sortbyname is identical with sortbyvote except for the if statement which specifies which field is used in comparisons.

It is a useful exercise to compare sortbyname with the parallelsort function of Section 4.5.4. In effect, both functions sort words in alphabetical order. But each 'word' has associated data which must be kept with the word. Observe that sortbyname (which uses a structure) is much simpler than parallelsort (which uses parallel arrays). What is also significant is that if there were a third (or further) data item in the structure, sortbyname will need no changes whereas parallelsort gets bigger for each parallel array that is added.

## 7.2 Pointers to structures

Just as it is possible to take the address of an int variable, so too can one take the address of a structure variable. Using the declaration :

```
typedef struct persondata {
    char name[NAMELENGTH];
    int age;
} PersonData;
```

consider

```
PersonData child, *ptr;
```

This declares child to be a structure variable with two fields. It also declares ptr to be a **pointer to** a structure of the type PersonData. In other words, the values which ptr can assume are addresses of variables of type PersonData. For example, the statement

```
ptr = &child;
```

is valid and assigns the **address** of the structure variable `child` to `ptr`. As with pointers to other types, `*ptr` refers to the object that `ptr` is pointing at. In this example, `*ptr` is a synonym for `child`. We can refer to the fields that `ptr` is pointing at by using the operator '.' as in

```
(*ptr).name and (*ptr).age
```

However, pointers to structures occur so frequently in C that a special alternative notation is available. If `ptr` is pointing at a structure of type `persondata`, then

ptr  -> name   refers to the 'name' field, and
ptr  -> age    refers to the 'age' field.

-> is a 'minus' sign followed by a 'greater than' sign.

### 7.3  Linked lists

When values are stored in a one-dimensional array ($x[0]$ to $x[n]$), say), they can be thought of as being organized as a 'linear list'. Consider each item in the array as a **node**. A linear list means that the nodes are arranged in a linear order such that

$x[0]$ is the first node;
$x[n]$ is the last node;
if $0 < k <= n$, then $x[k]$ is preceded by $x[k-1]$;
if $0 <= k < n$ then $x[k]$ is followed by $x[k+1]$.

Thus, given a node, the 'next' node is assumed to be in the next location (if any) in the array; the order of the nodes is the order in which they have been placed in the array. Consider the problem of inserting a new node between two existing nodes $x[k]$ and $x[k+1]$. This can be done only if $x[k+1]$ and the nodes after it are moved to make room for the new node. Similarly, the deletion of $x[k]$ involves the movement of the nodes $x[k+1]$, $x[k+2]$, etc. Accessing any given node is easy; all we have to do is provide the appropriate subscript.

In many situations, we use an array for representing a linear list. But we can also represent such a list by using an organization in which each node points explicitly to the next node. This new organization is referred to as a **linked list**.

In a (singly) linked list, each node contains a pointer which points to the next node in the list. We can think of each node as a cell with two fields:

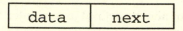

where `data` can actually be one or more fields (depending on what needs to be stored in a node), and `next` 'points to' the next node of the list. The `next` field of the last node is set to NULL; it does not point to anything. In addition to the cells of the list, we need a pointer variable (`top`, say) which points to the first item in the list. If the list is empty, the value of `top` is NULL.

Pictorially, we represent a linked list as follows:

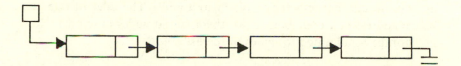

The symbol ⏚ is used to represent the NULL pointer.

How can we represent a linked list in a C program? Since each node consists of at least two fields, we will need to use a `struct` to define the format of a node. But what is the type of the `next` field? We know it's a pointer, but a pointer to what? It's a pointer to a structure of which it is a part! Thus the definition of the structure includes a field which points to the structure being defined. (This is usually called a self-referencing structure). As an example, suppose the data at each node is a positive integer. We can define a node as follows:

```
struct node {
    int num;
    struct node *next;
};
```

or using `typedef`:

```
typedef struct node {
    int num;
    struct node *next;
} Node, *NodePtr; /* we also declare a name for
                         'struct node *' */
```

The variable `top` can now be defined as a pointer to a node, thus:

```
Node *top;
```

or

```
NodePtr top;
```

As explained before, the `struct` declaration of `node` (as we have written it) does not allocate any storage for any variables. It simply specifies the form that such variables will take. However, the declaration of `top` does allocate storage, but only for a pointer to a node. The **value** of `top` can be the address of a node but, so far, there are no nodes in the list. How can storage be allocated to nodes of the list?

### 7.3.1 *Dynamic storage allocation – malloc, calloc, sizeof*

Consider the problem of reading positive integers (terminated by 0) and building a linked list which contains the numbers in the order in which they were read. One question which arises is how many nodes will there be in the list? This, of course, depends on how many numbers are supplied. One disadvantage of using an array for storing a linear list is that the size of the array must be specified beforehand. If we need to store more items than this size allows, the program may have to be aborted. With the linked list approach, whenever a new node must be added to the list, storage is allocated for the node and the appropriate pointers are set. Thus we allocate just the right amount of storage for the list – no more, no less. We do use extra storage for the pointers, but this is more than compensated for by more efficient use of storage as well as easy insertions and deletions. Allocating storage 'as needed' is usually referred to as **dynamic storage allocation**. (On the other hand, array storage is referred to as **static** storage allocation).

In C, storage can be allocated dynamically by using the standard functions `malloc` and `calloc`. In order to use these functions (and `free`, later), your program must be preceded by the header line

```
#include <stdlib.h>
```

The prototype for `malloc` is

```
void *malloc(size_t size);
```

where `size_t` is an implementation-defined unsigned integer type defined in the standard header `<stddef.h>`. Typically, `size_t` is `typedef`'d as `unsigned int` or `unsigned long int`.

`malloc` allocates `size` bytes of memory and returns a pointer to the first byte. The storage is uninitialized. If it is unable to find the requested amount of storage, `malloc` returns NULL. When your program calls `malloc`, it is important to verify that the requested storage has been successfully allocated. In order to use the storage allocated, the pointer returned must be assigned to a pointer variable of the appropriate type. As an example, assuming that `chptr` is a character pointer, the statement:

```
chptr = malloc(20);
```

allocates 20 bytes of storage and stores the address of the first byte in `chptr`. To be safe, the program should check that `chptr` is not NULL before continuing.

**Note**: In general, a pointer to one type may not be directly assigned to a pointer of another type; however, assignment is possible if an explicit cast is used. For example, given the declarations

```
int * intptr;
double * dbptr;
```

the assignment

```
intptr = dbptr;          /* wrong */
```

is invalid. However, it is valid to use

```
intptr = (int *) dbptr;  /* right */
```

On the other hand, pointers may be assigned to and from pointers of type void *, and may be compared with them. Thus, in the above example, no cast is required to assign the void * returned by malloc to the character pointer chptr.

The prototype for calloc is

```
void *calloc(size_t num, size_t size);
```

calloc allocates num * size bytes of memory and returns a pointer to the first byte. (Another way of looking at it is that calloc allocates enough memory for an array of num objects each of size size). All bytes returned are initialized to 0. If it is unable to find the requested amount of storage, calloc returns NULL. When your program calls calloc, it is important to verify that the requested storage has been successfully allocated. In order to use the storage allocated, the pointer returned must be assigned to a pointer variable of the appropriate type. As an example, assuming that chptr is a character pointer, the statement:

```
chptr = calloc(10, 20);
```

allocates $10 \times 20 = 200$ bytes of storage and stores the address of the first byte in chptr. To be safe, the program should check that chptr is not NULL before continuing.

calloc is useful for allocating storage for arrays. An example will be given after the discussion of sizeof.

### The sizeof *operator*

sizeof is a standard unary operator that returns the number of bytes needed for storing its argument. For example,

```
sizeof (int)
```

returns the number of bytes needed for storing an int variable. (Strictly speaking, the value returned by sizeof is of type size_t, defined in the standard header < stddef.h >). The argument to sizeof is either a type or a variable. If it is a type (like int or float or double), it must be enclosed in parentheses. If it is a variable, the parentheses are optional. For example, if root is a variable of type double, then both

```
sizeof root
```

and

```
sizeof (root)
```

are valid and return the number of bytes needed for storing root.

sizeof is used mainly for writing portable code, where the code depends on the number of bytes needed for storing various data types. For example, an integer may occupy 2 bytes on one machine but 4 bytes on another. Using sizeof(int) (instead of 2 or 4) in one's program ensures that the program will work on either machine. sizeof is used quite often with the functions malloc and calloc. For example, assuming that dbptr is a 'pointer to double', the statement:

```
dbptr = malloc(sizeof(double));
```

allocates enough storage for storing a double variable and assigns the address of the first byte to dbptr.

Another example is (assuming flptr is a 'pointer to float'):

```
flptr = calloc(10, sizeof(float));
```

Here, storage is allocated for 10 floats and the address of the first is stored in flptr.

One can also use type names defined with typedef as an argument to sizeof. Using the structure declarations above,

```
top = malloc(sizeof (Node));
```

allocates enough storage for one Node structure, and assigns the address of the structure to top.

The function free is related to malloc and calloc. It is used to free storage acquired by calls to malloc and calloc. Its prototype is

```
void free(void *ptr);
```

and it releases the storage pointed to by ptr. For example, to free the storage pointed to by top, above, one could use:

```
free(top);
```

Observe that even though free expects a void *, it is not **necessary** to explicitly cast top (a Node *) into a void * (see Note on page 205). Of course, it is perfectly acceptable to use

```
free((void *) top);
```

It is a **fatal error** to attempt to free storage not obtained by a call to malloc or calloc.

### 7.3.2 *Building a linked list – version 1*

Consider again the problem of building a linked list of positive integers in the order in which they arrive. If the incoming numbers are (0 terminates the data)

```
25 18 43 32 0
```

then the following list will be built:

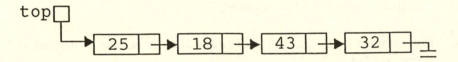

In our solution, we start with an empty list. Our program will reflect this with the statement

```
top = NULL;
```

(The symbolic constant NULL is defined in <stdio.h>).
    When a new number arrives, we must

(1) allocate storage for a node;
(2) put the number in the new node;
(3) make the new node the last one in the list.

For the first number, we must set top to point to the new node. But for each subsequent number, we must set the next field of current last node to point to the new node. But how do we find the last node of the existing list? One method is to start at the top of the list and follow the next pointers until we encounter NULL. This is time-consuming if we have to do it for each new number. A better approach is to keep a pointer (`last`, say) to the last node of the list. This pointer is updated as new nodes are added. Program P7.2 reads the numbers and creates the linked list as discussed.

---

**Program P7.2**

```c
#include <stdio.h>
#include <stdlib.h>

typedef struct node {
    int num;
    struct node *next;
} Node, *NodePtr;

main()
{
    int n;
    NodePtr top, new, last;

    top = NULL;
    if (scanf("%d", &n) != 1) n = 0;
    while (n != 0) {
        new = malloc(sizeof(Node));
        new -> num = n;
        new -> next = NULL;

        if (top == NULL) /* first number */
            top = last = new;
        else {
            last -> next = new;   /* set last node to
                                        point to new node */
            last = new; /* make the new node the
                            last node */
        }
        if (scanf("%d", &n) != 1) n = 0;
    }
}
```

---

Program P7.2 only builds the linked list. If, for example, we wanted to print the numbers from the list (**after** it is completely built), we could use the following function `printlist`:

```
void printlist(NodePtr top)
{
    while (top != NULL) { /* as long as there's a node */
        printf("%d\n", top -> num);
        top = top -> next; /* go on to the next node */
    }
}
```

### 7.3.3 *Some characteristics of linked lists*

A list with one pointer in each node is called a one-way linked list. One important characteristic of such a list is that, normally, access to the nodes is via the 'top of list' pointer and the pointer field in each node. (However, other explicit pointers may point to specific nodes in the list, for example, the pointer `last`, above, which pointed to the last node in the list). This means that access is restricted to being sequential. The only way to get to node 4, say, is via nodes 1, 2 and 3. Since we can't access the $k$th node directly, we will not be able, for instance, to perform a binary search on a linked list. The great advantage of a linked list is that it allows for easy insertions and deletions anywhere in the list.

Suppose we wanted to insert a new node between the second and third nodes. We can view this simply as insertion after the second node. Suppose p points to the second node and new points to the new node, then the insertion can be accomplished by:

```
new -> next = p -> next;
p -> next = new;
```

The first statement says 'let the new node point to whatever the second node is pointing at, i.e., the third node'. The second statement says 'let the second node point to the new node'. The net effect is that the new node is inserted between the second and the third. The new node becomes the third node and the original third node becomes the fourth node. This is illustrated by:

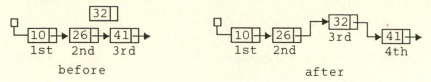

before                                    after

Does this code work if p were pointing at the last node? In this case, p –> next is NULL. The first statement sets new –> next to NULL and the second sets the last node to point to the new node. The code works for insertion after the last node. This is illustrated by:

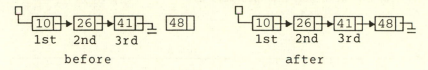

before                                    after

In many situations, it is required to insert a new node at the head of the list. That is, we want to make the new node the first node. Assuming that new points to the new node, it can be inserted at the head of the list with:

```
new -> next = top;
top = new;
```

The first statement sets the new node to point to whatever top is pointing at (that is, the first node), and the second statement updates top to point to the new node. This is illustrated by:

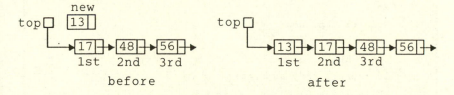

before                                    after

One should observe that the code works even if the list were initially empty (that is, if top were NULL).

### 7.3.4 Building a linked list – version 2

To illustrate insertion at the top of the list, consider the same problem as above, but now each new number is to be inserted at the top of the list.

If the incoming numbers are

    25 18 43 32 0

then the following list will be built:

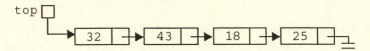

The program to build the list in reverse order is actually simpler than the previous one. It is shown as program P7.3.

---

**Program P7.3**

```c
#include <stdio.h>
#include <stdlib.h>

typedef struct node {
    int num;
    struct node *next;
} Node, *NodePtr;

main()
{
    int n;
    NodePtr top, new;

    top = NULL;
    if (scanf("%d", &n) != 1) n = 0;
    while (n != 0) {
        new = malloc(sizeof(Node));
        new -> num = n;
        new -> next = top;
        top = new;
        if (scanf("%d", &n) != 1) n = 0;
    }
}
```

The first program inserts incoming numbers at the end of the list. This is an example of adding an item to a **queue**. A queue is a linear list in which insertions occur at one end and deletions occur at the other end. The second program inserts incoming numbers at the top of the list. This is an example of adding an item to a **stack**. A stack is a linear list in which insertions and deletions occur at the same end. In stack terminology, we say an item is 'pushed' onto the stack. Deleting an item from a stack is referred to as 'popping' the stack.

### 7.3.5 Deletion from a linked list

Deleting a node from the top of a linked list is accomplished by

```
top = top -> next;
```

This says let `top` point to whatever the first node was pointing at. Of course, before we delete, we should check that there **is** something to delete, that `top` is not NULL.

To delete an arbitrary node from a linked list requires more information. Suppose p points to the node to be deleted. Deleting this node requires that we change the `next` field of the previous node. This means we must know the pointer to the previous node; suppose it is pp. Then deletion of node p can be accomplished by

```
pp -> next = p -> next;
```

This is illustrated by

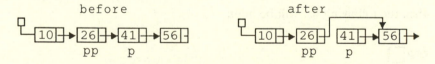

One may wonder what happens to nodes which have been deleted. In our explanations above, 'deletion' meant 'logical deletion', that is, as far as processing the list is concerned, the deleted nodes are not present. But the nodes are still in memory, occupying storage, even though we may have lost the pointers to them. If we have a large list in which many deletions have occurred, then there will be a lot of 'deleted' nodes scattered all over memory. These nodes occupy storage even though they will never need to be processed. C provides us with a function, free, to free the storage space occupied by nodes which are to be deleted. The space to be freed should have been obtained by a call to `malloc` or `calloc`. `free(p)` frees the space pointed to by p.

To illustrate its use, deleting the first node of the list can be accomplished by

```
old = top; /* save the pointer to the node to be
                deleted */
top = top -> next; /* set top to point to the 2nd
                        node, if any */
free(old); /* free the space occupied by the first
                node */
```

where `old` is the same kind of pointer as `top`.

To delete a node from elsewhere in the list where p points to the node to be deleted and pp points to the previous node, we can use:

```
pp -> next = p -> next; /* logical deletion */
free(p); /* free the space occupied by the
                deleted node */
```

### 7.3.6 *Building a linked list – version 3*

Finally, suppose we wanted to build the list of numbers so that it is always sorted in ascending order. For example, if the incoming numbers are

```
25 18 43 32 0
```

then the following list will be built:

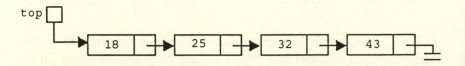

When a new number is read, it is inserted in the existing list (which is initially empty) in its proper place. The first number is simply added to the empty list. Each subsequent number is compared with the numbers in the existing list. As long as the new number is greater than a number in the list, we move down the list until the new number is smaller than an existing number or we come to the end of the list. To facilitate the insertion of the new number, before we leave a node we must save the pointer to it in case the new number must be inserted after this node. However, this can only be determined when we compare with the number in the next node. Our program P7.4 uses p to point to the current node and pp to point to the previous node. The insertion of a new node in its proper position in the list is delegated to the function `insertlist`; `insertlist` returns a pointer to the top of the modified list. We have also included the function `printlist` to print the numbers in the list.

---

**Program P7.4**

```c
#include <stdio.h>
#include <stdlib.h>

typedef struct node {
    int num;
    struct node *next;
} Node, *NodePtr;

main()
{
    int n;
    NodePtr top;
    NodePtr insertlist(NodePtr top, int n);
    void printlist(NodePtr top);

    top = NULL;
    if (scanf("%d", &n) != 1) n = 0;
    while (n != 0) { /* create linked list in
                        sorted order */
        top = insertlist(top, n);
        if (scanf("%d", &n) != 1) n = 0;
    }
    if (top == NULL)
        printf("\nNo numbers supplied\n");
    else {
        printf("\nThe numbers in ascending "
               "order\n\n");
```

---

```
            printlist(top);
        }
    }

NodePtr insertlist(NodePtr top, int n)
{   /* This function inserts n in its ordered
        position in a (possibly empty) list pointed to
        by top, and returns a pointer to the new
        list */
    NodePtr new, p, pp;

    new = malloc(sizeof(Node));
    new -> num = n;

    if (top == NULL) { /* first number */
        new -> next = NULL;
        return new; }    /* the new node is first in
                                the list */
    else { /* there is at least one number in the
                list */
        if (n <= top -> num) { /* insert at the top */
            new -> next = top;
            return new;    /* the new node is now the
                                first in the list */
        }
        else { /* find the proper place in the list */
            pp = top;
            p = top -> next;
            while (p != NULL && n > p -> num) {
                pp = p;
                p = p -> next;
            }
            /* insert after pp */
            pp -> next = new;
            new -> next = p;
            return top;    /* the top of the list has
                                not changed */
        }
    }
}
```

```
void printlist(NodePtr top)
{
    while (top != NULL) { /* as long as there's
                             a node */
        printf("%d\n", top -> num);
        top = top -> next; /* go on to the next
                              node */
    }
}
```

## Exercises 7

(1) Write typedef and struct declarations for each of the following.

   (a) employees in a company;
   (b) customers in a bank;
   (c) students in a high school;
   (d) library cataloguing information for books;
   (e) borrowers at a library;
   (f) playing cards;
   (g) time, measured in hours, minutes and seconds;
   (h) description of a car;
   (i) information on car parts sold by a dealer;
   (j) information on a cheque;
   (k) teams in a football league;
   (l) position of a chess piece on a board.

(2) Each line of data consists of a student's name followed by marks (out of 100) made in three assignments. Data is terminated by the name "END". Using structures, write a C program to read the data, and for each student, calculate the average mark obtained. Output your results under suitable headings. For each student, print the name, the three marks, the average and a message 'Pass' or 'Fail'. (A student passes if the average is greater than or equal to 50).

   At the end, print the number of students processed, the number who passed, the number who failed and the name of the student obtaining the highest average. (Ignore the possibility of a tie).

   Also determine the class average for each of the three assignments.

   Modify the program to list the students in (a) alphabetical order (b) in descending order by average mark.

(3) A survey of 10 pop records is made. Each person votes by specifying three values (each from 1 to 10), in order, representing their choice of first, second and third. First choice scores 4 points, second choice scores 2 points and third choice scores 1 point. Data consists of the titles of the 10 records followed by the voters' choices. Using structures, write a program to read

the data, process the votes and print the title of the most popular record. Appropriate validation should be done, for example, a person does not vote for the same record more than once.

(4)   C does not provide any built-in facilities for dealing with complex numbers (those with real and imaginary parts). Using structures, write the necessary declarations and functions to implement the addition, subtraction, multiplication and division of complex numbers.

(5)   Write functions to manipulate rational numbers of the form $a/b$ where $a$ and $b$ are integers and $b \neq 0$. Answers should always be reduced to lowest terms. In addition to others, you will need to write functions to:

- find the greatest common divisor of two integers;
- find the least common multiple of two integers;
- simplify a fraction.

(6)   The equation of a straight line can be determined from its slope, $m$, and one point $(x1, y1)$ on the line. Write the structure declaration for a line. Write a function which, given the information for a line, prints the equation of the line using the formula

$$y - y_1 = m(x - x_1)$$

(7)   Write a program to create the index for a book. Each section of data consists of a page number followed by the words or phrases to be indexed on that page. Choose a suitable character for separating consecutive words or phrases and an appropriate marker for ending each section of data. Output consists of an alphabetical listing of the words and phrases followed by the page numbers in which they appear.

(8)   Write a function to sort a linked list of integers as follows:

(a) Find the node with the smallest value in the list.
(b) Interchange its 'data' with that at the top of the list.
(c) Starting from what is now the second element, repeat (a) and interchange its 'data' with that of the second element.

Continue until the list is sorted.

(9)   Write a function to sort a linked list of integers as follows:

(a) Find the largest value in the list.
(b) Delete it from its position and insert it at the head of the list.
(c) Starting from what is now the second element, repeat (a) and (b).
(d) Starting from what is now the third element, repeat (a) and (b).

Continue until the list is sorted.

(10)   Write a function which, given pointers to two sorted linked lists of integers, merges the two lists into one sorted list. No new storage should be allocated for the merged list. The merged list should consist of the original cells of the given lists; only pointers should be changed. The function should return a pointer to the merged list.

(11)   The non-zero (real) elements of an $n \times n$ sparse matrix are to be stored in

a hash table. Data consists of

row, column, element

repeated as many times as there are non-zero elements. A row value of 0 terminates the data.

Assuming that there are no more than 100 elements to be stored, write a C program to store the matrix. Include validation tests for invalid row or column values, and repeated (row, column) pairs.

Write a function which, given $i$ and $j$, returns the value of the $(i, j)$th element of the matrix.

(12) Write a function which, given a pointer to a linked list, returns the number of nodes in the list.

(13) Write a function which, given a pointer to a linked list and key, searches for key in the list. If found, return a pointer to the node in which key is found; otherwise, return NULL.

(14) The letters of a word are stored in a linked list, one letter per node. Write C statements to reverse the letters of the word.

(15) Write a function which determines if the nodes in a list are in order.

(16) Write a function which, given a pointer to a linked list, returns a pointer to the last node of the list.

(17) A linked list is used to represent a polynomial, each element of the list representing one (non-zero) term of the polynomial. The 'data' for each term consists of a coefficient and an exponent. The terms are stored in order of **decreasing** exponent and no coefficient is 0.

Write a function to read (coefficient, exponent) pairs and create the linked list representing the polynomial.

Given that first and second each point to a polynomial, write C code to evaluate the sum of the polynomials, and store the sum in a newly created list pointed at by sum. (Be careful not to include terms with zero coefficient in the sum).

Write a function which, given a pointer to a polynomial and a value $x$, returns the value of the polynomial evaluated at $x$.

(18) A data file contains registration information for six courses – CS20A, CS21A, CS29A, CS30A, CS35A and CS36A. Each line of data consists of a 6-digit student registration number followed by a student name (ended with $) followed by six (ordered) values, each of which is 0 or 1. (A registration number of 0 terminates the data). A value of 1 indicates that the student is registered for the corresponding course; 0 means he is not. Thus 1 0 1 0 1 1 means that the student is registered for CS20A, CS29A, CS35A and CS36A, but not for CS21A and CS30A. You may assume that there are no more than 100 students.

Write a program to read the data and produce a class list for each of the six courses. Each list begins on a new page and consists of a heading, e.g., Class List For CS20A, followed by the registration numbers and names of those students taking the course.

Include options which allow the class list to be printed in order by registration number or in alphabetical order by name.

(19)  Write a program to read and store a thesaurus as follows.

   Data for the program consists of lines of input. Each line contains a (variable) number of distinct words, all of which are synonyms. The words are to be inserted in a hash table and synonyms are held on a **sorted** linked list. A word can appear on more than one line, but each word must be inserted only once in the table. (If a word appears on another line, then the words on that line would be inserted in an existing list). Data is terminated by a line containing ENDOFSYNONYMS.

   After the thesaurus has been built, selected words are read and printed with an alphabetic list of all their synonyms.

(20)  Write a program to read students' data and produce two listings as described below. Each line of data consists of a 5-digit student number, a name (terminated by *), a telephone number, and six numeric values – the first five are assignment marks (out of 25) and the sixth is an examination mark (out of 100). The assignments count for 25% of the final mark and the examination counts for 75%. The students' data are to be stored in an array of structures. For each student, the final numeric mark, $\alpha$, is calculated. The letter grade is then calculated as follows:

| $\alpha =$ Numeric score | Letter grade |
|---|---|
| $\alpha < \mu - 3\sigma/2$ | F |
| $\mu - 3\sigma/2 \leq \alpha < \mu - \sigma/2$ | D |
| $\mu - \sigma/2 \leq \alpha < \mu + \sigma/2$ | C |
| $\mu + \sigma/2 \leq \alpha < \mu + 3\sigma/2$ | B |
| $\mu + 3\sigma/2 \leq \alpha$ | A |

where $\mu$ is the mean numeric score and $\sigma$ is the standard deviation.

   The first listing to be produced consists of student's name, assignment marks, course-work mark (out of 25), examination mark (out of 100), examination percentage (out of 75), final numeric score and letter grade, arranged in alphabetical order by name.

   The second listing to be produced consists of the same information as above, but arranged so that the numeric scores are in descending order.

# 8

# Binary Trees and Other Structures

In the previous chapter, we discussed how to declare and use structures in C. We also discussed in some detail the data structure called a linear list, and showed how to implement it using C pointers. In this chapter, we introduce a very versatile data structure called a binary tree. The binary tree is a classic example of a non-linear data structure; compare a linear list where we identify a 'first' item, a 'next' item and a 'last' item. We show how to implement and manipulate a binary tree in a C program by developing a program to produce a cross-reference listing of the words in the input.

The chapter concludes with a discussion of nested structures, unions and bit-fields.

## 8.1 Binary trees

In the linked list structure discussed in the last chapter, each node of the list contained one pointer which 'pointed to' the next item in the list. But there is no reason why the node must contain one pointer only. There could also be another pointer which 'points to' the previous node in the list or one which 'points to' the first item in the list. In a **binary tree**, each node contains two pointers.

A binary tree can

(a) be empty, or
(b) consist of a root and two subtrees – a left and a right – each of which is itself a binary tree.

A consequence of the above (recursive) definition is that each node of a binary tree has exactly two subtrees with the proviso that any of these may be empty. Figure 8.1 shows several examples of binary trees.

(i) binary tree with 1 node, the root

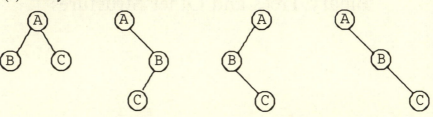

(ii) binary trees with 3 nodes

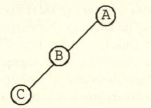

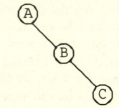

(iii) binary tree with all right subtrees       binary tree with all left
    empty                                       subtrees empty

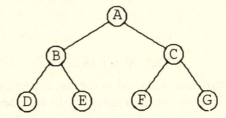

(iv) binary tree where each node, except the leaves (nodes with 0 subtrees),
    has exactly 2 subtrees (called a complete binary tree)

(v) a general binary tree

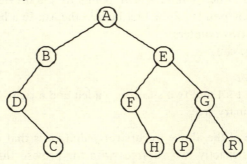

Figure 8.1. Examples of binary trees

If a node has one non-empty child (subtree), we make a distinction between an empty left and an empty right subtree. So, for instance,

(empty left) is a different binary tree from

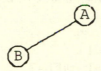

(empty right).

### Some terminology and observations

- Each node of a binary tree is the root of a subtree.
- Each node, except the root, has exactly one parent. In a diagram, this means that each node, except the root, has exactly one line leading into it.
- The **degree** of a node is the number of non-empty subtrees of the node.
- A node of degree 0 is called a **terminal node** or a **leaf**.
- A **branch** node is a non-terminal node. A branch node has at least one non-empty subtree.
- The **level** of a node is a measure of the depth of the node in the tree. The root is considered to be at level 0. The level of any other node is the number of branches which must be traversed in the most direct path from the root to the node.

For example, given the following binary tree,

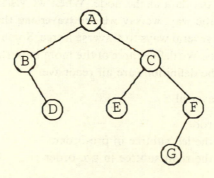

we have

$$degree(A) = degree(C) = 2$$
$$degree(B) = degree(F) = 1$$
$$degree(D) = degree(E) = degree(G) = 0$$

There are three terminal nodes (leaves): D, E and G.

There are four branch nodes: A, B, C and F.

$$level(A) = 0$$
$$level(B) = level(C) = 1$$
$$level(D) = level(E) = level(F) = 2$$
$$level(G) = 3$$

### *Traversing a binary tree*

Given a binary tree, we may 'visit' the nodes of the tree in several orders. For example, the nodes of the tree

may be 'visited' in the order A B C, or B A C, or B C A or even C A B. (In fact, for a binary tree of $n$ nodes, there are $n!$ ways to 'visit' the nodes, assuming that each node is visited once). By 'visit' here, we mean 'do whatever needs to be done' when we get to a node. It may mean simply printing the information at the node, or performing some more involved processing with the data at the node. When we visit the nodes of a tree in some systematic way, we say we are **traversing** the tree. As indicated above, there are several ways to traverse a tree. Some traversals are more useful than others. We define three of the more important ways to traverse a binary tree. The definitions are all recursive.

(1) Pre-order traversal

    (a)  visit the root;
    (b)  traverse the left subtree in pre-order;
    (c)  traverse the right subtree in pre-order.

The pre-order traversal of the binary tree

is A B C.

The pre-order traversal of

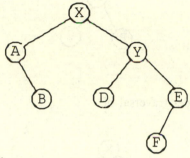

is X A B Y D E F.

(2) In-order traversal

(a) traverse the left subtree in in-order;
(b) visit the root;
(c) traverse the right subtree in in-order.

The in-order traversal of

is B A C.

The in-order traversal of

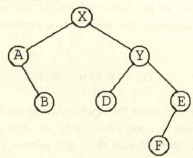

is A B X D Y F E.

(3) Post-order traversal

    (a) traverse the left subtree in post-order;
    (b) traverse the right subtree in post-order.
    (c) visit the root;

The post-order traversal of

is B C A.

    The post-order traversal of

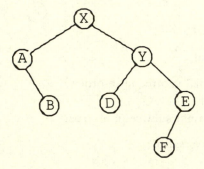

    is B A D F E Y X.

Note that the traversals derive their names from the place where we visit the root relative to the traversals of the left and right subtrees. As another example, consider the binary tree representing the arithmetic expression

$$(12+18)*(36-48/16)$$

The leaves of the tree contain the operands and the branch nodes contain the operators. Given a node containing an operator, the left subtree represents the first operand and the right subtree represents the second operand.

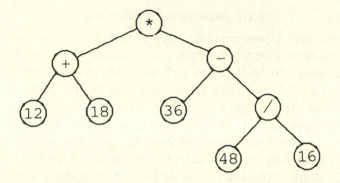

The pre-order traversal is      * + 12 18 − 36 / 48 16
The in-order traversal is       12 + 18 * 36 − 48 / 16
The post-order traversal is     12 18 + 36 48 16 / − *

The post-order traversal can be used (in conjunction with a stack) to evaluate an arithmetic expression. The steps are as follows:

(1) Get the next item, $X$.
(2) If $X$ is an operand (a variable or constant), push it onto the stack.
(3) If $X$ is an operator, pop its operand(s) from the stack, apply the operator to the item(s) popped and push the result back onto the stack.

These steps are repeated until the end of the traversal. At the end, the result of the expression is the value at the top of the stack. Using the post-order traversal above, the expression is evaluated as follows:

- 12 and 18 are pushed on the stack;
- + causes 18 and 12 to be popped; 12 + 18 is evaluated, giving 30, which is pushed on the stack;
- 36, 48 and 16 are then pushed, so the stack now contains 30, 36, 48, 16;
- / causes 16 and 48 (in that order) to be popped; 48/16 is evaluated, giving 3, which is pushed. The stack now contains 30, 36, 3;
- − causes 3 and 36 (in that order) to be popped; 36 − 3 is evaluated, giving 33, which is pushed. The stack now contains 30, 33;
- * causes 30 and 33 to be popped; 30 * 33 is evaluated, giving 990, which is pushed;
- the traversal is completed and the stack contains 990, the result of the expression.

The in-order traversal is useful when dealing with **binary search trees** (Section 8.1.2).

### 8.1.1 Representing a binary tree

Firstly, we need a pointer (`root`, say) which points to the node at the root of the tree. If the tree is empty, `root` is set to NULL. In addition to the information to be stored at each node, we will need two pointers, `left` and `right`, say; `left` points to the left subtree of the node and `right` points to the right subtree of the node. A pointer is set to NULL if the corresponding subtree does not exist (is empty). But what kind of pointers are these? As with linked lists, they point to structures which have the same form as the structure to which they belong. To give an example, suppose the data to be stored at each node is a word. The following declarations may be used to specify the binary tree:

```
typedef struct treenode {
   char word[MAXWORDSIZE];
   struct treenode *left, *right;
} TreeNode, *TreePtr;
TreePtr root;
```

Note that the declaration of `treenode` contains, not an instance of itself (which is illegal) but, rather, a **pointer** to an instance of itself. In the next section, we will see how these declarations can be used to build a binary tree.

### 8.1.2 Binary search trees

Consider one possible binary tree built with the following three-letter words:

gem run hex bee pie tea dot

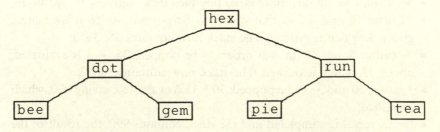

The above is a special kind of binary tree. It has the property that, given any node, the word(s) in the left subtree is (are) 'smaller' and the word(s) in the right subtree is (are) 'greater' than the word at the node. (Here, 'smaller' and 'greater' refer to alphabetical order). Such a tree is called a **binary search tree**. This is because it facilitates the search for a given key. The method of searching is very similar to the binary search using arrays (Section 2.5.2).

Consider the search for pie. Starting at the root, pie is compared with hex. Since pie is greater (in alphabetical order) then hex, we can conclude that if it is in the tree, it must be in the right subtree. Following the right subtree of hex, we next compare pie with run. Since pie is smaller than run, we must follow the left subtree of run. We then compare pie with pie, and the search ends successfully.

But what if we were searching for cue?

- cue is smaller than hex, so we go left;
- cue is smaller than dot, so we go left again;
- cue is greater than bee, so we must go right.

But since the right subtree of bee is empty, we can conclude that cue is not in the tree. If it is necessary to add cue to the tree, note that we have also found the place where it must be added. It must be added as the right subtree of bee, thus:

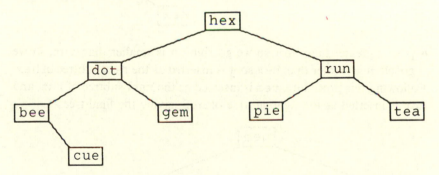

Thus the binary search tree not only facilitates searching, but if an item is not found, it can be easily inserted. It combines the speed advantage of a binary search with the easy insertion of linked lists.

The tree drawn above is the optimal binary search tree for the seven given words. This means that it is the 'best possible' tree for these words in the sense that it gives the same 'number of comparisons' as a binary search on a linear array. But this is not the only possible search tree for these words. Suppose the words came in one at a time and, as each word came in, it was added to the tree in such a way that the tree remained a binary search tree. The final tree built will depend on the order in which the words came in. For example, suppose the words came in the order:

gem run hex bee pie tea dot

Initially the tree is empty. When gem comes in, it becomes the root of the tree.

- run comes next and is compared with gem. Since run is greater, it is inserted as the right subtree of gem.
- hex is greater than gem, so we go right; hex is smaller than run so it is inserted as the left subtree of run.
- bee is smaller than gem, so it is inserted as the left subtree of gem.

The tree built so far is

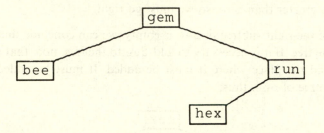

- pie is greater than gem, so we go right; it is smaller than run, so we go left; it is greater than hex so it is inserted as the right subtree of hex. Following this procedure, tea is inserted as the right subtree of run, and dot is inserted as the right subtree of bee, giving the final tree:

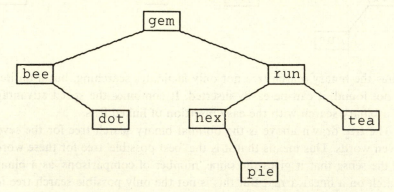

Note that the tree obtained is quite different from the optimal search tree. The number of comparisons required to find a given word has also changed. For instance, pie now requires four comparisons; it required three previously. dot now requires three as opposed to two previously. But bee now requires two as opposed to three previously.

It can be proved that if the words come in random order, then the average search time for a given word is approximately 1.4 times the average for the optimal search tree. But what about the worst case? If the words come in alphabetical order, then the tree built will be:

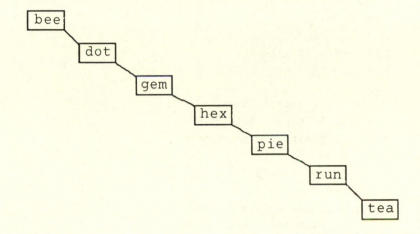

Searching such a tree is reduced to a sequential search of a linked list. This kind of tree is called a **degenerate** tree. Certain orders of the words will give some very unbalanced trees. As an exercise, draw the trees obtained for the following orders of the words:

(a) tea run pie hex gem dot bee
(b) bee tea dot run gem pie hex
(c) tea bee dot run pie gem hex
(d) dot gem tea run bee pie hex

We now consider an algorithm for finding or inserting an item in a binary search tree. Assume the following:

- root points to the root of a binary search tree; initially, root is NULL.
- if p points to a given node, we use the notation data(p), left(p) and right(p) to refer to the fields of the node.

The following pseudocode algorithm searches the tree for key; if it is not found, it is inserted in the tree in its appropriate place.

```
  if root = NULL then
     /* this is the first key. Get a node; assume
        new points to it */
     getnode(new);
     data(new) = key;
     left(new) = NULL:
     right(new) = NULL;
     root = new;
  else
     positionfound = FALSE;
     p = root;
     repeat
        if key < data(p) then
           if left(p) = NULL then
              positionfound = TRUE
           else
              p = left(p)
           endif
        else if key > data(p) then
           if right(p) = NULL then
              positionfound = TRUE
           else
              p = right(p)
           endif
        endif
     until key = data(p) or positionfound;
     if key = data(p) then
        "key found at node p"
     else /* key is not in the tree; insert it */
        /* get a node; assume new points to it */
        getnode(new);
        data(new) = key;
        left(new) = NULL:
        right(new) = NULL;
        if key < data(p) then left(p) = new
        else right(p) = new;
     endif
  endif
```

Consider once again the problem of doing a frequency count of the words in the input (Section 4.5). Three methods were discussed for solving this 'search and insert' problem. Briefly, they were:

(1) sequential search and add at the end: this has the advantage of simplicity, but gets slower as the table size increases.
(2) binary search, but this requires that new words must be inserted in such a way that the table is always sorted. Searching is fast, but inserting words can be time-consuming.
(3) hashing – this gives fast lookup and easy insertion. One possible disadvantage is that the table is not in order.

A fourth possibility involves using a binary search tree. The tree is searched for each incoming word. If the word is not found, it is added to the tree and its frequency count is set to 1. If the word is found, then its frequency count is incremented by 1. At the end of the input, an in-order traversal of the tree gives the words in alphabetical order. (See next section for a function which does an in-order traversal of a tree). We could use the following declaration for the nodes of the tree:

```
typedef struct treenode {
    char word[MAXWORDSIZE];
    int frequency;
    struct treenode *left, *right;
    } TreeNode, *TreePtr;
```

A similar declaration would be used in the solution of the problem discussed in the next section.

## 8.2 A cross-reference program

For variety, we will discuss the solution of a slightly more difficult problem than the 'frequency count' problem. We want to write a program to produce a cross-reference listing of the words in the input. More specifically, the output consists of the lines in the input, numbered starting at 1; this is followed by an alphabetical listing of the words, and each word is followed by the line number(s) in which it appears. If it appears more than once on a given line, the line number is repeated.

We will use a binary search tree to store the words. This will facilitate searching for a word as well as printing the words in alphabetical order. The major new problem here is how to store the line numbers. What complicates matters is that some words may appear on several lines while others may appear on just one or two. Our solution is to keep a linked list of line numbers for each word. Thus each node of the tree will contain a pointer to the 'cell' containing the first line number in which the word occurs. The line number 'cells' will have the format

| line number | next |
|---|---|

where `next` points to the cell containing the next line number in which the word occurs (NULL, if none). The declarations for the line number cells and the tree nodes are:

```
typedef struct linenumcell {
    int linenumber;
    struct linenumcell *next;
} LineNumCell, *CellPtr;
typedef struct treenode {
    char word[MAXWORDSIZE];
    CellPtr firstline;
    struct treenode *left, *right;
} TreeNode, *TreePtr;
```

Observe the declarations of `next` and `firstline`. They are both of the same type; however, we cannot use `CellPtr` to declare `next` since, at that stage, `CellPtr` is unknown to the compiler. Similarly, `TreePtr` cannot be used to declare `left` and `right`.

The following illustrates the data structure for the word 'simple', assuming it appears on lines 5, 13 and 16.

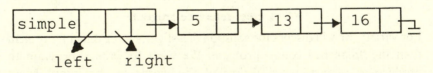

        `left`     `right`

The program is based on the following outline:

```
while there is a word
    find or insert word /* see below */
endwhile
perform an in-order traversal of the tree; as each node is visited, the
word and its line numbers are printed
stop
```

'find or insert word' could be expanded to

> search for word
> if this is a new word then
>> add it to the tree (create a new tree node)
>> create and link first line number cell for this word
> else
>> create a new line number cell
>> add it to the end of the list of cells for this word
> endif

In program P8.1, we assume that the data is stored in a disk file which is designated as the standard input. Alternatively, if the data is being typed at the keyboard, we assume that the terminal operates in such a way that characters are read only after 'return' is pressed – they are not read immediately they are typed.

---

### Program P8.1

```
#include <stdio.h>
#include <stdlib.h>
#include <ctype.h>
#include <string.h>

#define TRUE 1
#define FALSE 0
#define INPUTEXHAUSTED 0
#define WORDFOUND 1
#define MAXWORDSIZE 20

typedef struct linenumcell {
    int linenumber;
    struct linenumcell *next;
} LineNumCell, *CellPtr;
typedef struct treenode {
    char word[MAXWORDSIZE];
    CellPtr firstline;
    struct treenode *left, *right;
} TreeNode, *TreePtr;
```

```
int currentline = 0;
main()
{   char newword[MAXWORDSIZE];
    TreePtr root, findOrInsert(TreePtr root,
                                    char word[]);
    int getword(char word[], int max);
    void inorderTraversal(TreePtr root);

    root = NULL;
    while (getword(newword, MAXWORDSIZE) == WORDFOUND)
        root = findOrInsert(root, newword);
    inorderTraversal(root);
}


/* getputchar returns the next character in
   the input. It also echoes the input,
   numbering the lines */

int getputchar(void)
{
    extern int currentline;
    int ch;
    static int writelinenum = TRUE;

    if ((ch = getchar()) != EOF) {
        if (writelinenum) {
            printf("%3d. ", ++currentline);
            writelinenum = FALSE;
        }
        putchar(ch);
        if (ch == '\n') writelinenum = TRUE;
    }
    return ch ;
}


/* getword stores the next word in word */

int getword(char word[], int maxwordsize)
{
    int ch, next;
    int getputchar(void);
```

```
    do
        ch = getputchar();
    while (!isalpha(ch) && ch != EOF);

    if (ch == EOF) return INPUTEXHAUSTED;

    /* The first letter of the word has been
       found */
    next = 0;
    word[next++] = ch;
    while (--maxwordsize > 0) {
        word[next++] = ch = getputchar();
        if (!isalpha(ch)) break;
    }
    word[next -1] = '\0';
    return WORDFOUND;
}


/* findOrInsert searches the tree for inword.
   If it is not found, createTreeNode is
   called. If it is found, anotherOccurrence
   is called. */


TreePtr findOrInsert(TreePtr root, char inword[])
{
    TreePtr p, new, createTreeNode(char word[]);
    void anotherOccurrence(TreePtr);
    int compare;

    if (root == NULL)
        root = createTreeNode(inword);
    else {
        p = root;
        do {
            if ((compare = strcmp(inword,
                                  p -> word)) < 0)
                if (p -> left == NULL) break;
                else p = p -> left;
```

```
                else if (compare > 0)
                    if (p —> right == NULL) break;
                    else p = p —> right;
            } while (compare != 0);
        if (compare != 0) { /* NULL ptr encountered;
                                insert word */
            new = createTreeNode(inword);
            if (compare < 0) p —> left = new;
            else p —> right = new; }
        else anotherOccurrence(p);
    }
    return root;
}


/* createTreeNode gets storage for a tree node, sets the
   fields, and returns a pointer to the new node */

TreePtr createTreeNode(char newword[])
{
    TreePtr new;
    CellPtr createLineCell(void);

    new = malloc(sizeof(TreeNode));
    new —> left = NULL;
    new —> right = NULL;
    new —> firstline = createLineCell();
    strcpy(new —> word, newword);
    return new;
}


/* createLineCell creates a cell to hold a line number;
   it sets the fields and returns a pointer to the cell */

CellPtr createLineCell(void)
{
    extern int currentline;
    CellPtr new;
    new = malloc(sizeof(LineNumCell));
    new —> linenumber = currentline;
```

```
    new -> next = NULL;
    return new;
}


/* anotherOccurrence is called when a word is already in
   the tree. It finds the last node in the list of line
   numbers for the word, calls createLineCell, and adds
   the new cell at the end of the list. */

void anotherOccurrence(TreePtr nodeptr)
{
    CellPtr p;
    CellPtr createLineCell(void);

    p = nodeptr -> firstline;
    while (p -> next != NULL) p = p -> next;
    /* p is now pointing at the last cell */
    p -> next = createLineCell();
}


void inorderTraversal(TreePtr root)
{
    void visit(TreePtr nodeptr);

    if (root != NULL) {
        inorderTraversal(root -> left);
        visit(root);
        inorderTraversal(root -> right);
    }
}


/* visit prints a word followed by the line numbers in
   which it appears */

void visit(TreePtr nodeptr)
{
    CellPtr p;
    printf("%-20s ", nodeptr -> word);
    p = nodeptr -> firstline;
```

```
    /* the 'while' loop prints a line number followed
       by a comma for each line number except the last. On
       exit from the 'while', the last number is printed,
       followed by a 'newline' */
    while (p -> next != NULL) {
        printf("%3d,", p -> linenumber);
        p = p -> next;
    }
    printf("%3d\n", p -> linenumber);
}
```

Figure 8.2 shows some sample output produced by the program. Note that words which begin with uppercase letters appear first in the table since uppercase letters come before lowercase letters in the ASCII character set.

```
 1.      Farewell to you and the youth I have
 2. spent with you.
 3.      It was but yesterday we met in a dream.
 4.      You have sung to me in my aloneness,
 5. and I of your longings have built a tower
 6. in the sky.
 7.      But now our sleep has fled and our dream
 8. is over, and it is no longer dawn.
 9.      The noontide is upon us and our half
10. waking has turned to fuller day, and we
11. must part.
12.      If in the twilight of memory we should
13. meet once more, we shall speak again together
14. and you shall sing to me a deeper song.
15.      And if our hands should meet in another
16. dream we shall build another tower in the
17. sky.
```

And                    15
But                     7                          *continued*

```
Farewell           1
I                  1, 5
If                 12
It                 3
The                9
You                4
a                  3, 5, 14
again              13
aloneness          4
and                1, 5, 7, 8, 9, 10, 14
another            15, 16
build              16
built              5
but                3
dawn               8
day                10
deeper             14
dream              3, 7, 16
fled               7
fuller             10
half               9
hands              15
has                7, 10
have               1, 4, 5
if                 15
in                 3, 4, 6, 12, 15, 16
is                 8, 8, 9
it                 8
longer             8
longings           5
me                 4, 14
meet               13, 15
memory 12
met                3
more               13
must               11
my                 4
no                 8
noontide           9
```

*continued*

| | |
|---|---|
| now | 7 |
| of | 5, 12 |
| once | 13 |
| our | 7, 7, 9, 15 |
| over | 8 |
| part | 11 |
| shall | 13, 14, 16 |
| should | 12, 15 |
| sing | 14 |
| sky | 6, 17 |
| sleep | 7 |
| song | 14 |
| speak | 13 |
| spent | 2 |
| sung | 4 |
| the | 1, 6, 12, 16 |
| to | 1, 4, 10, 14 |
| together | 13 |
| tower | 5, 16 |
| turned | 10 |
| twilight | 12 |
| upon | 9 |
| us | 9 |
| waking | 10 |
| was | 3 |
| we | 3, 10, 12, 13, 16 |
| with | 2 |
| yesterday | 3 |
| you | 1, 2, 14 |
| your | 5 |
| youth | 1 |

Figure 8.2. Sample output of cross-reference program

## Comments on the cross-reference program

The variable `currentline` is declared as a global variable. In C, a variable is 'global' if it is declared outside of any function. Generally, it is placed before `main`. In this program, `currentline` may be used in any function without having to declare it in that function. For example, it is used in `getputchar` and `createLineCell`. You will observe that, in each of these two functions, there is a declaration

```
extern int currentline;
```

Strictly speaking, these declarations are not required provided that **the functions appear in the same file** as the first declaration (the definition) of `currentline`. It is here that storage is allocated to the variable and, in this case, initialized to 0. In contrast, the **declarations** in `getputchar` and `createLineCell` simply announce the properties of the variable, without allocating any storage. In effect, these declarations say that the variable is not being newly defined at this point, but that it is declared elsewhere and this is a reference to that declaration. Even though, in this case, the declarations are not **necessary**, it is good programming practice to include them, since one should account for all the variables a function uses. This makes it easier to understand the way a function communicates with its environment.

In the function `getputchar`, note the declaration

```
static int writelinenum = TRUE;
```

Here the word `static` ensures that the storage occupied by `writelinenum` is retained between calls to the function. Conceptually, when the function is first called, storage is allocated to `writelinenum` and it is initialized to TRUE. Subsequent calls to the function use the same storage originally allocated to `writelinenum` and the value left in it from the previous call.

The procedure `findOrInsert` follows the structure of the algorithm on page 232, except that the creation of a new node has been delegated to the function `createTreeNode` which returns a pointer to the node created. Also, use is made of the `break` statement to terminate the search when a NULL pointer is encountered. This does the job of the boolean variable `positionfound` in the algorithm.

## 8.3 Initialization of an array of structures

An array of structures may be initialized in a similar way to a two-dimensional array (Section 6.6.3). The initializers for each individual structure are enclosed in braces, as in the following example:

```
struct letterfrequency {
        char letter;
        int frequency;
};
struct letterfrequency vowels[] = {
        {'a', 25},
        {'e', 30},
        {'i', 20},
        {'o', 15},
        {'u', 10}
};
```

Since all initial values are supplied, this could be shortened to:

```
struct letterfrequency vowels[] =
        {'a', 25, 'e', 30, 'i', 20, 'o', 15, 'u', 10};
```

If we wanted to set frequency to 0 for each vowel, we could have used:

```
struct letterfrequency vowels[] = {
        {'a'},
        {'e'},
        {'i'},
        {'o'},
        {'u'}
};
```

Here the braces are all required. However, in this particular example, setting the frequencies to 0 is more easily (and more clearly) accomplished by:

```
struct letterfrequency vowels[] =
        {'a', 0, 'e', 0, 'i', 0, 'o', 0, 'u', 0};
```

## 8.4 Nested structures

We have mentioned that a member of a structure cannot be the same as the structure being defined. However, we have seen examples where a member can be a pointer to the structure being defined or a pointer to another structure. A member is also permitted to be a structure other than the one being defined. For example, given the declaration

```
struct nametype {
    char first[20];    /* first name */
    char middle;       /* middle initial */
    char last[20];     /* last name */
};
```

one could then declare

```
struct persondata {
    struct nametype name;
    int age, numchild;
    float salary;
        etc.
} person;
```

which contains a structure within a structure – a nested structure.

person.name refers to a structure of the form nametype;
person.name.first refers to the person's first name and
person.name.last[0] refers to the first letter of the last name.

The 'member of structure' operator – the dot '.' operator – associates from left to right. Thus

```
person.name.last[0]
```

is equivalent to

```
(person.name).last[0]
```

## 8.5 Unions

Sometimes it is convenient to be able to store different types of values in the same memory location. But because a variable must be declared to contain values of one specific type, it is not usually possible to store a different type of value in the variable. However, this can be done by declaring a variable to be a union. (Of course, it can hold only one type of value at a time). As an example, consider

```
union numtype {
     int inum;
     float fnum;
};
```

The form of the declaration is similar to that of a structure except that the word structure is replaced by the word union. As given, the above only conveys information about the types of values which may be stored in the union; it does not declare any variables. To do this, we could say

```
union numtype intflo;
```

or, if we preferred,

```
union numtype {
     int inum;
     float fnum;
} intflo;
```

or, even

```
union {
     int inum;
     float fnum;
} intflo;
```

(In this last case, though, we couldn't declare other variables later without repeating the entire declaration). To make life easier, we could also use a typedef, as in

```
typedef union numtype {
     int inum;
     float fnum;
} UnumType;
```

and then say

```
UnumType intflo;
```

Regardless of which format is used to declare `intflo`, enough storage is allocated to it to enable it to hold any of the types of values declared. In the example, if an `int` occupies 2 bytes and a `float` occupies 4 bytes, then the amount of storage allocated to `intflo` is 4 bytes.

A member of a union is accessed in the same way as for a structure. Thus we could say

```
intflo.inum = 12;
```

or

```
intflo.fnum = 3.14;
```

It is the programmer's responsibility to ensure that the type of the value retrieved from a union is the type most recently stored in it. Unpredictable results will occur if a value is stored as one type and retrieved as another. For example, if the most recent value assigned to `intflo` was via

```
intflo.inum = 12;
```

then

```
printf("%f", intflo.fnum);
```

will print some meaningless value.

Also, one should not try to guess where a particular member is stored within the union. In the above example, if `intflo` occupies 4 bytes and `intflo.inum` occupies 2 bytes, it is wrong to assume that `intflo.inum` is stored, for instance, in the first 2 bytes.

It is also possible to have 'pointers to unions'. These are declared and used in an identical manner to 'pointers to structures'. For example, given

```
UnumType *numptr;
```

the following are permissible:

```
numptr = &intflo; /* you can take the address of a
                     union */
numptr -> inum = 12;
numptr -> fnum = 3.14;
printf("%f", numptr -> fnum);
```

As an example of a situation in which a union may be useful, consider a compiler wishing to store

identifier, type, value

for identifiers in a program. The identifiers can be stored as strings (or character pointers), the type can be an integer (e.g. 1 = int, 2 = float, etc), but there's a problem with the values, since these can be of varying types. One solution is to declare the value as a union. For simplicity, suppose each value can be one of int, long, float or double. The following declaration can be used for each element of the table:

```
struct TableEntry{
    char *idptr;
    int type;
    union {
        int inum;
        long lnum;
        float fnum;
        double dnum;
    } value;
};
```

and

```
struct TableEntry table[100];
```

declares a table of size 100, where each element in the table is a structure. To refer to the float field, say, of table[j], one can use table[j].value.fnum.

Suppose the valid values of type are 0 (undefined), 1 (int), 2 (long), 3 (float) and 4 (double), and we wanted to print the value of the identifier in table[j]. We could do this with:

```
if (table[j].type == 0)
    printf("undefined variable\n");
else if (table[j].type == 1)
    printf("%d\n", table[j].value.inum);
else if (table[j].type == 2)
    printf("%ld\n", table[j].value.lnum);
    /* % ell d, Section 9.4.3 */
```

```
else if (table[j].type == 3)
   printf("%f\n", table[j].value.fnum);
else if (table[j].type == 4)
   printf("%f\n", table[j].value.dnum);
```

In passing, note that in a well-written program, the 'magic' numbers 0, 1, 2, 3 and 4 should be replaced by symbolic constants, e. g. UNDEFINED, INT, etc.

The above example illustrated a union within a structure. It is also possible to have a structure (or an array) within a union. For example,

```
union {
    int age;
    struct {
        int day;
        int month;
        int year;
    } birthdate;
} persondata;
```

or, simply

```
union {
    int age;
    struct {
        int day, month, year;
    } birthdate;
} persondata;
```

declares a union which can hold either a single integer value (representing the person's age) or a three-valued structure (representing the date of birth). To refer to the year in which the person was born, one could use persondata.birthdate.year. Enough storage is allocated to persondata to hold either the structure or an integer.

An example of an array within a union is:

```
union {
    int code;
    char message[40];
} descr;
```

Here, the amount of storage allocated to `descr` is 40 bytes – the size of its longest member. Element `j` of the array is referred to by `descr.message[j]`.

## 8.6 Bit-fields

In some applications, storage space can be minimized if several values can be packed in a single word or byte. In declaring a member of a structure, it is permissible to specify the number of **bits** which the member may occupy. When this is done, the member is referred to as a **bit-field**. For example,

```
struct machinetype {
    opcode : 5;
    reg : 2;
    address : 9;
} instruction;
```

declares `instruction` to be a structure variable with three bit-fields. In the usual case, a bit-field declaration consists of a name, a colon and the number of bits. A bit-field is usually considered as an unsigned integer, and the name could be preceded by `unsigned` to emphasize this fact. However, it is also possible to specify a bit-field as `signed`; the exception to this rule is a bit-field of length 1.

The above declaration could be used, for instance, to simulate 16-bit machine instructions where each instruction consists of a 5-bit operation code, a 2-bit field to specify one of four registers and a 9-bit address field. Suppose we wanted to store the instruction

```
ADD 1, 175 /* add the contents of location 175 to
              register 1 */
```

and the code for ADD is $10011_2 = 23_8$ and $175_{10} = 257_8$. We could use the following to do this:

```
instruction.opcode = 023; /* octal constant */
instruction.reg = 01;
instruction.address = 0257;
```

A bit-field is treated as a small, unsigned integer. We could make the above declaration more explicit, but equivalent, by writing:

```
struct machinetype {
    unsigned opcode : 5;
    unsigned reg : 2;
    unsigned address : 9;
} instruction;
```

A bit-field is a set of adjacent bits within a single 'storage unit'. This 'storage unit' is implementation-dependent but is almost invariably the amount of storage occupied by an int. Whether or not a bit-field can span the boundary between two 'storage units' is implementation-dependent. The ordering (whether left-to-right or right-to-left) of bit-fields in memory is also implementation-dependent.

For the remainder of this section, we assume that a 'storage unit' is the amount of storage occupied by an int and that a field cannot span the boundary between two int's.

To give another example, suppose we wanted to store the data obtained by a survey. The data to be stored consists of:

- name (up to 20 characters);
- age at last birthday;
- sex (male or female);
- marital status (one of single, married, widowed, divorced);
- number of children (up to 15);
- resident or non-resident;
- salary range (one of 10 categories);
- homeowner or not;

Apart from the name, we could use bit-fields for the other data, for instance,

- 7 bits for age (can store up to age 127);
- 1 bit for each of sex, resident status, homeowner status;
- 2 bits for marital status;
- 4 bits for each of number of children and salary range.

One possible declaration is:

```
typedef struct persondata {
    char name[20];
    age : 7;
    sex : 1;
```

```
    maritalstatus : 2;
    numchild : 4;
    resident : 1;
    salary : 4;
    homeowner : 1;
} PERSONDATA;
```

As before, the bit-fields could be declared explicitly as unsigned. Using a 16-bit int, age, sex, maritalstatus, numchild and resident (a total of 15 bits) will be stored in one int, and salary and homeowner will be stored in the next int, leaving a 1-bit 'hole' at the end of the first int.

In declaring a bit-field, it is permitted to omit the name of the field. This option is usually used for 'padding'. For example, suppose an int was stored using 16 bits, and we wanted to store a and b (using 3 bits each), skip 2 bits and then store c using 8 bits. We could do this with

```
struct {
    a : 3;
    b : 3;
      : 2;
    c : 8;
} abc;
```

The special field width of 0, used with an unnamed bit-field, can be used to force the next bit-field to begin on an int boundary. Thus,

```
struct {
    a : 3;
    b : 3;
      : 0;
    c : 8;
} abc;
```

ensures that c will be stored beginning at an int boundary.

Finally, a word of caution: A bit-field has no address so it is illegal to apply the 'address-of' operator '&' to it. One implication of this is that a value cannot be read into a bit-field using scanf.

# Exercises 8

(1)  Give the preorder, inorder and postorder traversals of the following binary trees:

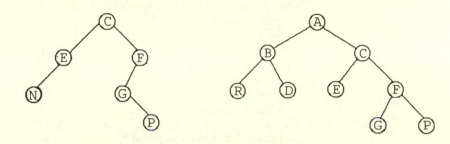

(2)  Draw the binary tree for the expression $(a-b-c)*(d+e/f+g)/(x+y)$ and give the pre-order, in-order and post-order traversals.

(3)  Assuming that **double-order** traversal is defined by:

(a)  visit the root;
(b)  traverse the left subtree in double-order;
(c)  visit the root;
(d)  traverse the right subtree in double-order.

list the nodes of the trees in questions (1) and (2) in double-order.

(4)  Write a recursive function which, given root pointing to the root of a binary tree, returns the height of the tree. (The **height** of a tree is the number of levels in the tree).

(5)  Write a recursive function which, given **root** pointing to the root of a binary tree, returns the number of leaves in the tree.

(6)  Write a recursive function which, given root pointing to the root of a binary tree, returns the number of nodes in the tree.

(7)  Write a function to traverse a binary tree level by level; that is, visit the root, then visit the nodes at level 1 (from left to right), then visit the nodes at level 2 (from left to right), etc. Hint: use a queue.

(8)  Write a function which makes a **copy** of a binary tree. Obtain the necessary new nodes from the system and copy the information fields from the existing tree to the new one.

(9)  Draw the binary search trees given that the following words come in the order shown:

- Bert Jeff Gary Inga Abel Olga Nora Mary Vera Jill
- Vera Abel Olga Bert Nora Gary Mary Inga Jill Jeff
- Jeff Nora Gary Bert Olga Vera Abel Mary Jill Inga

(10)  The following algorithm traverses a binary tree in in-order and prints the information at each node. root points to the root of the tree and the fields of a node pointed to by p are designated by left(p), info(p) and right(p).

Write a C function to implement it.

```
set stack, S, to empty
set p to root
repeat
    while p ≠ null
        push p onto S
        set p to left(p)
    endwhile
    if S is not empty then
        pop S into p
        print info(p)
        set p to right(p)
    else
        return /* traversal completed */
    endif
forever
```

(11) Write a program to maintain information about authors and the books they have written. The authors are inserted in a binary search tree and the books by a given author are held on a sorted linked list. The tree and linked lists are to be implemented using dynamic storage allocation, and are maintained according to the following commands.

  Each command consists of an asterisk followed by two letters. The parameters (p1, p2) are strings enclosed in double quotation marks (").

*AU p1 – add the author to the tree.

*AB p1 p2 ... – p1 is an author followed by an arbitrary number of books. If the author is already stored, the books are added to his existing list. If he is not stored, he is added to the tree and the books are put on his list.

*DA p1 – delete an author from the tree. An author can be deleted only if there are no books on his list.

*DB p1 p2... – delete the books (specified in the command) from the given author, p1.

*PB p1 – list all the books by the given author.

*PA – list the authors in alphabetical order.

*PL – print the author tree, level by level.

*PT – print the names of the authors in alphabetical order; each author is followed by a list of his books.

(12) A floating point number is to be stored in a 16-bit word using the following scheme:

> 1 bit for the sign (0 for positive, 1 for negative);
> 5 bits for the exponent (a positive or negative power of 2);
> 10 bits for the mantissa.

The exponent is stored as a 5-bit two's complement integer. As an example, the bit pattern

$$0\ 00101\ 1011011100$$

is interpreted as the binary number

$$0.1011011100_2 \times 2^5 = 10110.111_2 = 22.875_{10}$$

Write functions to add, subtract, multiply and divide numbers stored in the above format.

# 9

# Standard Input/Output

In this chapter, we discuss many of the issues pertaining to the input and output of data in C using the 'standard' input/output streams. The C language does not define input/output per se. Rather, input/output is performed using libraries of routines. Some of these libraries contain routines which can be used in any environment while others contain routines geared to the specific environment in which the compiler is being used. The function prototypes, symbolic constants, macro definitions and other declarations are contained in the header file `stdio.h`. Any program that uses any of these functions must be preceded by:

```
#include <stdio.h>
```

## 9.1 `stdin, stdout, stderr`

When a C program begins execution, three predefined I/O streams are automatically opened. These are:

- `stdin` – the standard input; generally, this is the keyboard, but often operating systems will allow it to be redirected to a specified disk file. So 'reading the standard input' could mean reading from the keyboard or from a specified disk file.
- `stdout` – the standard output; generally, this is the screen but it could also be redirected to a specified disk file or the printer.
- `stderr` – the standard error output; in general, this stream refers to the screen, even if `stdout` is redirected.

To be more precise, `stdin`, `stdout` and `stderr` are variables of type FILE * (file pointer). File pointers are discussed in Chapter 10.

## 9.2 I/O routines

I/O routines in C can be roughly divided into two categories:

(i) those which read/write the standard input/output streams and
(ii) those which read/write specified streams. The specified streams are usually disk files, but could also be `stdin`, `stdout` or `stderr`. Our terminology will, in general, refer to files.

Routines in the first category include:

`getchar` – read a character
`putchar` – write a character
`gets` – read a string up to, and including, the next newline character; the newline character is not stored as part of the string.
`puts` – write a string
`printf` – write data according to a specified format
`scanf` – read data according to a specified format

Those in the second category include:

`getc` – read a character from a specified file
`putc` – write a character to a specified file
`fgets` – read a string, possibly including newline, from a specified file
`fputs` – write a string to a specified file
`fscanf` – read formatted data from a specified file
`fprintf` – write formatted data to a specified file
`fread` – read a block of binary data from a specified file
`fwrite` – write a block of binary data to a specified file
`fseek` – go to a specified position in a file
`fopen` – open a file, specifying the 'mode' of operation
`fclose` – close a file
`feof` – returns TRUE if end-of-file is reached
`ferror` – returns TRUE if an error has occurred
`rewind` – reset the file 'pointer' to the beginning of the file

Strictly speaking, the routines in the first category are special cases of the corresponding routines in the second category. Those in the first category will be discussed in this chapter while those in the second will be discussed in Chapter 10.

Many compiler implementations will include additional routines not specified here. Please check your compiler manual for details.

## 9.3 Text and binary files

In C, all data is treated as a sequence of bytes. However, for the purposes of input/output, we distinguish between two kinds of files – **text** files and **binary** files.

A **text** file is a sequence of characters organized into lines. Conceptually, we think of each line as being terminated by a newline character. However, depending on the host environment, certain character translations may occur. For example, if we wrote the newline character '\n' to a file, it could be translated into two characters – a carriage return and a linefeed character. Thus, there is not necessarily a one-to-one correspondence between characters written and those stored on an external device. Similarly, there may not be a one-to-one correspondence between the number of characters stored in a file and the number read.

A **binary** file is simply a sequence of bytes, with no character translations occurring on input or output. Thus there **is** a one-to-one correspondence between what is read or written and what is stored in the file.

Apart from possible character translations, there are conceptual differences between text and binary files. To illustrate, suppose that an integer is stored using 2 bytes (16 bits); the number 3371 is stored as 00001101 00101011.

If we were to write this number to a text file, it would be written as the character '3', followed by the character '3', followed by '7', followed by '1', occupying 4 bytes in all. On the other hand, we could simply write the two bytes 'as is' to a binary file. Even though we could still think of them as a sequence of two 'characters', the values they contain may not represent any valid characters. In fact, in this case, the decimal values of the two bytes are 13 and 43 which, interpreted as two ASCII characters, are the carriage return control character (CR) and '+'. Another way to look at it is that, in general, each byte in a text file contains a human-readable character whereas, in general, a binary file contains an arbitrary bit pattern in each byte. Binary files are important for writing data directly from its internal representation to an external device, usually a disk file.

The standard input and output are considered text files. A disk file may be opened as a text file or as a binary file. In the next section, we discuss functions which operate on the standard input/output. The first part of Chapter 10 discusses input/output of files in general and Section 10.8 deals specifically with binary files.

## 9.4 Functions for standard input/output

In this section, we discuss the functions which read/write the standard input/output. For completeness, some material is repeated from previous chapters.

### *9.4.1* getchar *and* putchar

getchar is used to read characters from the standard input. Its prototype is

```
int getchar(void);
```

getchar returns (the integer value of) the next character from stdin. On end-of-file, EOF (defined in stdio.h) is returned. Since EOF must be distinguishable from any possible character that can be returned, it cannot be the 'value' of any character. Hence the reason why getchar returns int rather than char; the value of EOF is an integer value (usually 0) which must not be the value of any character. Even though we think of getchar as a function, it is really a macro defined in terms of the more general function getc (Section 10.3) as:

```
#define getchar() getc(stdin)
```

putchar is used to write characters to the standard output. Its prototype is:

```
int putchar(int ch);
```

putchar writes the character contained in the least significant byte of ch to stdout. The value returned is the value of the character written unless an error occurs, in which case EOF is returned. putchar is also a macro defined in terms of the more general putc (Section 10.3) as:

```
#define putchar(ch) putc(ch, stdout)
```

### *9.4.2* gets *and* puts

gets is used to read a line of data from stdin. Its prototype is:

```
char *gets(char line[]);
        /* same as 'char *gets(char *line)' */
```

gets reads and stores characters in the array line until a newline is encountered. The newline is stored and then replaced by \0. In other words, 'newline' is never part of the string returned. It is up to the programmer to ensure that line is large enough to hold the string.

If successful, gets returns line – in effect, a pointer to the characters read. If an error occurs or EOF is reached, gets returns NULL (the null pointer, defined in stdio.h). If it is necessary to know which condition occurred, the functions feof and ferror (Section 10.5) must be used. An example of the use of gets is given after puts (next).

gets is useful for reading strings which may contain blanks or tabs. Recall that the '%s' option of scanf cannot be used to read a string containing any whitespace characters, since a whitespace character indicates the end of the input field.

puts writes a string to stdout. Its prototype is:

```
int puts(char *str);
```

puts writes the characters pointed to by str to the standard output. The terminating NULL character (\0) of the string is replaced by a newline character in the output.

If successful, puts returns a non-negative value ('\n' on many systems); if it fails, it returns EOF.

The following code segment prompts for a name using puts, reads the name using gets and prints a greeting using printf. On input, the user must signify the end of the name by pressing 'return'. In the example, the name must not be longer than 19 characters, since one character is reserved for \0.

```
char name[20];

puts("Hi, what's your name?");
gets(name);
printf("Delighted to meet you, %s\n", name);
```

### 9.4.3 printf

Many of our programs so far have used printf for producing output. We have introduced and explained relevant features of printf when needed. We now give a more formal and precise explanation of printf.

`printf` is a function which takes a variable number of arguments, formats them according to certain specifications and produces output on `stdout`. In the simplest case, there is one argument – a string to be printed. For example,

```
printf("The quality of mercy is not strained;");
```

will produce

```
The quality of mercy is not strained;
```

However, `printf` does not automatically terminate a line so that, in this case, subsequent output will be added on the same line. For instance, the statements:

```
printf("The quality of mercy is not strained;");
printf("It droppeth as the gentle rain from heaven");
```

will produce

```
The quality of mercy is not strained;It droppeth as the gentle
rain from heaven
```

To force termination of a line, the newline character, \n, must be included in the string. The statements:

```
printf("The quality of mercy is not strained;\n");
printf("It droppeth as the gentle rain from heaven\n");
```

will produce

```
The quality of mercy is not strained;
It droppeth as the gentle rain from heaven
```

If we wanted to print a blank line between the two lines, we could accomplish this with:

```
printf("The quality of mercy is not strained;\n\n");
                                          /* two \n */
printf("It droppeth as the gentle rain from heaven\n");
```

or

```
printf("The quality of mercy is not strained;\n");
printf("\nIt droppeth as the gentle rain from heaven\n");
```

or, even

```
printf("The quality of mercy is not strained;");
printf("\n\n");
printf("It droppeth as the gentle rain from heaven\n");
```

\n is usually referred to as an 'escape sequence'. It is C's way of specifying 'hard-to-specify' characters. A complete list of escape sequences is given in Section 4.1.

In the general case, printf can be written

```
printf(<format string>, <arg1>, <arg2>, ...);
```

where ⟨format string⟩ is a string enclosed in double quotes and ⟨arg1⟩, ⟨arg2⟩, ... are items whose values are to be printed. The format string must contain **format specifications** which specify **how** the values are to be printed. Each ⟨arg⟩ can be a constant, a variable, an expression with operators or even a function call. More formally, the prototype for printf is

```
int printf(char *format, ...);
```

where '...' indicates an unspecified number of arguments. If an error occurs, printf returns a negative value; otherwise, it returns the number of characters written.

In the simplest case, a format specification consists of a percentage sign (%) and a single letter (the specification letter). Normally, the letter specifies the type of the corresponding argument. There must be **one** format specification for **each** argument. The first format specification matches ⟨arg1⟩, the second matches ⟨arg2⟩, etc. The allowable format specifications and the data type they normally match are:

%c        a single character (type char or int)
%d, %i    an integer value (type int)
%e, %E    a floating point value (type float or double) to be printed

using exponential notation, e.g. `2.736528E+03`. The general form is `[-]m.ddddddE±xx` or `[-]m.ddddddE±xx` where the number of d's is specified by the precision (p. 266); the default precision is 6.

`%f`  a floating point value (type `float` or `double`) to be printed in normal fractional notation, e.g. `2736.528`

`%g, %G`  a floating point value (type `float` or `double`); `%e` or `%E` is used if the exponent is less than −4 or greater than or equal to the precision (see p. 266); otherwise, `%f` is used. Trailing zeros and a trailing decimal point are not printed.

`%n`  the argument must be an `int` **pointer**; the number of characters written so far by this call to `printf` is written into the argument.

`%o`  print the unsigned octal equivalent (without a leading 0) of the value of the argument.

`%p`  a pointer value (memory address) – the actual printed value may depend on the underlying machine.

`%s`  a string; characters from the string are printed until the NULL character (`\0`) is encountered (but see **Specifying precision**, p. 266).

`%u`  the argument is treated as an unsigned decimal integer.

`%x, %X`  the argument is converted to an unsigned hexadecimal number (without a leading `0x` or `0X`). `abcdef` is used for `%x` and `ABCDEF` is used for `%X`.

`%%`  no argument is converted; `%` is printed.

The 'length modifiers' h, l (ell) or L may also be used between `%` and the specification letter. For h, the corresponding argument is printed as a `short int` or `unsigned short int`. For l, the corresponding argument is printed as a `long int` or `unsigned long int`. For L, the corresponding argument is printed as a `long double`.

The 'alternate output' modifier `#` may also be used between `%` and the specification letter.

- `%#o` prints an octal number with a leading 0;
- `%#x` or `%#X` prints a (non-zero) hexadecimal number with a leading `0x` or `0X`, respectively.
- `%#e` or `%#E` or `%#f` ensures that the number is always printed with a decimal point.
- `%#g` or `%#G` ensures that the number is always printed with a decimal point. In addition, trailing zeros will not be removed.

If the type of the argument does not match exactly with its corresponding format specification, then C will attempt to make an appropriate conversion. For example, if num is an integer variable, then:

```
printf("%c", num);
```

will interpret the value of num as a character and, if possible, print that character – which character, of course, depends on the underlying character set.

When a printf statement is executed, the format string is printed with the format specification(s) replaced by the value(s) of the corresponding argument(s). Thus if num is 75, the statement

```
printf("Number of students = %d\n", num);
```

will produce

```
Number of students = 75
```

and if ch contains the character 'E', then

```
printf("%c occurred %d times\n", ch, num);
```

will print

```
E occurred 75 times
```

The specification %d (as well as the others) prints the corresponding argument using just as many print positions as it needs. For example, if num is 75, then two print positions are used but if num is 4375 then four print positions are used.

### Specifying a field width

To obtain more precise control of the formatting of output, a 'field width' may be specified between % and the specification letter. For example, the specification "%4d" says to print the integer argument in a **minimum** field width of 4. If the number has **fewer** than 4 digits, it is right justified in the field by padding on the left with blanks. If the number has **more** than 4 digits, it is printed using whatever field width is necessary.

In general, if the field width is w and the argument to be printed contains less than *w* characters, it is padded on the left with blanks to make up the field width. If the argument contains more than *w* characters, it is printed using whatever field width is necessary.

If the field width is specified with a leading zero then, if padding is necessary, 0's are used. For example, if num = 75, then

```
printf("Pay this amount: $%04d\n", num);
```

will produce

```
Pay this amount: $0075
```

Given the declaration:

```
char word[] = "congratulations"; /* 15 letters */
```

the following explains how word would be printed for various specifications:

%10s    since the field width, 10, is smaller than the number of characters (15) to be printed, the entire word is printed in a field width of 15.

%20s    since the field width, 20, is greater than the number of characters (15) to be printed, the word is printed in a field width of 20 padded on the left with 5 blanks, thus (◇ denotes a blank): ◇◇◇◇◇congratulations

%020s  since the field width, 20, is greater than the number of characters (15) to be printed, the word is printed in a field width of 20 padded on the left with 5 0's, thus: 00000congratulations

### Left justification

As discussed above, arguments are printed right justified in the specified field width. If left justification is required, then the field width must be preceded by a minus sign (−), as in "%−20s". For this specification, the above word would be printed in a field width of 20, padded on the right with 5 blanks, thus (◇ denotes a blank): congratulations◇◇◇◇◇

If the field width is written with a leading 0, then the padding character is 0. Left justification is usually required for the printing of strings. One must be careful in specifying left justification for numbers when the padding character is 0. For example, if num = 75, then

```
printf("Pay this amount: $%-04d\n", num);
```

will produce

```
Pay this amount: $7500
```

You may not mind this if you are receiving the payment, but it is certainly unacceptable if you have to pay.

### Specifying precision

For the printing of strings and floating point values, the field width may be followed by a point (.) and another number specifying **precision**, as in "%20.12s" or "%7.2f". The precision alone may be specified, as in "%.12s" or "%.2f". In the case of a string, the precision specifies the maximum number of characters to be printed from the string. In the case of a floating point number, it specifies the number of digits to be printed after the decimal point. The following illustrates the various possibilities:

%20.12s     print a maximum of 12 characters from the string, **right** justified in a field width of 20. If the string contains less than 12 characters, then that amount is printed. For the 15-letter **word**, above, the first 12 letters 'congratulati' would be printed in a field width of 20, with 8 leading blanks, thus (◇ denotes a blank): ◇◇◇◇◇◇◇◇congratulati

%-20.12s    print a maximum of 12 characters from the string, **left** justified in a field width of 20. If the string contains less than 12 characters, then that amount is printed. For the 15-letter **word**, above, the first 12 letters 'congratulati' would be printed in a field width of 20, with 8 trailing blanks, thus (◇ denotes a blank): congratulati◇◇◇◇◇◇◇◇

%.12s       print a maximum of 12 characters from the string. If the string contains less than 12 characters, then that amount is printed. Since the field width is not specified, use whatever width is necessary. For the 15-letter word, above, the first 12 letters 'congratulati' would be printed in a field width of 12. For a

5-letter word, say, the five letters would be printed in a field width of 5.

In the following, assume that the value to be printed is 53.6287, and ◇ denotes a blank.

%7.2f      print the value rounded to two digits after the decimal point, right justified in a field width of 7, thus: ◇◇53.63

%-7.2f      print the value rounded to two digits after the decimal point, left justified in a field width of 7, thus: 53.63◇◇

%7.0f      print the value rounded to the nearest whole number, right justified in a field width of 7, thus: ◇◇◇◇◇54

%07.0f      print the value rounded to the nearest whole number, right justified in a field width of 7, and pad with 0's, thus: 0000054

%.2f      print the value rounded to two digits after the decimal point, using whatever field width is necessary, thus: 53.63

%.0f      print the value rounded to the nearest whole number, thus: 54

In the case of %e or %E, the number is printed using exponential notation, for example, 5.36287E+01. The precision determines how many digits are printed after the decimal point. When specifying the field width, one should cater for the exponent part which uses four print positions. The exponent is printed with e or E depending on which one is used in the specification. If the field width specified is too small to hold the value to be printed, C uses whatever field width is necessary for printing the value. In the following, assume that the value to be printed is 53.6287, and ◇ denotes a blank.

%12.6e      print the value rounded to six digits after the decimal point, right justified in a field width of 12, thus: 5.362870e+01 (the printed value occupies exactly 12 positions).

%12.3E      print the value rounded to three digits after the decimal point, right justified in a field width of 12, thus: ◇◇◇5.363E+01

%-12.3E      print the value rounded to three digits after the decimal point, left justified in a field width of 12, thus: 5.363E+01◇◇◇

%12.0E    print the value rounded to 0 digits after the decimal point, right justified in a field width of 12, thus: ◇◇◇◇◇◇◇◇5E+01

%015.7E   print the value rounded to seven digits after the decimal point, right justified in a field width of 15, and pad with 0's, thus: 005.3628700E+01

%.5E      print the value rounded to five digits after the decimal point, using whatever field width is necessary, thus: 5.36287E+01

%5.4E     print the value rounded to four digits after the decimal point, using whatever field width is necessary (since the field width specified is too small), thus: 5.3629E+01

### *Printing %*

If % appears in a format string and what follows it cannot be interpreted as a valid specification, then the behaviour is undefined. However, to print a percent sign, one can use %% in the format string. For example, if incr = 25, then

```
printf("Percentage increase in price = %d%%\n", incr);
```

would produce

```
Percentage increase in price = 25%
```

Finally, it is worthwhile to remember that printf uses the specifications in the format string to determine how many arguments should follow. If **fewer** arguments are supplied than printf expects, an error would occur, either producing meaningless results or causing an abrupt termination of the program. If **more** arguments are supplied than printf expects, then no error results, but the extraneous arguments are ignored.

### *9.4.4* scanf

In the following discussion, the term 'whitespace character' is taken to mean either a blank, a tab, a newline, a carriage return, a vertical tab or a formfeed character.

The function scanf is used for reading data from the standard input.

The general form is

```
scanf(<conversion string>, <addr1>, <addr2>,...);
```

where ⟨conversion string⟩ is a string enclosed in double quotes and containing **conversion specifications**. {More formally, the prototype for scanf is

```
int scanf(char * format, ...);
```

where '...' indicates an unspecified number of arguments}.

In the simplest case, a conversion specification consists of % followed by a single letter (e.g. %d or %s), similar to the format specifications of printf. ⟨addr1⟩, ⟨addr2⟩,... are **pointers** (memory addresses). The values read will be stored at these addresses. As with printf, it is an error to have **fewer** addresses than conversion specifications, but it is not an error to have **more**. However, nothing will be stored at the extraneous addresses.

scanf gets a value from the input, converts it according to the next conversion specification, and stores that value at the next specified address. This is repeated until the conversion string is exhausted or until some input fails to match the conversion specification (for example, a letter is encountered instead of a digit).

The value returned by scanf is the number of successfully assigned input items. Normally, this value is ignored but it can be used for error checking; for example, if the number of assigned items is not the same as the number expected to be assigned, then there must be some error in the data.

On end of file or error, scanf returns EOF provided that no value has, as yet, been assigned; otherwise, it returns the number of assigned items. Thus, if scanf is called to read two numbers and only one is supplied before the end-of-file, the value returned by scanf is 1, not EOF.

For example, assume the declarations:

```
int aint;
float aflt;
```

The statement

```
scanf("%d %f", &aint, &aflt);
```

contains two conversion specifications (%d and %f) and two pointers – the addresses of the integer variable aint and the floating point variable aflt. The next items in the input stream should be an integer followed by a floating point number. If the next input line contains, say,

253 7.28 472

then the characters '2', '5', '3' are converted to the decimal integer 253 and stored in aint, and the characters '7', '.' '2', '8' are converted to the floating point number 7.28 and stored in aflt. Subsequent input would be read starting with the blank after '8'. Observe that %d matches with an int pointer and %f matches with a float pointer. The blank between %d and %f (in the conversion string) says that, in the data, any amount (> 0) of whitespace characters could be used to separate the two numbers. (Strictly speaking, this blank isn't necessary, but it makes the specification more readable. If it is omitted, one or more whitespace characters must still separate the numbers in the data).

The letters which may be used in a conversion specification (conversion letters) are almost identical to those used for format specifications in printf. The following are the valid specifications and their meanings:

%c       used for reading a single character and must be matched with a char **pointer**. The next input character is stored at the specified address.

%d       used for reading an integer and must be matched with an int **pointer.** An integer (string of decimal digits) should come next in the input stream.

%e       same as %f (next).

%f       used for reading a floating point number and must be matched with a float **pointer**. A valid floating point number consists of an optional sign, a string of digits possibly containing a decimal point, and an optional exponent part consisting of the letter E (or e) followed by a possibly signed integer. Examples of valid floating point numbers are 25, −25, −25.73, 5.731E 2, 0.731E−2.

%g       same as %f (above).

%i      used for reading an integer and must be matched with an `int` **pointer**. The integer may be in octal (leading O) or hexadecimal (leading Ox or OX).

%n     must be matched with an `int` **pointer**; the number of characters read so far by this call to `scanf` is written into the argument. No input is read, and the count of assigned items is not incremented.

%o     used for reading an octal integer (with or without a leading O) and must be matched with an `int` **pointer**.

%p     used for reading a pointer value and must be matched with a `void *`. Valid input is implementation-dependent, but is of the form printed by `printf("%p")`.

%s     used for reading a string of characters not containing any whitespace characters, and must be matched with a **character pointer** pointing to an array of characters large enough to hold the string and \0 which is added automatically at the end. Beginning with the next non-whitespace character, characters are stored (starting at the specified address) until the next whitespace character is encountered. Because a whitespace character ends the reading of a string, %s cannot be used to read a string containing blanks. For such strings, the standard function `fgets` can be used (see Section 10.6)

%u     used for reading an unsigned decimal integer and must be matched with an `unsigned int` **pointer**.

%x     used for reading a hexadecimal integer (with or without a leading Ox) and must be matched with an `int` **pointer**.

The conversion letters d, i, n, o, u and x must be preceded by h if the argument is a `short int` **pointer**, or by l (ell) if the argument is a `long int` **pointer**. The conversion letters e, f and g must be preceded by l (ell) if the argument is a `double` **pointer**, or by L if the argument is a `long double` **pointer**.

Except for %c, all the above specifications will skip over whitespace characters, if necessary, looking for the start of the next data item. This means that `scanf` will skip over blanks, tabs and even blank lines looking for the next data item. `%c` stores the next character (whatever it may be) in its argument; no `\0` is added. To read the next non-whitespace character, `%1s` (percent one s) may be used; however, in this case, `\0` is appended to the character read.

In addition to the above, the special specifications `%[<str>]` and `%[∧<str>]` are allowed where `<str>` represents an unquoted string of characters, for example, `%[aeiou]` or `%[∧aeiou]`. Both specifications must be matched with a `char` **pointer**. `%[<str>]` is used for reading the longest non-empty string of input characters which match characters from `<str>`. Thus `%[aeiou]` matches the longest string consisting of the letters a, e, i, o, u; any other character stops the matching process. The matched string is stored in the argument and is properly terminated by `\0`. As usual, the input field begins with the next non-whitespace character. `%[∧<str>]` matches the longest non-empty string of characters **not** belonging to `<str>`. Thus `%[∧aeiou]` will match a string starting at the next non-whitespace character and terminated by any of the letters a, e, i, o or u. As another example `%[∧$]` will match any string of characters terminated by $.

As in the case of `printf`, an optional field width, *w*, may be specified between `%` and the conversion letter, e.g. `%3d`. If *w* is present, it specifies the **maximum** field width in which to look for the next data item, starting with the next non-whitespace character. Thus, except for `%c`, the following holds:

- If a field width is not specified, the **maximum** input field extends from the next non-whitespace character until the next whitespace character.
- If a field width is specified, the **maximum** input field extends from the next non-whitespace character until the next whitespace character or until the field width is exhausted, whichever comes first.
- Within the maximum input field, the reading of a data item may be terminated by a non-whitespace character. For example, a numeric field can be terminated by any character which cannot form part of the number being read. For example, if the input field contains 53kgs, the specification `%d` will read 53 as the next integer; subsequent reading of the input starts at 'k'. As another example, the string read by `%[∧$]` is terminated by $. See also the following subsection on **Ordinary characters in conversion string**.

The following illustrates some possibilities (◇ denotes a space):

Table 9.1

| Input line | x | a | b |
| --- | --- | --- | --- |
| 354.759127682 | 354.75 | 912 | 76 |
| 2.1◊45◊7265 | 2.1 | 45 | 72 |
| 2.14◊5726532 | 2.14 | 572 | 65 |
| ◊◊◊2.1457◊3613◊5 | 2.1457 | 361 | 3 |
| ◊◊123◊45◊◊◊6789 | 123.0 | 45 | 67 |

Given the statement:

```
scanf("%6f %3d %2d", &x, &a, &b);
```

Table 9.1 shows the values assigned to x, a and b for various input data lines.

### *Assignment suppression*

Sometimes it is necessary to skip over certain data items in the input. Perhaps the data has been stored beforehand and the present application needs to process only some of that data. For instance, there may be five data items per line and the present application needs only items 1, 3 and 5. For these situations, the assignment suppression character * may be used after %. For example, the statement:

```
scanf("%d %*s %d", &a, &b);
```

says to read an integer into a, skip over a string of non-whitespace characters, then read another integer into b.

If required, a field width may be specified with *, as in

```
scanf("%*5f %d", &a);
```

This says to locate the start of the next data item, skipping over whitespace characters, if necessary. The next data item should be a floating point number; read characters up to the next whitespace character or until 5 characters have been read, whichever comes first. The * causes these characters to be ignored. Starting from this point, the next integer is read and assigned to a. Table 9.2 shows the values assigned to a for various input lines (◇ denotes a space):

Table 9.2

| Input line | a |
|---|---|
| 12345678◊9 | 678 |
| ◊◊◊1.2345◊7◊8 | 5 |
| ◊◊12.3◊456◊78 | 456 |
| 1◊23◊45678 | 23 |

Note that the value returned by scanf does not include the count of assignment-suppressed data items. Thus, in the above example, the value returned by scanf is 1, not 2.

### Ordinary characters in conversion string

Normally, the conversion string contains conversion specifications, perhaps separated by blanks, tabs or even newlines. If any whitespace characters are present, they are ignored. It is also possible for the conversion string to contain ordinary characters, except %. (However, %% in the conversion string matches a single % in the input). If it does, then these characters are expected to match corresponding characters in the input stream. For example, in the statement:

```
scanf("%d, %d", &a, &b);
```

the comma in the conversion string is expected to match a comma in the input stream. This simply means that the two integers in the input must be separated by a comma. If the data is supplied as, say,

```
29 17
```

then an error would result. However, one must be careful even if a comma is supplied. In the above conversion string, the comma follows immediately after the (first) letter 'd'. In the data, the comma must appear immediately after the first integer. Thus,

```
29,◊◊◊17
```

and even

    29,17

are okay, but

    29◇,◇17

would cause an error because of the space after '29'.

As another example, consider the statement (◇ denotes a space):

    scanf("a◇=◇%d,◇b=%d", &a, &b);

The data for a and b must conform to the following:

- The input line must start with an a; there must be no leading blanks otherwise an error would result;
- the next space in the conversion string matches zero or more spaces in the input. In general, one or more whitespace characters in the conversion string will match zero or more whitespace characters in the input.
- the next non-whitespace character in the input must be '='. This may be separated from the first number by zero or more spaces.
- the first number must be followed immediately by a comma.
- the next non-whitespace character must be 'b'; this must be followed immediately by '='.
- zero or more whitespace characters may then precede the next number.

The following input lines would all successfully match the above specification:

    a=5,b=6
    a◇=◇◇◇5,◇◇◇b=◇◇◇6
    a◇◇◇◇=5,◇◇b=6

The following would all generate errors:

    ◇a◇=◇5,◇b◇=  6        no leading space allowed
    a◇=◇5◇,◇b=6          no space allowed between 5 and ,
    a=5,b◇=6             no space allowed between b and =

A very subtle error could arise if the above (`scanf`) statement were being executed repeatedly (as part of a `while`, say). In this case, it would seem reasonable to supply data in the following manner:

```
a=5,  b=6
a=12,  b=35
a=23,  b=13
    etc,
```

But this won't work since, immediately after the second number, `scanf` expects to find 'a'. In this case, `scanf` finds the newline character. The problem can be solved by putting a blank at the end of the conversion string, as in:

```
scanf("a◇=◇%d,◇b=%d◇", &a, &b);
```

or at the beginning of the conversion string, as in:

```
scanf("◇a◇=◇%d,◇b=%d", &a, &b);
```

In the first case, the **first** input line **must** start with 'a', but subsequent lines may have leading blanks since the blank at the end of the conversion string will now match any number of whitespace characters. In the second case, **all** input lines may have leading blanks.

Another subtle point arises with putting the blank at the **end** of the conversion string, especially if the data is being typed interactively at the keyboard. After the value has been assigned to b, `scanf` attempts to match this blank with 0 or more whitespace characters in the input. The matching stops when the next non-whitespace character is encountered. Thus `scanf` will return only when that character (presumably 'a') is typed. To illustrate, suppose we type

```
a=6,  b= 7
```

and press "return". We would expect `scanf` to assign 6 to a and 7 to b and the program to go on to the next statement. But `scanf` doesn't terminate until we type the 'a' of the next set of input values. This, of course, can be done on the same line or on a subsequent line.

For these reasons, it is best, in this example, to put a blank at the **start** of the conversion string and to put none at the end.

## Exercises 9

(1) Distinguish between text and binary files.
(2) Give the internal 16-bit representation of the integer 8259. Interpreting this 16-bit value as two 8-bit bytes, what are the two ASCII characters represented?
(3) Distinguish between `gets` and `fgets`.
(4) Distinguish between `puts` and `fputs`.
(5) How will the numbers 842, −375 and 765432 be printed by each of the following format specifications?

    (a) `%5d`
    (b) `%05d`
    (c) `%-5d`
    (d) `%-05d`

(6) How will the string "land of steelband and calypso" (29 characters) be printed by each of the following format specifications?

    (a) `%20s`
    (b) `%40s`
    (c) `%040s`
    (d) `%30.15s`
    (e) `%-30.15s`
    (f) `%.15s`

(7) How will the numbers 123.4567 and −9.87654 be printed by each of the following format specifications?

    (a) `%5f`
    (b) `%10f`
    (c) `%-10f`
    (d) `%-010f`
    (e) `%010.3f`
    (f) `%7.0f`
    (g) `%10e`

(8) How can one print a percentage sign as part of an output string?
(9) Carefully explain what value is returned by `scanf`.
(10) Why can the specification `%s` not be used to read the name 'Jim Slim'?
(11) What is the difference between `%5d` as an **output** specification and `%5d` as an **input** specification?
    In general, what is the difference between a field width on output and a field width on input?
(12) The specification `%10s` will correctly read the name `Jim Slim` – true or false?
(13) The input stream contains the line

    `435, 276`

The specification `"%d %d"` will correctly read the two integers – true or false?

(14)  The input stream contains the line

```
435 276
```

The specification "%d, %d" will correctly read the two integers – true or false?

(15)  The input stream contains the lines

```
435
276
```

The specification "%d %d" will correctly read the two integers – true or false?

(16)  Is an 'assignment suppressed' item counted in the value returned by scanf?

(17)  Given the statement

```
scanf("%2d %5f %3d", &a, &x, &b);
```

what values are assigned to a, x and b for the following input lines (◇ denotes a space)?

```
123456789 12345
1◇◇◇◇456.789◇◇◇43
◇◇◇◇4375◇213◇564
◇◇3◇◇5.8◇◇2◇◇59
```

# 10

# File Input/Output

In the previous chapter we discussed the reading and writing of data from and to the 'standard' input/output streams. In this chapter we discuss how data can be read from and written to named files. The treatment is divided into two parts – the first deals with text files and the other with binary files. (See Section 9.3 for the distinction between text and binary files.)

All our programs so far have read data from the standard input file (the keyboard or a specified file) and written output to the standard output file (the screen, the printer or a specified file). The important point about these programs is that they read data from one source only and sent output to one destination only. But consider the following scenario.

We have some data in a file which we would like to process. Thus our program must read data from this file. However, we would also like to enter a few values interactively from the keyboard. Our program must read data from this source as well. We could use the keyboard as the standard input, but how do we then get the program to read the data from the file? In C, a program can read and write data to named files using a host of standard functions. Many of these – for example, `fscanf` and `fprintf` – operate in an identical manner to those dealing with standard I/O, except that there's a new argument – a **file pointer** – indicating which file is to be read or written. Before we look at the details, some preliminary discussion is necessary.

## 10.1 Internal vs external file name

The usual way of using a computer is via its operating system. We normally create and edit files using the system **editor**. When we create a file, we give it a name which we use whenever we need to do anything with the

279

file. This is the name by which the file is known to the operating system. We will refer to such a name as an **external** file name. (The term **external** is used here to mean 'external to a C program'). When we are writing a program, we may want to specify, say, the reading of data from a file. The program will need to use a file name but, for several reasons, this name should not be an external file name. The major reasons are:

- The file to be read may not have been created as yet.
- If the external name is tied to the program, the program will be able to read a file with that name only. If the data is in a file with a different name, either the program will have to be changed or the file renamed.
- The program will be less portable since different operating systems have different file-naming conventions. A valid external file name on one system may be invalid on another one.

For these reasons, the program should use an **internal** file name, and, at some later stage, this internal name would be associated with a real file – one with an external name. In C, the internal name is actually a **file pointer**. This pointer points to an area of memory which contains information about the file, things like whether it's an input or output file, the address of the buffer associated with the file, the position of the next character to be read or written, etc. The structure containing the file information is a predefined type FILE (defined in stdio.h). In order to use a file, we must

(1) declare a pointer to the file;
(2) **open** the file using the standard function fopen.

## 10.2 fopen **and** fclose

As an example, suppose we were writing a program to process payroll data for a number of employees. In the program, we could refer to the file containing the data as paydata. {This could be (and usually is) quite different from the name of the external file in which the data is actually stored. For instance, the file might be named payroll.nov.dat.} paydata is declared as:

```
FILE *paydata;
```

This declares paydata as a pointer to a FILE. As discussed above, it is a pointer to a structure which will contain information about the external file associated with the internal name paydata.

The standard function `fopen` returns a pointer to a `FILE`, and its prototype is declared in `stdio.h` as:

```
FILE *fopen(char name[], char mode[]);
```

or

```
FILE *fopen(char *name, char *mode);
```

or

```
FILE *fopen(char *, char *);
```

Both parameters are character strings (or, more accurately, pointers to strings). The first specifies an external file name and the second specifies the manner in which the file is to be used, for example, whether text or binary or whether for reading or writing. The valid modes are as follows:

| | |
|---|---|
| "r" | open text file for reading; file must exist. |
| "w" | create text file for writing; if file exists, its contents are destroyed, otherwise it is created, if possible. |
| "a" | open text file for appending (writing at the end); if file does not exist, it is created if possible (but some systems may report error). |
| "r+" | open text file for both reading and writing; file must exist. |
| "w+" | create text file for both reading and writing; if file exists, its contents are destroyed, otherwise it is created, if possible. |
| "a+" | open text file for reading and appending; if the file exists, its contents are retained; if the file does not exist, it is created if possible (but some systems may report error). |

A file opened for reading ("r" or "r+") must exist. If it doesn't, then `fopen` returns NULL. As indicated above, certain modes (e.g., "w" or "a") require that a file be created. If it cannot be created (for example, the user may have exceeded the allotted disk space or the disk may be write-protected), then `fopen` returns NULL. If the external file exists, then opening it for 'writing' causes the old contents to be destroyed.

If a file is opened with "a" or "a+", all write operations occur at the end of the file. This holds even if the file pointer is repositioned with `fseek` or `rewind` (Section 10.9.1). When a write operation is about to occur, the file pointer is positioned at the end of the file. This ensures that existing data cannot be overwritten.

When 'b' is added to the above modes, the files are treated as binary, rather than text. Thus the following are also valid modes:

"rb"     open binary file for reading; file must exist.
"wb"     create binary file for writing; if file exists, its contents are destroyed, otherwise it is created, if possible.
"ab"     open binary file for appending (writing at the end); if file does not exist, it is created if possible (but some systems may report error).
"rb+"    open binary file for both reading and writing; file must exist.
"wb+"    create binary file for both reading and writing; if file exists, its contents are destroyed, otherwise it is created, if possible.
"ab+"    open binary file for reading and appending; if the file exists, its contents are retained; if the file does not exist, it is created if possible (but some systems may report error).

Observe that the basic modes are reading ("r"), writing ("w") and appending ("a"). Adding "+" allows both reading and writing, and adding "b" specifies that the file is to be treated as a binary file. The modes "rb+", "wb+" and "ab+" could also be written as "r+b", "w+b" and "a+b", respectively.

Consider the statement:

```
paydata = fopen("payroll.nov.dat", "r");
```

This says to open the external file `payroll.nov.dat` for reading. If such a file does not exist, an error results and `fopen` returns NULL. If the file exists, then `fopen` returns the address of the place in memory where information about the file would be kept. In the example, this address is assigned to `paydata`, thus establishing a connection between the external file name `payroll.nov.dat` and the internal name `paydata`. Subsequent accesses to the external file are done via the internal name only. Once the file has been opened, we can read data from it using `fscanf`, say. For example, the statement:

```
fscanf(paydata, "%s %f %f", name, &hours, &rate);
```

says to read values for `name`, `hours` and `rate` from the file associated

with `paydata`. `fscanf` is used in exactly the same way as `scanf`, except
that the first argument is now a file pointer.

When we are finished using the file, we must **close** it. This is done via
the standard function `fclose`. The above file may be closed with

```
fclose(paydata);
```

Note that the argument to `fclose` is a file pointer. In the example, this
statement severs the association between the internal name `paydata` and
the external file `payroll.nov.dat`. If required, the name `paydata` can
now be used with another external file.

It is important to close all files before your program terminates. Failure
to do so could result in output being lost or a file becoming corrupted.

As used above, the name of the external file `payroll.nov.dat` is
tied to the program, since it is used in the `fopen` statement. If the data
to be processed is in another file `payroll.dec.dat`, say, then the
statement to open the file must be changed to:

```
paydata = fopen("payroll.dec.dat", "r");
```

or the name of the file must be changed to `payroll.nov.dat`, which
may not be desirable. A more flexible approach is to let the user supply
the name of the external file at run time. For instance, if `payfile` is an
array of characters large enough to hold the name of the file, then we can
use:

```
printf("Enter payroll data file name: ");
scanf("%s", payfile);
paydata = fopen(payfile, "r");
```

Just in case the user types the file name incorrectly or forgot to create
the file, we can use the fact that `fopen` will return NULL to check for
this, as in:

```
do {
    printf("Enter payroll data file name: ");
    scanf("%s", payfile);
    paydata = fopen(payfile, "r");
    if (paydata == NULL) printf("File does not exist\n");
} while (paydata == NULL);
```

Now, exit from the do...while takes place only when an existing file name is entered. As usual, the assignment and test of paydata (against NULL) can be done in one statement such as:

```
if ((paydata = fopen(payfile, "r")) == NULL)
    printf("File does not exist\n");
```

To pursue the example, suppose we wanted to write the payroll report onto an external file called payreport.nov. Suppose payout is declared as:

```
FILE *payout;
```

then the statement:

```
payout = fopen("payreport.nov", "w");
```

can be used to associate the internal name payout with the external file name payreport.nov. Output can then be sent to the file using fprintf, say, as in:

```
fprintf(payout,"Name: %s, Net pay: $%7.2f\n",
        name, salary);
```

fprintf is identical to printf, except that the first argument is now a file pointer, indicating where the output is to be sent.

As above, it is best to let the user supply the name of the file at run time and to use a character array variable as the first argument to fopen.

### 10.3 getc **and** putc

We have used getchar to read a character from the standard input and putchar to send a character to the standard output. To read a character from a named file, we use getc, as in:

```
ch = getc(fileptr);
```

where ch is an int and fileptr is the pointer to the file from which characters are being read. To write a character to a file, we can use putc, as in:

```
putc(ch, fileptr);
```

Note that the file pointer is the **second** argument to putc.

In C, the file pointers stdin and stdout are predefined to point to the standard input and output, respectively. Thus,

```
getchar() is equivalent to getc(stdin)
```

and

```
putchar(ch) is equivalent to putc(ch, stdout).
```

### 10.4  File processing example – telephone charges

We will illustrate the ideas behind the reading and writing of named files with the solution to the following problem.

*Problem:*   Write a program to calculate the telephone charges for a number of customers. The data for each customer consists of

name, previous meter reading, present meter reading

and is stored in a file. The difference between the two readings gives the number of units used by the customer for the period under consideration. The amount due for each customer is calculated by

units used × rate + rental charge

The 'rate' and 'rental charge' are supplied to the program at run time. These values are assumed to be the same for all customers and must be entered once only.

The program should

- Request the rate and rental charge;
- Read the data for each customer and calculate the amount due, provided that the previous reading is less than or equal

to the present reading. If the previous reading is greater, then this customer's data is written to an 'error' file.
- For valid data, the customer's data together with the amount payable should be written to a 'billing' file.

This program will need to read two input streams – the standard input for the rate and rental charge and the file containing the customers' data. It will also need to write three output streams – the standard output for prompting for the rate and rental charge, the 'billing' file and the 'error' file. Our program P10.1 uses the following file pointers:

```
cusdata    –  input file of customers' data
errfile    –  output file of customers with invalid data
billfile   –  output file of customers with valid data
```

and is based on the following outline:

```
open files
get the rate and rental charge (using the standard input/output)
while there is data in cusdata
    get a customer's data
    if data is valid
        process and write to billfile
    else
        write to errfile
    endif
endwhile
close files
```

In the interest of brevity, the external names of the files will be embedded in our program. But, as discussed above, a more flexible approach is to let the user supply the names at run time. The names used are `customers.dat`, `billreport` and `errors.dat`.

As a sample run, given that `customers.dat` contains the following data (the names are joined because %s cannot read a string containing blanks):

```
JohnBrown        245      572
MaryFischer      550      850
SusanSpicer      425      375
AlanJones        700      1200
```

**Program P10.1**

```c
#include <stdio.h>

FILE *cusdata, *billfile, *errfile;

main()
{
    float rate, rental;
    int oldread, newread;
    char name[20];

    void producebill(char [], int, int, float,
                     float);
    void reporterror(char [], int, int);

    cusdata = fopen("customers.dat", "r");
    billfile = fopen("billreport", "w");
    errfile = fopen("errors.dat", "w");

    printf("Rate per unit: ");
    scanf("%f", &rate);
    printf("Rental charge: ");
    scanf("%f", &rental);

    while (fscanf(cusdata, "%s %d %d", name,
           &oldread, &newread) == 3) {
        if (oldread <= newread)
            producebill(name, oldread, newread,
                        rate, rental);
        else
            reporterror(name, oldread, newread);
    }
    fclose(cusdata);
    fclose(billfile);
    fclose(errfile);
    printf("\n\n***End of run***\n");
}
```

```
     void producebill(char name[], int old, int new,
                      float rate, float rental)
     {
        int units;
        float amtdue;

        units = new - old;
        amtdue = units * rate + rental;
        fprintf(billfile, "\nName: %s\n", name);
        fprintf(billfile, "Previous meter reading: "
                          "%d\n", old);
        fprintf(billfile, "Present meter reading: "
                          "%d\n", new);
        fprintf(billfile, "Units used: %d\n", units);
        fprintf(billfile, "Pay this amount: "
                          "$%6.2f\n", amtdue);
     }

     void reporterror(char name[], int old, int new)
     {
        fprintf(errfile, "\nCustomer %s not "
                         "processed\n", name);
        fprintf(errfile, "Invalid meter readings: "
                         "%d, %d\n", old, new);
     }
```

and the following values are supplied:

```
Rate per unit: 0.25
Rental charge: 50.00
```

when the program terminates, `billreport` contains the following output:

```
Name: JohnBrown
Previous meter reading: 245
Present meter reading: 572
Units used: 327
Pay this amount: $131.75
```

```
Name: MaryFischer
Previous meter reading: 550
Present meter reading: 850
Units used: 300
Pay this amount: $125.00

Name: AlanJones
Previous meter reading: 700
Present meter reading: 1200
Units used: 500
Pay this amount: $175.00
```

and `errors.dat` contains the following:

```
Customer SusanSpicer not processed
Invalid meter readings: 425, 375
```

In our program the file pointers have been declared as **external** variables. If we wished, we could have passed them as arguments to the appropriate functions. For example, we could have written the function heading of `reporterror` as:

```
void reporterror(FILE *errfile, char name[], int old,
                 int new)
```

and, in `main`, called it with:

```
reporterror(errfile, name, oldread, newread);
```

Of course, the formal parameter could have a different name from the actual argument.

A useful utility is one which copies one file to another. The following assumes that the files are opened and closed in the calling routine.

```
void copyfile(FILE *fromfile, FILE *tofile)
{
    int ch;

    while ((ch = getc(fromfile)) != EOF) putc(ch, tofile);
}
```

If, for instance, we wanted to copy the 'error' file to the standard output, we would have to:

- close it as a 'write' file;
- reopen it as a 'read' file;
- use the statement:

```
copyfile(errfile, stdout);
```

  to write the error file to the standard output;
- close the error file.

## 10.5 `feof` **and** `ferror`

When data is being read from a file, several possible conditions can arise.

(1) The data could be read successfully.
(2) An attempt may be made to read beyond the end of the file.
(3) A 'read error' could occur; for example, the disk may be damaged.

The functions which read data return EOF if an attempt has been made to read beyond the end of the file. However, many of these functions also return EOF if an error is encountered (for example, trying to write to a file opened for reading only). How can a program determine which condition obtained?

The function `feof` can be used to check the end-of-file condition on a file. Its prototype is

```
int feof(FILE *fp);
```

The argument to `feof` is a file pointer, `fp`, say. `feof` returns non-zero (TRUE) if the end of the file associated with `fp` has been reached; otherwise, it returns zero (FALSE). For example, to copy a file (pointed to by `fp`) to the standard output, one could use:

```
while (!feof(fp)) putchar(getc(fp));
```

Of course, the code could also be written as (`ch` is an `int`):

```
while ((ch = getc(fp)) != EOF) putchar(ch);
```

Testing for end-of-file with EOF is fine for text files. This is because C guarantees that the (integer) value of EOF is different from that of any other character. Thus EOF could be returned only when the end of the file is actually reached. Unfortunately, the same does not hold for binary files. This is because a binary file consists of arbitrary bit patterns (as opposed to bit patterns representing characters). Thus it is entirely possible that the value of an arbitrary byte could be the same as the value of EOF. Testing such a byte against EOF would lead to the erroneous conclusion that the end of the file had been reached. For binary files, therefore, the safest way to test for end-of-file is to use the function feof.

The function ferror accepts a file pointer – fp, say – and returns non-zero (TRUE) if an error occurred during the last file operation attempted; otherwise, it returns zero (FALSE). Its prototype is:

```
int ferror(FILE *fp);
```

and can be used as in the following example (chfile is a FILE *):

```
fscanf(chfile, "%d %f", &age, &allowance);
                            /* int age; float allowance; */
if (ferror(chfile))
    fprintf(stderr, "Error reading age, allowance\n");
```

Since the error indication (for a given file) could be set by any file operation, it is important to test for it immediately after a given operation. If this is not done, an error may be lost. For example, suppose two scanf's are done and then ferror is called. If it returns TRUE, we would not know whether the error was due to the first or the second call to scanf.

## 10.6 fgets **and** fputs

These are two standard functions which can be used with arbitrary files. fgets is used to read an entire string (up to, and including, the next newline) and fputs is used to output a string which may or may not contain a newline.

The prototype of fgets is:

```
char *fgets(char line[], int max, FILE *infile);
```

The character array line must have at least max elements. Characters are read from `infile` and stored in `line` until 'newline' is encountered or 'max-1' characters have been stored, whichever comes first. If 'newline' is encountered and 'max-1' characters have not yet been stored, `\n` is added to `line`. In either case, `line` is terminated with `\0`. If at least one character (other than `\0`) is stored in `line`, `fgets` returns `line` (which is, in effect, a pointer to the characters stored). If end-of-file is encountered and no characters have been stored in `line`, `fgets` returns `NULL`. If an error occurs, `fgets` also returns `NULL`. Since `NULL` is returned for both end-of-file and error conditions, the functions `feof` and/or `ferror` must be used to determine which one occurred. Note that the file pointer is the last argument, not the first as in `fscanf` or `fprintf`.

`fgets` is useful for reading strings which may contain blanks or tabs. Recall that the '`%s`' option of `fscanf` cannot be used to read a string containing blanks or tabs.

The prototype for `fputs` is:

```
void fputs(char string[], FILE *outfile);
```

`string` contains the string (properly terminated by `\0`) to be written to `outfile`. It may contain **any** characters, including newlines. The terminating `\0` is not written. If successful, `fputs` returns a non-negative value; if unsuccessful, it returns `EOF`.

### *Example – comparing two files*

This example uses `fgets` to compare two files, printing the first lines, if any, where they differ.

The program P10.2 reads lines from both files (using `fgets`) until a mismatch is found or one of the files comes to an end. It also illustrates one way of verifying the filename that a user enters, using the function `getfilename`.

The following points are for noting:

- The maximum filename catered for is MAXNAME − 1;
- The maximum linelength (including `\n`) catered for is MAXLINE − 1;
- The filename is read using `gets`, so it may contain blanks. Since the user will normally press 'return' after typing the filename, we cannot use

```
fgets(name, MAXNAME, stdin);
```

since, in this case, the newline character (`\n`) becomes part of the string

**Program P10.2**

```c
#include <stdio.h>

#define MAXNAME 20
#define MAXLINE 101

main()
{
    char name1[MAXNAME], name2[MAXNAME];
    char line1[MAXLINE], line2[MAXLINE];
    FILE *file1, *file2;
    FILE *getfilename(char *, char *);
    char *eof1, *eof2;

    int linenum = 0;

    file1 = getfilename("First file?", name1);
    file2 = getfilename("Second file?", name2);

    while ((((eof1 = fgets(line1, MAXLINE, file1))
            != NULL) &&
        ((eof2 = fgets(line2, MAXLINE, file2))
            != NULL) &&
        (strcmp(line1, line2) == 0))
      linenum++;
    /* at this stage, linenum is the number of
       matching lines found */
    if (eof1 == NULL) /* then first file came to an
                         end */
        if (fgets(line2, MAXLINE, file2) == NULL)
                            /* second also ended */
            printf("\nFiles are identical\n\n");
        else     /* first file ended, second file not
                    ended */
            printf("\n%s, with %d line(s), is a "
                 "subset of %s\n\n",
                  name1, linenum, name2);
    else if (eof2 == NULL) /* first file not ended,
                              second file ended */
```

```
                printf("\n%s, with %d line(s), is a "
                       "subset of %s\n\n",
                       name2, linenum, name1);
        else { /* mismatch found */
            printf("\nThe files differ at line number "
                   "%d\n\n", ++linenum);
            printf("The lines are \n %s\n and \n %s\n",
                   line1, line2);
        }
        fclose(file1);
        fclose(file2);
    }


FILE * getfilename(char *prompt, char *name)
/* store the filename in 'name' and return the
   pointer to the file */
{
    FILE *fileptr;

    do {
        printf("%s ", prompt);
        gets(name);
        if ((fileptr = fopen(name, "r")) == NULL)
            printf("File does not exist or access "
                   "denied\n");
    } while (fileptr == NULL);
    return fileptr;
}
```

stored and will be considered part of the filename. Recall that with gets, \n is never part of the string returned.
- Recall that the evaluation of a boolean expression ceases as soon as its truth value is determined. Thus, for instance, if the end of the first file is reached, the while statement exits immediately without a line being read from the second file.

- In the interest of brevity and simplicity, we assume that no errors in reading the files occur – the files are read until one or the other comes to an end. To cater for errors, we could use ferror to determine if a reading error caused fgets to return NULL. Alternatively, we could use feof to determine if the end-of-file was actually reached.

## 10.7 sprintf **and** sscanf

These functions enable output to be sent to a string and input to be read from a string.

sprintf is similar to printf except that it sends output to a string. The general form is

```
sprintf(⟨string⟩, ⟨format string⟩, ⟨arg1⟩, ⟨arg2⟩, ...);
```

The output produced is stored in the character array ⟨string⟩. It is the programmer's responsibility to ensure that ⟨string⟩ is large enough to hold the output. For example, given:

```
char buffer[50];
int a = 12;
float x = 7.50;
```

The statement:

```
sprintf(buffer, "age = %d, allowance = $%f\n", a, x);
```

stores the string

```
age = 12, allowance = $7.50\n
```

in buffer, adding \0 at the end. sprintf returns the number of characters stored in buffer, not counting the terminating \0.

sscanf is similar to scanf except that it gets its input from a string. The general form is

```
sscanf(⟨string⟩, ⟨conversion string⟩, ⟨addr1⟩, ⟨addr2⟩, ...);
```

where the values to be stored in ⟨addr1⟩, ⟨addr2⟩, etc. are obtained from the character array ⟨string⟩. For example, using the above declarations, the statement:

```
sscanf("    25    3.14   ", "%d %f", &a, &x);
```

will search the first string for values for a and x. In this case, a is assigned 25 and x is assigned 3.14.

A useful example of this function is given in Section 11.2.

### 10.8 Input/output for binary files

As discussed before, a binary file contains data in a form which corresponds exactly with the internal representation of the data. For example, if a float variable occupies 4 bytes of memory, writing it to a binary file simply involves making an exact copy of the 4 bytes. (On the other hand, writing it to a text file causes it to be converted to character form and the characters obtained are stored in the file). Normally, a binary file can be created only from within a program and its contents can be read only by a program. Listing a binary file, for example, only produces 'garbage' and, sometimes, generates an error. (Compare a text file which can be created by typing into it and whose contents can be listed and read by a human). However, a binary file does have the following advantages:

- the values of data types such as arrays and structures can be written to a binary file. (For a text file, individual elements must be written).
- data can be transferred to and from a binary file much faster than for a text file since no data conversions are necessary; the data is read and written 'as is'.
- data stored in a binary file usually occupies less space than the same data stored in a text file. For example, the integer −25367 (six characters) occupies 6 bytes in a text file but only 2 bytes in a binary file.

ANSI C provides the functions fread and fwrite for use on binary files.

### *10.8.1* fread *and* fwrite

Consider the problem of reading integers from the standard input and writing them, in their internal form, to a (binary) file. Assume that the numbers are to be stored in the external file num.dat. This could be done with:

```
#include <stdio.h>

main()
{
    FILE *intfile;
    int num;

    if ((intfile = fopen("num.dat","wb")) == NULL) {
        printf("Cannot open file\n");
        return;
    }
    while (scanf("%d", &num) == 1)
        fwrite(&num, sizeof(int), 1, intfile);

    fclose (intfile);
}
```

In the program, num.dat is opened with "wb" which means 'open a binary file for writing'. If the file cannot be opened, a message is printed and the program is stopped. (A return statement in main returns control to the operating system). The while loop reads a number from the standard input and writes it to the file. In the statement:

```
fwrite(&num, sizeof(int), 1, intfile);
```

- &num specifies the address of the item(s) to be written;
- sizeof(int) specifies the size of each item to be written;
- 1 specifies that one item is to be written;
- intfile specifies the file to which the items are to be written.

In general, fwrite writes a specified number of items to a binary file. Its prototype is:

```
size_t fwrite(void *buffer, size_t unitsize,
              size_t numitems, FILE *fp);
```

where

- buffer is the address of the item(s) to be written;
- unitsize is the size of each item;
- numitems is the number of items to be written;
- fp is the file pointer.

fwrite returns the number of full items written; this could be less than numitems if an error occurs. unitsize is usually specified using the sizeof operator. This is particularly useful for structures as well as to ensure portability. As another example, if poly is a double array of size 20, then:

```
fwrite(poly, sizeof(double), 20, fp);
```

writes the entire array to the file specified by fp. Recall that an array name is a synonym for the address of its first element.

Given the declaration:

```
struct child {
    char name[20];
    int age;
    char sex;
    float allowance;
} susan;
```

we could write the entire structure susan to a file with:

```
fwrite(&susan, sizeof(struct child), 1, fp);
```

If class is an array of structures defined as:

```
struct child class[100];
```

then the 100 structure elements could be written to a file with:

```
fwrite(class, sizeof(struct child), 100, fp);
```

The function fread has the same format as fwrite, and is used for reading a specified number of items from a binary file. Its prototype is:

```
size_t fread(void *buffer, size_t unitsize,
                size_t numitems, FILE *fp);
```

where

- `buffer` is the address where the items read are to be stored;
- `unitsize` is the size of each item;
- `numitems` is the number of items to be written;
- `fp` is the file pointer.

`fread` returns the number of full items actually read; this could be less than `numitems` if an error occurs or if the end of the file is reached before `numitems` are read. The functions `feof` or `ferror` may be used to distinguish between a read error and an end-of-file condition.

The following program reads the file of integers created above and prints them on the standard output. The file is opened with "`rb`" which means 'open a binary file for reading'. Each time a number is read, the return value of `fread` should be 1; if it isn't, then either the end-of-file was reached or an error occurred.

```c
#include <stdio.h>

main()
{
    FILE *intfile;
    int num;

    if ((intfile = fopen("num.dat","rb")) == NULL) {
        printf("Cannot open file\n");
        return;
    }

    while (fread(&num, sizeof(int), 1, intfile) == 1)
            printf("%d\n", num);

    if feof(intfile) printf("\nEnd of list\n");
    else printf("\nError reading file\n");

    fclose(intfile);
}
```

### 10.9  Random access files

In the normal mode of operation, data is read from a file in the order in which it is stored. When a file is opened, one can think of an imaginary pointer positioned at the beginning of the file. (This is not to be confused with the data type FILE * discussed previously). As items are read from the file, this pointer moves along by the number of bytes read. Put another way, this pointer indicates where the next read (or write) operation would occur. Normally, this pointer is moved implicitly by a read or write operation. However, C provides facilities for moving the pointer explicitly to any position in the file. We discuss the functions rewind and fseek. While rewind can be used on either text or binary files, fseek is recommended for use with binary files only. For a text file, character translations (such as converting 'newline' to 'carriage return' and 'line feed') would cause fseek to give unexpected results.

### *10.9.1* rewind *and* fseek

The function rewind positions the pointer at the beginning of the file. Its prototype is:

```
void rewind(FILE *fp);
```

rewind does not return a value. If the end-of-file or error condition was set for a file, a call to rewind clears the condition.

The function fseek allows more flexible movement within a file. Its prototype is:

```
int fseek(FILE *fp, long offset, int origin);
```

and it moves the file pointer to a position which is offset bytes from origin. If successful, fseek returns zero; otherwise, it returns non-zero.

origin must be one of the following predefined constants (defined in stdio.h):

| | |
|---|---|
| SEEK_SET | Beginning of the file |
| SEEK_CUR | Current position of file pointer |
| SEEK_END | End of the file |

offset is a long integer; if the actual argument is not a long integer, then the function prototype causes automatic coercion to long. For example,

```
fseek(intfile, 32, SEEK_SET);
```

moves the file pointer to a position which is 32 bytes from the beginning of the file, that is, to the beginning of the 33rd byte. Since 32 is an `int`, it is automatically converted to `long int` before being passed to `fseek`. We could also have used 32L.

One of the most common uses of `fseek` is to retrieve the records of a file in random order. This is illustrated by the next example.

Consider the declaration:

```
struct partrecord {
    char partnum[7];      /* part number */
    char name[25];        /* name of part */
    int amtinstock;       /* quantity in stock */
    float unitprice;      /* unit selling price */
};
```

and suppose we wanted to create a file containing the records for several parts. The data for each part will be read from the standard input, stored in a temporary structure and then written, as one unit, to a binary file. Suppose that a part number is a six-character string (e. g. LNS020) and a part name is a maximum of 24 characters long. (The extra character declared is used for storing \0). For simplicity, we assume that a part name does not contain any spaces. Some sample data are shown below:

| LNS020 | Park-Lens | 8 | 6.50 |
| BLJ375 | Ball-Joints | 12 | 11.95 |
| FLT015 | Oil-Filter | 23 | 4.95 |

Program P10.3 reads the data and stores it in a binary file `parts.dat`. The data are stored in the order in which they arrive.

The program confirms that a given part record has been written successfully to the parts file by checking the return value of `fwrite`. If successful, `fwrite` should return 1, in this example.

To understand how `fseek` may be used on the parts file, think of the records as being numbered consecutively from 1 and suppose that each

## Program P10.3

```
#include <stdio.h>

typedef struct partrecord {
    char partnum[7];
    char name[25];
    int amtinstock;
    float unitprice;
} PartRecord;

main()
{
    FILE *partfile;
    PartRecord part;

    if ((partfile = fopen("parts.dat","wb")) == NULL) {
        printf("Cannot open file\n");
        return;
    }

    while (scanf("%s %s %d %f", part.partnum, part.name,
                    &part.amtinstock, &part.unitprice) == 4)
        if (fwrite(&part, sizeof(PartRecord), 1,
                    partfile) != 1) {
            printf("Error in writing file\n");
            return;
        }
    /* end while */
    fclose(partfile);
}
```

record is 40 bytes long. If the records are stored in the file starting at byte 0:

Record 1 occupies bytes 0 – 39;
Record 2 occupies bytes 40 – 79;
Record 3 occupies bytes 80 – 119;

and, in general,

Record *n* starts at byte number (*n* − 1)*40 and occupies the next 40 bytes.

Now, suppose we wanted to read record *n*; we must

(1) position the file pointer at the beginning of the *n*th record;
(2) read a number of bytes equal to the size of a record.

This can be done with:

```
fseek(partfile, (n - 1)*sizeof(PartRecord), SEEK_SET);
fread(&part, sizeof(PartRecord), 1, partfile);
```

As usual, we could check the return values to ensure successful completion of the operations. The following code requests a record number, reads the record from the file and prints the record information on the screen. It assumes that the record number supplied is a valid one.

```
printf("Enter record number: ");
scanf("%d", &n);

fseek(partfile, (n - 1)*sizeof(PartRecord), SEEK_SET);
fread(&part, sizeof(PartRecord), 1, partfile);
        /* PartRecord part */

printf("\nPart number: %s\n", part.partnum);
printf("Part name: %s\n", part.name);
printf("Quantity in stock: %d\n", part.amtinstock);
printf("Unit price: $%-6.2f\n", part.unitprice);
```

### 10.9.2 Indexed files

The above showed how to retrieve a part record given the record number. But this is not the most natural way to retrieve records. More likely than not, we would want to retrieve records based on some **key**, in this case, the part number. Thus it is more natural to ask, 'How many of BLJ375 do we have?' rather than 'How many of record 2 do we have?'. The problem then is how to retrieve a record given the part number.

One approach is to use an **index**. Just like a book index, a file index enables us to find records in a file quickly. The index is created as the file is loaded. Later on, it must be updated as records are added to, or deleted from, the file. In our example, an index entry will consist of a part number and a record number. The declaration for an index entry could be:

```
struct indexentry {
    char pnum[7];
    int recnum;
};
```

and an array of such structures could be used to hold the entire index. For example, if we wanted to cater for up to 100 items, we could use:

```
struct indexentry index[100];
```

The index will be kept in order by part number. Let us illustrate the creation of an index for the following records:

| | | | |
|---|---|---|---|
| LNS020 | Park-Lens | 8 | 6.50 |
| BLJ375 | Ball-Joints | 12 | 11.95 |
| FLT015 | Oil-Filter | 23 | 4.95 |
| PNT217 | Contact-Points | 10 | 3.75 |
| GLT555 | Fuel-Filter | 7 | 2.50 |

We assume that the records are stored in the file in the given order. When the first record is read and stored, the index will be:

LNS020          1

meaning that the record for LNS020 is record number 1 in the parts file. After the second record is read and stored, the index will be:

BLJ375          2
LNS020          1

since the index is in order by part number. After the third record is read and stored, the index will be:

| | |
|---|---|
| BLJ375 | 2 |
| FLT015 | 3 |
| LNS020 | 1 |

After the fourth record is read and stored, the index will be:

| | |
|---|---|
| BLJ375 | 2 |
| FLT015 | 3 |
| LNS020 | 1 |
| PNT217 | 4 |

and after the fifth record is read and stored, the index will be:

| | |
|---|---|
| BLJ375 | 2 |
| FLT015 | 3 |
| GLT555 | 5 |
| LNS020 | 1 |
| PNT217 | 4 |

The next program, P10.4, illustrates how an index can be created as described above. As each record is read, it is stored in the parts file, parts.dat. A count is kept (in numrecords) of the number of records read. The part number and the record number are then inserted in the proper place in the index (an array of structures).

In order to simplify the search of the index, index entries are stored from index[1] to index[numrecords], and index[0].pnum is set to the null string. This ensures that any valid part number would be greater than whatever is in index[0].pnum. Since the index is always sorted, we use a (modified) binary search to search for the location in which the new entry must be inserted.

When all the part records have been stored, the index itself is stored in the file index.dat. In order to retrieve and use the index the next time, we need to store its size (MAXRECORDS + 1) as well as the number of entries actually used (numrecords). We store numrecords in index[0].recnum and, in the file, we store the value of (MAXRECORDS + 1) followed by index[0] up to index[MAXRECORDS].

Also, note the use of the standard function exit (defined in stdlib.h) in the functions createmaster and saveindex. exit is used to

## Program P10.4

```c
#include <stdio.h>
#include <stdlib.h>
#include <string.h>

#define KEYSIZE 6
#define MAXNAME 24
#define MAXRECORDS 100

typedef struct partrecord {
    char partnum[KEYSIZE + 1];
    char name[MAXNAME + 1];
    int amtinstock;
    float unitprice;
} PartRecord;

typedef struct indexentry {
    char pnum[KEYSIZE + 1];
    int recnum;
} IndexEntry;

main()
{
    IndexEntry index[MAXRECORDS + 1];
    void createmaster(char *filename, IndexEntry
                      index[], int max);
    void saveindex(char *filename, IndexEntry
                   index[], int max);

    createmaster("parts.dat", index, MAXRECORDS);
    saveindex("index.dat", index, MAXRECORDS + 1);

}

void createmaster(char *filename, IndexEntry
                  index[], int maxrecords)
/* stores records in partfile; caters for maxrecords
   index entries; sets index[0].recnum to the
```

```
    number of index entries (same as the number of
    records stored) */
{

    FILE *partfile;
    PartRecord part;
    IndexEntry newentry;
    int searchresult;
    int keysearch(char key[], IndexEntry index[], int max);
    void insertindex(IndexEntry, IndexEntry index[],
                     int, int);


    int numrecords = 0;

    if ((partfile = fopen(filename,"wb")) == NULL) {
       printf("Cannot open file %s\n", filename);
       exit(1);
    }

    strcpy(index[0].pnum, "");
     /* null string, simplifies function keysearch */

    while (scanf("%s %s %d %f", part.partnum,
          part.name, &part.amtinstock,
          &part.unitprice) == 4)
    {
       searchresult = keysearch(part.partnum, index,
                                numrecords);
       if (searchresult < 0) /* this is a new part
                               number */
          if (numrecords == maxrecords) {
             printf("Too many records: only %d "
                    "allowed\n", maxrecords);
             exit(1); }
          else { /* the index has room */
             strcpy(newentry.pnum, part.partnum);
             newentry.recnum = ++numrecords;
             insertindex(newentry, index,
                         -searchresult,
                         numrecords - 1);
```

```
            if (fwrite(&part, sizeof(PartRecord), 1,
                      partfile) != 1) {
              printf("Error in writing file\n");
              exit(1);
            }
         }
      else printf("Duplicate part number: "
               "%s - record ignored\n",
               part.partnum);
   }
   index[0].recnum = numrecords;
   fclose(partfile);
}


int keysearch(char key[], IndexEntry index[],
              int max)
/* searches for key from index[1] to index[max]
   using a binary search. If found, it returns the
   location; otherwise it returns the negative of
   the location in which key should be inserted.
   Uses the fact that index[0].pnum = "" */
{
   int mid, compare;
   int lo = 1;
   int hi = max;

   do {
      mid = (lo + hi) / 2;
      if ((compare = strcmp(key, index[mid].pnum))
                 < 0) {
         hi = mid - 1;
         if (lo > hi) return (-mid); }
      else if (compare > 0) {
         lo = mid + 1;
         if (lo > hi) return (-lo);
      }
   } while (compare != 0);
   return mid;
}
```

```
void insertindex(IndexEntry newitem, IndexEntry
                 index[], int slot, int max)
/* inserts newitem in index[slot], first moving
   elements from 'slot' to 'max' one place down */
{
    int j;

    for (j = max; j >= slot; j--)
        index[j + 1] = index[j];
    index[slot] = newitem;
}

void saveindex(char *filename, IndexEntry index[],
               int max)
/* saves the index in filename; max is the size of
   index. */
{
    FILE *indexfile;

    if ((indexfile = fopen(filename, "wb")) == NULL) {
        printf("Cannot open file %s. Index "
               "not saved\n", filename);
        exit(1);
    }

    fwrite(&max, sizeof(int), 1, indexfile);
                       /* save the index size first*/
    fwrite(index, sizeof(IndexEntry), max, indexfile);
                       /* save the index */
    fclose(indexfile);
}
```

terminate execution of a program and return control to the operating system. It is conventional to use exit(0) to indicate normal termination; other arguments are used to indicate some sort of error.

Program P10.4 loads the 'part records' into the parts file and, at the same time, creates an index for the file. The index is in ascending order by the key, part number. However, the records are stored in the file in the order of arrival, which is not necessarily the same as ascending order by part number.

Consider the problem of printing the records in the file in order by part number. This can be done by retrieving the records in the order in which the part numbers appear in the index. In general,

index[i].pnum gives the *i*th part number, and
index[i].recnum gives the position (record number) of the record in the file.

Program P10.5

- retrieves the index from the file index.dat. Recall that this file contains the size of the index array followed by the index and that
  index[0].recnum contains the number of records in the file.
- prints the records in order by part number.

---

**Program P10.5**

```
#include <stdio.h>
#include <stdlib.h>
#include <string.h>

#define KEYSIZE 6
#define MAXNAME 24
#define MAXRECORDS 100

typedef struct partrecord {
    char partnum[KEYSIZE + 1];
    char name[MAXNAME + 1];
    int amtinstock;
    float unitprice;
} PartRecord;

typedef struct indexentry {
    char pnum[KEYSIZE + 1];
    int recnum;
} IndexEntry;

main ()
```

```
{
    FILE *partfile;
    PartRecord part;
    IndexEntry index[MAXRECORDS + 1];
    int numrecords;
    void retrieveindex(char *filename,
                       IndexEntry index[]);
    void printfile(char *filename, IndexEntry
                   index[], int);
    retrieveindex("index.dat", index);
    numrecords = index[0].recnum;
    printfile("parts.dat", index, numrecords);
}
void retrieveindex(char *filename, IndexEntry
                   index[])
{
    FILE *indexfile;
    int max;

    if ((indexfile = fopen(filename,"rb")) == NULL){
        printf("cannot open index file.\n");
        exit(1);
    }

    fread(&max, sizeof(int), 1, indexfile);
    fread(index, sizeof(IndexEntry), max, indexfile);
    fclose(indexfile);
}


void printfile(char *filename, IndexEntry index[],
               int amount)
{
    FILE *partfile;
    int j;
    PartRecord part;

    if ((partfile = fopen(filename,"rb")) == NULL) {
        printf("cannot open parts file \n");
        exit(1);
    }
```

```
    for (j = 1; j <= amount; j++) {
        fseek(partfile, (index[j].recnum - 1)
            * sizeof(PartRecord), SEEK_SET);
        fread(&part, sizeof(PartRecord), 1, partfile);

        printf("\nPart number: %s\n", part.partnum);
        printf("Part name: %s\n", part.name);
        printf("Quantity in stock: %d\n",
            part.amtinstock);
        printf("Unit price: $%-6.2f\n",
            part.unitprice);
    }
    fclose(partfile);
}
```

Now suppose we wanted to retrieve a random record, given the part number (key, say). Since the index is in order, we could use a fast search method (for example, binary search) to locate key. If it is found in location j, then index[j].recnum is the record number in the file. The record could then be retrieved with:

```
fseek(partfile, (index[j].recnum - 1)
    * sizeof(PartRecord), SEEK_SET);
fread(&part, sizeof(PartRecord), 1, partfile);
```

This idea is expanded in the next subsection.

### 10.9.3 *Updating a random access file*

The information in a file is not usually static. It must be updated from time to time. For our parts file, we may want to update it to reflect the new 'quantity in stock' as items are sold or to reflect a change in price. We may decide to stock new parts so we must add records to the file, and we may discontinue selling certain items so their records must be deleted from the file. Adding new records is done in a similar manner to loading the file in the first place. We can delete a record logically by marking it as deleted in the index, or simply removing it from the index. Later, when the file is reorganized, the record could be deleted physically (that is, not present in the new file). But how can we change the information in an existing record? To do this, we must:

- locate the record in the file;
- read it into memory;
- change the desired fields;
- write the updated record to the same position in the file from which it came.

This means that our file must be opened for both reading and writing. Assuming that the file already exists, it must be opened with mode "rb+". We explain how to update a record whose part number is stored in key.

First we search the index for key. If it is not found, no record exists for this part. Suppose it is found in location j. Then index[j].recnum gives its record number (n, say) in the parts file. We then proceed as follows (omitting error checking in the interest of clarity):

```
fseek(partfile, (n - 1)*sizeof(PartRecord), SEEK_SET);
fread(&part, sizeof(PartRecord), 1, partfile);
```

The record is now in memory in the structure variable part. Suppose we needed to subtract amtsold from the amount in stock. This could be done with:

```
if (amtsold > part.amtinstock)
    printf("Cannot sell more than you have\n");
else
    part.amtinstock -= amtsold;
```

Other fields (except the key, since the key is used to identify the record) could be updated similarly. When all changes have been made, the updated record is in memory in the structure variable part. It must now be written back to the file in the same position from which it came. This could be done with:

```
fseek(partfile, (n - 1)*sizeof(PartRecord), SEEK_SET);
fwrite(&part, sizeof(PartRecord), 1, partfile);
```

Note that we must call fseek again since, after the previous fread, the file is positioned at the beginning of the next record; we must re-position it at the beginning of the record just read. The net effect is that the updated record overwrites the old record.

Program P10.6 updates the `amtinstock` field of records in the parts file. The user is asked to enter a part number and the amount sold. The program searches the index for the part number using a binary search. If found, the record is retrieved from the file, updated in memory, and written back to the file. This is repeated until the user enters a dummy part number "$$$".

---

### Program P10.6

```c
#include <stdio.h>
#include <stdlib.h>
#include <string.h>

#define KEYSIZE 6
#define MAXNAME 24
#define MAXRECORDS 100
#define ENDOFDATA 0
#define DATAGIVEN 1
#define DUMMYPART "$$$"

typedef struct partrecord {
    char partnum[KEYSIZE + 1];
    char name[MAXNAME + 1];
    int amtinstock;
    float unitprice;
} PartRecord;

typedef struct indexentry {
    char pnum[KEYSIZE + 1];
    int recnum;
} IndexEntry;

main()
{
    FILE *partfile;
    PartRecord part;
    IndexEntry index[MAXRECORDS + 1];
```

```
        char key[KEYSIZE + 1];
        int numrecords, amtsold;
        void retrieveindex(char *filename, IndexEntry
                            index[]);
        int searchresult;
        int keysearch(char key[], IndexEntry index[], int max);
        int getinfo(char *, int *);
        void updaterecord(FILE *, int n, int amtsold);

        if ((partfile = fopen("parts.dat", "rb+"))
                        == NULL) {
        printf("cannot open parts file \n");
        exit(1);
    }
    retrieveindex("index.dat", index);
    numrecords = index[0].recnum;

    while (getinfo(key, &amtsold) != ENDOFDATA)
        if ((searchresult = keysearch(key, index,
                            numrecords)) < 0)
            printf("\nPart %s not found\n", key);
        else
            updaterecord(partfile,
                        index[searchresult].recnum, amtsold);
    /*endwhile*/
    }


    void retrieveindex(char *filename, IndexEntry
                        index[])
    {
        FILE *indexfile;
        int max;

        if ((indexfile = fopen(filename,"rb")) == NULL){
            printf("cannot open index file.\n");
            exit(1);
        }
```

```c
    fread(&max, sizeof(int), 1, indexfile);
    fread(index, sizeof(IndexEntry), max, indexfile);
    fclose(indexfile);
}

int getinfo(char *key, int *amtptr)
{
    char reply[20]; /* caters for a y/n reply of up
                       to 19 characters */

    do {
        printf("Part number (%s to end)?", DUMMYPART);
        scanf("%s", key);
        if (strcmp(key, DUMMYPART) == 0)
            return ENDOFDATA;
        printf("Amount sold?");
        scanf("%d", amtptr);
        printf("ok? y or n:");
        scanf("%s", reply);
    } while (strncmp(reply, "y", 1) != 0 &&
             strncmp(reply, "Y", 1) != 0);
    return DATAGIVEN;
}

void updaterecord(FILE *partfile, int num, int
                  amtsold)
/* subtracts amtsold from amtinstock field of record
   num */
{
    PartRecord part;

    fseek(partfile, (num - 1) * sizeof(PartRecord),
        SEEK_SET);
    fread(&part, sizeof(PartRecord), 1, partfile);
    printf("Amount in stock = %d\n",
        part.amtinstock);
    printf("Amount sold = %d\n", amtsold);

    if (amtsold > part.amtinstock)
        printf("Cannot sell more than you have: "
            "transaction ignored\n");
```

```
    else {
        part.amtinstock -= amtsold;
        printf("Amount remaining = %d\n",
                part.amtinstock);
        fseek(partfile, (num - 1) *
                sizeof(PartRecord), SEEK_SET);
        if (fwrite(&part, sizeof(PartRecord), 1,
                    partfile) != 1) {
            printf("error in writing file\n");
            exit(1);
        }
    }
}


int keysearch(char key[], IndexEntry index[],
              int max)
/* searches for key from index[1] to index[max]
   using a binary search. If found, it returns the
   location; otherwise it returns the negative of
   the location in which key should be inserted.
   Uses the fact that index[0].pnum = "" */
{
    int mid, compare;
    int lo = 1;
    int hi = max;

    do {
        mid = (lo + hi) / 2;
        if ((compare = strcmp(key, index[mid].pnum))
                    < 0) {
            hi = mid - 1;
            if (lo > hi) return (-mid); }
        else if (compare > 0) {
            lo = mid + 1;
            if (lo > hi) return (-lo);
        }
    } while (compare != 0);
    return mid;
}
```

## *Observations on program P10.6*

- The function `getinfo` gives the user the chance to confirm that the data entered is correct. When asked the question:

  `ok? y or n:`

  the user is supposed to type only one character ('y' or 'n'), but the program caters for up to 19 characters. Only the first character typed is used in the comparison against "y" (and "Y") and only when the user enters y (or Y) does the program attempt to process the data entered. The function `strncmp` (defined in `string.h`) is similar to `strcmp`, except that a third argument is used to specify the maximum number of characters to compare from each string. For example,

  `strncmp(s1, s2, n);`

  compares string `s1` with string `s2` up to a limit of n characters. The strings are compared character by character until the result of the comparison is known (corresponding characters are different), one of the strings comes to an end or n pairs of characters have been compared, whichever comes first.
- In `updaterecord`, if the amount sold is greater than the amount in stock, a message is issued and the transaction ignored; the record in the file remains unchanged.
- Any number of transactions may be done on any record. However, for each transaction, the part number and the amount sold must be entered.

## Exercises 10

(1) What is the difference between a file opened with "r+" and one opened with "w+"?

(2) Write a program to determine if two binary files are identical. If they are different, print the first byte number at which they differ.

(3) Write a program to read a (binary) file of integers, sort the integers and write them back to the same file. Assume that all the numbers can be stored in an array.

(4) Repeat (3) but assume that only 20 numbers can be stored in memory (in an array) at any one time. Hint: you will need to use at least 2 additional files for temporary output.

(5) Write a program to read two sorted files of integers and merge the values to a third sorted file.

(6) Write a program to read a text file and produce another text file in which all lines are less than some given length. Make sure and break lines in sensible places, for example, avoid breaking words or putting isolated punctuation marks at the beginning of a line.

(7) What is the purpose of creating an index for a file?

The following are some records from an employee file. The fields are employee number (the key), name, job title, telephone number, monthly salary and tax to be deducted.

```
STF425, Julie Johnson, Secretary, 623-3321, 2500, 600
COM319, Ian McLean, Programmer, 676-1319, 3200, 800
SYS777, Jean Kendall, Systems Analyst, 671-2025, 4200, 1100
JNR591, Lincoln Kadoo, Operator, 657-0266, 2800, 700
MSN815, Camille Kelly, Clerical Assistant, 652-5345, 2100, 500
STF273, Anella Bayne, Data Entry Manager, 632-5324, 3500, 850
SYS925, Riaz Ali, Senior Programmer, 636-8679, 4800, 1300
```

Assume that the records are stored in a binary file in the order given.

(a) How can a record be retrieved given the record number?

(b) How can a record be retrieved given the key of the number?

(c) As the file is loaded, create an index in which the keys are in the order given. How is such an index searched for a given key?

(d) As the file is loaded, create an index in which the keys are sorted. Given a key, how is the corresponding record retrieved?

Discuss what changes must be made to the index when records are added to and deleted from the file.

(8) For the 'parts file' application discussed in this chapter, write functions for (i) adding new records and (ii) deleting records.

# 11

# Miscellaneous Topics

When a C program is submitted for compiling, it is first processed by the C preprocessor. The output from the C preprocessor is then input to the compiler proper. In this chapter, we discuss the statements recognized by the C preprocessor. We then discuss:

- command line arguments, a means of passing arguments to `main`.
- two-dimensional arrays, expanding on our earlier treatment in Chapter 3. Our examples include matrix multiplication and the creation of magic squares.
- enumerated types, introducing the C keyword `enum`.
- the `goto` statement.
- the type modifiers `const` and `volatile`.

## 11.1 The C preprocessor

Many of our programs so far have used the `#define` 'directive' to specify symbolic or manifest constants. For example, if the directive

```
#define MAXLEN 25
```

appears at the beginning of a program, then whenever MAXLEN appears in the program, it is substituted by 25. (This substitution does not take place if MAXLEN appears within a character string such as "The value of MAXLEN is " or if it forms part of a longer word such as MAXLENGTH). This substitution is one of the facilities provided by the C preprocessor.

The preprocessor is called (automatically) as the first phase of compilation. 'Directives' to the preprocessor all begin with # and this must by the first non-whitespace character on the line. There can be zero or more whitespace characters between # and the first letter of the directive.

Preprocessor directives can appear anywhere in a source file, but they apply only to the remainder of the source file in which they appear. The main directives and the facilities provided by the preprocessor are:

- #define – simple text substitution; replace tokens in the program by 'replacement text'.
- #define – macro substitution with parameters; this provides a more elaborate mechanism for replacing text.
- #include – insert the contents of other files into the source file.
- #if, #elif, #else, #endif – allows a selection of statements to be compiled; this is usually referred to as 'conditional compilation'.

In addition, there are three special-purpose operators:

- # – the 'stringizing' (making into a string) operator;
- ## – the 'token-pasting' (joining separate tokens to form one) operator;
- defined – used to determine if an identifier is currently defined.

'#' and '##' are used mainly with macros which take arguments. defined is used in conjunction with #if, #elif, etc.

### *11.1.1 The* #define *directive*

The simplest form of #define is

```
#define <id> <replacement text>
```

where ⟨id⟩ is an identifier. Whenever ⟨id⟩ appears in the source file, it is replaced by ⟨replacement text⟩. However, the replacement is not done if ⟨id⟩ appears within a character string or if it forms part of a longer identifier. This form of #define has been used in most of our programs so far. One of the major uses of #define is for declaring symbolic constants. But, in theory, ⟨replacement text⟩ can be any set of characters, including none. For instance,

```
#define then
```

causes all occurrences of then to be deleted from the source file. This allows a programmer to write, for example:

```
if (a > b) then
    max = a;
else
    max = b;
```

Normally, this will generate a compilation error since then is not allowed in C. But with the #define, above, then will be removed from the code which will then compile properly.

The statement

```
#define EXCLAIM "My Goodness!"
```

is another example of a valid use of #define, and can be used, for example, in

```
printf("%s\n", EXCLAIM);
```

which would be expanded into

```
printf("%s\n", "My Goodness!");
```

However, consider

```
#define EXCLAIM My Goodness!
```

If we tried to use the statement

```
printf("%s\n", "EXCLAIM");
```

the result is that the word EXCLAIM would be printed; since EXCLAIM appears within a string, it is not replaced by its 'replacement text'.

⟨replacement text⟩ can be continued onto the next line by putting a backslash (\) at the end of the line to be continued.

⟨replacement text⟩ may contain previously #define identifiers, as in:

```
#define MAXLEN 25
#define MAXLEN1 (MAXLEN - 1)
```

One must be careful when the ⟨replacement text⟩ is an arithmetic expression, especially if the defined identifier is to be used in other expressions. For example, suppose the program contained the statement:

```
maxsize = MAXLEN1 * 2;
```

Using the above definition, this would be expanded to

```
maxsize = (MAXLEN - 1) * 2;
```

which, in turn, would be expanded to

```
maxsize = (25 - 1) * 2;
```

which would assign the value 48 to maxsize. However, if we had used

```
#define MAXLEN1 MAXLEN - 1
```

(without the brackets), then the statement

```
maxsize = MAXLEN1 * 2;
```

would be expanded to

```
maxsize = MAXLEN - 1 * 2;
```

which would assign the value 23 to maxsize.

As another example, consider a C compiler parsing a source program. When an identifier is encountered, it is looked up in the 'symbol table' of identifiers met so far. Suppose this table also contains the C keywords. Usually, the look-up routine returns the table location of the identifier if it is found. If the table is organized as a hash table, the keywords could be scattered all over the table. For example, the following five keywords could be in the locations indicated:

| keyword | location |
|---------|----------|
| for     | 23       |
| int     | 29       |
| case    | 45       |
| while   | 52       |
| static  | 63       |

In order to determine what action to take next, the compiler must test the returned value (symbol, say) to determine if the identifier is a keyword. For the above example, the test could be done with a structure such as:

```
switch (symbol) {

    case  23:    /* for */
    case  29:    /* int */
    case  45:    /* case */
    case  52:    /* while */
    case  63:    /* static */
}
```

However, the program would be much more readable if symbolic constants were defined as follows:

```
#define   CASE      45
#define   FOR       23
#define   INT       29
#define   STATIC    63
#define   WHILE     52
```

and the switch statement changed to:

```
switch (symbol) {

    case  CASE:

    case  FOR:

    case  INT:

    case  STATIC:

    case  WHILE:
}
```

Now we could also arrange the case constants in alphabetical order for even more readability. Note that since C distinguishes between upper and lower case, the symbolic constant FOR, say, is different from the keyword for.

### Macros with parameters

It is also possible to put a parameter list after the identifier being defined. The general form is

```
#define ⟨id⟩(⟨parameter list⟩) ⟨replacement text⟩
```

where ⟨parameter list⟩ consists of zero or more formal parameter names separated by commas. The brackets enclosing the ⟨parameter list⟩ are required and there must be **no** spaces between ⟨id⟩ and '('. (If there are spaces, the '(' would be taken as the first character of the replacement text.) For example, consider the following (first, but not correct) attempt to define a macro called square which takes one argument:

```
#define square(n) n * n
```

The program statement

```
y = square(x);
```

will be converted into the statement

```
y = x * x;
```

by preprocessing. Again, one must be careful in using this particular definition. Consider

```
y = square(x + 1);
```

The preprocessor will expand this into

```
y = x + 1 * x + 1;
```

which, in effect, is $2x+1$, not the square of $(x+1)$. To overcome this problem, brackets must be used, as in the following (second, but still not correct) attempt:

```
#define square(n) (n) * (n)
```

Now,

```
y = square(x + 1);
```

will be expanded into

```
y = (x + 1) * (x + 1);
```

which will yield the correct calculation.

But even these brackets may not be enough. Consider:

```
square(a)/square(b)
```

This will be expanded into:

```
(a) * (a) / (b) * (b)
```

but because * and / have the same precedence, it will simply evaluate to $a^2$ (since it is evaluated as $a * \dfrac{a}{b} * b$ and the $b$'s cancel each other). What is really needed is an extra set of brackets around the entire expression, as in:

```
#define square(n) ((n) * (n))
```

Now,

```
square(a)/square(b)
```

expands into

```
((a) * (a)) / ((b) * (b))
```

which gives the correct result.

Other examples are:

```
#define reciprocal(x)    (1.0 / (x))
#define cube(a)          ((a) * (a) * (a))
#define isdigit(ch)      (ch >= '0' && ch <= '9')
#define isupper(ch)      (ch >= 'A' && ch <= 'Z')
#define getchar()        getc(stdin)
#define putchar(ch)      putc(ch, stdout)
```

The definition of isdigit is valid for those character sets where the digits are assigned consecutive codes (e.g. ASCII and EBCDIC). The definition of isupper is valid for those character sets where the uppercase letters are assigned consecutive codes (e. g. ASCII but not EBCDIC).

An instance of the use of isupper is

```
while isupper(nextch) ⟨statement⟩
```

which will be expanded into

```
while (nextch >= 'A' && nextch <= 'Z') ⟨statement⟩
```

An example of a macro with two parameters is

```
#define factorial(n, nfac) for (nfac = 1; n > 0; n--) nfac *= n
```

Due to the nature of the expansion of factorial, both arguments must be variables. The statement

```
factorial(k, kf);
```

will be expanded into

```
for (kf = 1; k > 0; k--) kf *= k;
```

in effect putting k! into kf. Note, of course, that this changes the value of k as well.

From the above examples, it is seen that each occurrence of a formal parameter in the ⟨replacement string⟩ is replaced by the corresponding argument in the macro call. Another way of looking at this is that a formal parameter marks a place in the ⟨replacement text⟩ where actual values will be substituted when the macro is used. The number of actual arguments must be the same as the number of formal parameters. Each parameter name can appear more than once in ⟨replacement text⟩ and the names can appear in any order. (For example, in factorial, above, nfac is the second parameter but it appears first in the replacement text).

It is possible that an actual argument may itself contain one or more macros. In this case, any macros in an actual argument are expanded before the argument replaces the formal parameter. For example, in the statement

```
alpha = reciprocal(b + square(x));
```

the argument to reciprocal contains the macro square. The latter is expanded first to give:

```
alpha = reciprocal(b + ((x) * (x)));
```

This is then expanded to give:

```
alpha = (1.0 / (b + (x) * (x)));
```

Finally, if the name of the macro being defined appears in ⟨replacement text⟩, it is not expanded. This rule holds even if the name appears as the result of another macro expansion. In other words, 'recursive' macros are not allowed.

### *Macros vs functions*

For the most part, a macro can be used in the same way as a function. In our discussions so far, we have never really needed to distinguish between them. However, in certain situations, the differences could be important, and we highlight the major ones below.

(1) A macro is expanded 'in-line' before the program is compiled. **Each** occurrence of a macro name is replaced by the 'body' of the macro. On the other hand, the 'body' of a function is defined once no matter how many times it is called. However, each call of a function has some overhead associated with it (for instance, the stacking and unstacking of arguments). The result is that, in general, macros execute faster but increase the size of a program, especially if used in several places.

(2) A function name is a synonym for the address of the function, and can be used in contexts requiring a pointer. A macro name does not evaluate to an address. For example, if a macro name is used as an argument in a function call, the **value** of the macro is passed; if a function name is used as an argument, the address of the function is passed.

(3) Macros cannot be declared the way that functions are. Similarly, pointers to macro names cannot be declared the way that pointers to functions are. Hence type checking cannot be performed on macro arguments.

(4) In certain situations, macros may treat arguments with side-effects incorrectly, especially when an argument is evaluated more than once. Consider, again, the macro square defined above as:

```
#define square(n) ((n) * (n))
```

Assume $a = 5$ and consider the statement

```
y = square(++a);
```

This is expanded into

```
y = ((++a) * (++a));
```

and is evaluated as $y = (6)*(7) = 42$. Presumably, this is not what was intended. But if square were defined as a function, the argument ++a would be evaluated **once**, giving 6. This value is then passed to the function which evaluates $6*6 = 36$, the correct result.

### The 'stringizing' operator – #

This operator is used with macros which take arguments. If it precedes a formal parameter in ⟨replacement text⟩ then the corresponding actual argument is enclosed in double quotes and treated as a string constant. The resulting string constant becomes the actual argument and replaces #⟨parameter⟩. As an example, given

```
#define fun(x) printf(#x)
```

the statement

```
fun(This must be fun);
```

is expanded into

```
printf("This must be fun");
```

When an actual argument is 'stringized', it is automatically concatenated with any adjacent string constants separated from it by whitespace only. Given

```
#define fun(x) printf(#x "\n")
```

the statement

```
fun(This must be fun);
```

is first expanded into

```
printf("This must be fun" "\n");
```

The two strings are then concatenated, giving

```
printf("This must be fun\n");
```

If a character appearing in the actual argument normally requires an escape sequence when it appears in a string, the necessary escape \ is automatically inserted before the character. Given

```
#define fun(x) printf(#x "\n")
```

the statement

```
fun("This must be fun"); /* Quotes are now part of the
                                    argument */
```

is first expanded into

```
printf("\"This must be fun\"" "\n");
```

and then into

```
printf("\"This must be fun\"\n");
```

When executed, this will print

```
"This must be fun"
```

As another example, the statement

```
fun(Do's and don'ts);
```

will be expanded into

```
printf("Do\'s and don\'ts\n");
```

It is important to note that the actual argument is made into a string **without** any expansion being done. For example, given

```
#define EXCLAIM "My Goodness!"
#define fun(x) printf(#x "\n")
```

the statement

```
fun(EXCLAIM);
```

will be expanded into

```
printf("EXCLAIM\n");
```

and, as usual, identifiers within quotes are not expanded.

### The 'token-pasting' operator – ##

This operator can also be used with macros which take arguments. It enables two or more tokens to be joined to form a single token. Consider

```
#define maketemp(n) temp##n = 0
```

The statement

```
maketemp(3);
```

will be expanded into

```
temp3 = 0;
```

and

```
maketemp(orary);
```

will become

```
temporary = 0;
```

If a formal parameter in ⟨replacement text⟩ is preceded by ##, then each occurrence of ##⟨parameter⟩ is immediately replaced by the **unexpanded** actual argument, which is then concatenated with the preceding token. Thus

```
⟨token⟩##⟨parameter⟩
```

becomes

```
<token><actual argument>
```

The resulting token must be valid. If it is, it is rescanned for possible expansion if it is a macro name. For example, given

```
#define EXCLAIM "My Goodness!"
#define makeword(suffix) EX##suffix
```

the statement

```
printf("%s", makeword(CLAIM));
```

will be first expanded into

```
printf("%s", EXCLAIM);
```

and then into

```
printf("%s", "My Goodness!");
```

If a formal parameter in ⟨replacement text⟩ is followed by ##, then each occurrence of ⟨parameter⟩## is immediately replaced by the **unexpanded** actual argument, which is then concatenated with the following token. Thus

```
<parameter>##<token>
```

becomes

```
<actual argument><token>
```

The resulting token must be valid. If it is, it is rescanned for possible expansion if it is a macro name.

Finally, note that because ## joins two tokens together, it cannot be the first or last token in ⟨replacement text⟩.

### *11.1.2 The* #undef *directive*

Once an identifier has been defined using #define, it cannot be redefined to a different value without first removing the original definition. The #undef directive removes an identifier from the list of defined identifiers. Once an identifier has been undefined, it could subsequently be redefined with another value. (However, an identifier can be redefined with the **same** original value without first removing it with #undef). For example,

```
#undef EXCLAIM
```

removes 'EXCLAIM' from the list of defined identifiers.

To remove a macro name which takes arguments, only the name (and not the parameter list) must be specified.

The defined operator can be used to determine whether or not an identifier has been the subject of a #define directive.

defined(⟨id⟩) is true if ⟨id⟩ is currently defined, and false, otherwise. After ⟨id⟩ has been undefined, defined(⟨id⟩) is false.

defined is used mainly in conjunction with the 'conditional compilation' directives (see Section 11.1.4).

### *11.1.3 The* #include *directive*

This directive enables the contents of another file to be inserted in the position where the directive appears. The basic format is

```
#include "filename"
```

where the quotes are required.

For example, commonly used definitions, declarations or functions can be stored in one file. These can be easily inserted into any program by using an appropriate #include directive.

The exact details of what could follow #include depend on the particular implementation.

### *11.1.4 Conditional compilation –* #if, #elif, #else, #endif *directives*

These directives can be used to select particular statements for further compilation. As an example, consider the situation where we wish to 'comment out' a portion of a program, that is, we do not wish to have that portion compiled. It may not be possible to use the comment delimiters

/* and */ if the portion to be omitted itself contains a comment. (Since C does not allow nested comments, the */ of the inner comment would be deemed to end the 'comment' beginning with the first /*). In this situation, one could use the following (where OMIT is 0):

```
#if OMIT

    /* portion to be omitted */

#endif
```

Since OMIT is 0, the preprocessor treats this as false, and skips the portion of the program up to, and including #endif. What follows #if must be a constant expression. It is considered TRUE if it evaluates to non-zero, and FALSE if it evaluates to zero. In this example, we could achieve the same effect by using something like

```
#if defined(COMPILE)

    /* portion to be omitted */

#endif
```

If COMPILE has been #defined, then the portion is included for compilation. If COMPILE has not been #defined, then the portion is skipped.

    #else can be used to specify an alternative portion for compilation, as in

```
#if defined(GIVERULES)

    /* Compile these statements if GIVERULES is defined */

#else

    /* Compile these statements if GIVERULES is not defined */

#endif
```

#elif must be used if there are more than two alternatives from which to choose. Consider:

```
#if DIFF == 1
    #define MAXSIZE 100
#elif DIFF == 2
    #define MAXSIZE 400
#else
    #define MAXSIZE 1000
#endif
```

Here, the 'statements' are themselves preprocessor directives. Which one is selected for processing depends on the value of (a predefined constant) DIFF.

In general, there can be any number of #elif's, but there can be at most one #else. If present, #else must be the last directive before #endif.

## 11.2 Command-line arguments – argc and argv

In all our programs so far, main has been defined with an empty parameter list, thus:

```
main()
```

However, it is possible to pass arguments to main when the program is invoked for execution. These arguments are referred to as 'command-line arguments'.

When main is called to begin execution, two arguments – conventionally called argc (argument count) and argv (argument vector) – are passed to it. The function prototype for main can be thought of as:

```
main(int argc, char *argv[])
{

}
```

where argc is the number of command-line arguments with which the program was invoked and argv is an array of character pointers. Each pointer points to one of the arguments.

`argv[0]` points to the name by which the program was invoked;
`argv[1]` points to the first argument;
`argv[2]` points to the second argument;
        etc.

The last argument is stored in `argv[argc - 1]`. In addition, in ANSI C, `argv[argc]` is set to NULL. The name of the program is included in the count of arguments. Thus `argc` is 1 if no command-line arguments are supplied.

As an example, suppose we wanted to write a program called `add` which, when invoked, prints the sum of its command-line arguments. Thus

```
add 23 12 17
```

will print

```
52
```

To concentrate on the main issues, program P11.1 does not check that the arguments are indeed numbers. For the above example,

`argc` will be 4;
`argv[0]` will point to "add";
`argv[1]` will point to "23";
`argv[2]` will point to "12";
`argv[3]` will point to "17".
`argv[4]` will contain NULL.

The `for` loop steps through the arguments supplied. Note the use of `sscanf` to 'read' a number from a string. The net effect is that each command-line argument is added to `sum`.

Instead of the `sscanf` statement, one could have used:

```
num = atof(argv[j]);
```

`atof()` is a standard function which takes a character pointer (`chptr`, say) as its argument and returns the `double` equivalent of the string pointed to by `chptr`.

The specific method for invoking `add` depends on the operating system environment and/or the particular compiler. You will need to check the appropriate manual for details.

---

**Program P11.1**

```
#include <stdio.h>

main(int argc, char *argv[])
{
    int j;
    float num, sum;

    sum = 0;
    for (j = 1; j < argc; j++) {
        sscanf(argv[j], "%f", &num);
        sum += num;
    }
    printf("%f\n", sum);
}
```

---

## 11.3 Two-dimensional arrays

So far, we have dealt predominantly with one-dimensional arrays. Perhaps the most common example is an array of char for storing a string. We've also seen one-dimensional arrays of numbers or pointers and, in Chapter 7, we used a one-dimensional array of structures. One-dimensional arrays are, by far, the most common array type used in C programs. However, there are many situations in which it is natural to use a two-dimensional array. These include:

- storing and manipulating matrices;
- processing data which can be arranged in rows and columns;
- board games, where the board has a rectangular layout, for example, chess, checkers (draughts) or tic-tac-toe (noughts and crosses).

In Chapter 4, we saw an example of a two-dimensional array used for holding a table of words. We noted the following points then:

- A two-dimensional array is declared by specifying 2 subscript values within 2 sets of square brackets. For example,

```
int matrix[6][10];
```

declares `matrix` as a 6 by 10 array, that is, 6 rows and 10 columns. The rows are numbered 0 to 5 and the columns are numbered 0 to 9. In C, an array subscript always starts at 0.

- In the declaration, the subscript values must be constant expressions, that is, capable of being evaluated at compile time. For flexibility, it is usual to use symbolic constants as in:

```
int matrix[MAXROW][MAXCOL];
```

- If a two-dimensional array is used as a formal parameter of a function, the size of the **second** dimension **must** be specified, but the size of the first is optional. If the first is omitted, the square brackets must still be present, as in:

```
void fun(int matrix[][MAXCOL]);
```

We now discuss some other examples involving two-dimensional arrays.

It is quite common to use `for` statements to process the elements of an array. Suppose we wanted to read values into the above matrix. Assuming:

```
#define MAXROW 6
#define MAXCOL 10

    int r, c;
```

this could be done with:

```
for (r = 0; r < MAXROW; r++)
   for (c = 0; c < MAXCOL; c++)
      scanf("%d", &matrix[r][c]);
```

Here, for a given value of r, c runs through the values from 0 to MAXCOL − 1. This implies that the values for the matrix must be supplied in row order. If the values are supplied in column order, they could be read into the matrix with:

```
for (c = 0; c < MAXCOL; c++)
  for (r = 0; r < MAXROW; r++)
     scanf("%d", &matrix[r][c]);
```

### *11.3.1 Matrix multiplication*

Consider the problem of multiplying a matrix *A* by another matrix *B*. The matrix product is defined only if the number of columns of *A* is the same as the number of rows of *B*; in this case, the matrices are said to be **conformant**. Suppose

$$A \text{ is } m \times p$$

and

$$B \text{ is } p \times n$$

Then the product matrix, *C*, is $m \times n$ and element $C_{ij}$ is obtained by 'multiplying the *i*th row of *A* by the *j*th column of *B*'; this is done by multiplying each element of the *i*th row of *A* by the corresponding element of the *j*th column of *B* and adding the results. For example, if the *i*th row of *A* is

$$5 \ 7 \ 0 \ 4$$

and the *j*th column of *B* is

$$\begin{matrix} 2 \\ 0 \\ 6 \\ 3 \end{matrix}$$

element $C_{ij}$ of the product is obtained by

$$C_{ij} = 5 \times 2 + 7 \times 0 + 0 \times 6 + 4 \times 3 = 22$$

Assuming that the arrays (and other variables used below) have been declared and that the matrices are conformant, the following code finds $C = A \times B$:

```
for (i = 0; i < m; i ++)
    for (j = 0; j < n; j++)
    {
        sum = 0;
        for (k = 0; k < p; k++)
            sum += A[i][k] * B[k][j];
        C[i][j] = sum;
    }
```

The portion of code within the braces 'multiplies the $i$th row of $A$ by the $j$th column of $B$' and assigns the result to $C[i][j]$.

### 11.3.2 Magic squares

A magic square is an $n \times n$ matrix in which the numbers 1 to $n^2$ are placed in such a way that all rows, columns and diagonals add up to the same number. The $3 \times 3$ magic square is:

$$
\begin{array}{ccc}
8 & 1 & 6 \\
3 & 5 & 7 \\
4 & 9 & 2
\end{array}
$$

If $n$ is even, the algorithm for producing the magic square is very involved. However, if $n$ is odd, the following algorithm can be used, thinking of the square as made up of $n^2$ cells:

(1) Place 1 in the middle cell of the top row.

Repeat (2) until all the numbers have been placed.
(2) Assume the number $k$ has just been placed; the following places the number $k + 1$:

> If $k$ has been placed in the upper-right-hand corner, place $k + 1$ immediately below $k$
> else
>> attempt to place the number $k + 1$ by moving one cell up and one cell right.
>> If this move takes you above the top row in the $j$th column, place the number at the bottom of the $j$th column
>> else if this moves takes you beyond the right side of the square in the $i$th row, place the number at the left of the $i$th row
>> else if this move takes you to an already filled square, place the number immediately below $k$.
> endif

We want to read a value for $n$ and produce the corresponding magic square. Our program caters for values of $n$ up to a maximum defined by NMAX.

For a given value of $n$, the rows and columns are numbered from 0 to $n - 1$. Assume $m = n - 1$. The top row is row 0 and the bottom row is row *m.* 'Moving one row up' is done by **decreasing** the row subscript. We have gone 'above the top row' if the row subscript is less than 0. Similarly, the leftmost column is column 0 and the rightmost column is column *m*. 'Moving one cell to the right' is done by **increasing** the column subscript. We have gone 'beyond the rightmost column' if the column subscript is greater than *m*. To distinguish an 'already filled square' from an empty one, we initialize all cells to 0 (empty). Program P11.2 requests a value for *n*, validates it, and produces an $n \times n$ magic square.

---

**Program P11.2**

```c
#include <stdio.h>

#define NMAX 13

main()
{
    int square[NMAX][NMAX];
    int i, j, n, invalid;

    void createmagic(int square[NMAX][NMAX], int n);
    void printmagic(int square[NMAX][NMAX], int n);

    do {
        printf("Size of magic square (up to %d)?",
               NMAX);
        scanf("%d", &n);
        invalid = (n < 1 || n > NMAX || n % 2 == 0);
        if (invalid) printf("\nMust be positive, odd "
                            "and not bigger than "
                            "%d\n",NMAX);
    } while (invalid);

    /* set all cells to 0 */
    for (i = 0; i < n; i++)
        for (j = 0; j < n; j++)
            square[i][j] = 0;
```

---

```
      createmagic(square, n);
      printmagic(square, n);
}

void createmagic(int square[NMAX][NMAX], int n)
{
    int k;

    int m = n - 1;      /* maximum row, column
                               subscript */
    int i = 0;          /* row subscript */
    int j = n / 2 ;     /* column subscript */

    square[i][j] = 1; /* place 1 in the middle of the
                               top row */
    for (k = 2; k <= n * n; k++)
                        /* place the other numbers */
    {
       if (i == 0 && j == m) i = 1;
                          /* top-right-hand corner */
       else
       {
          --i;          /* move up one row */
          ++j;          /* move right one column */

          if (i < 0) i = m;   /* above the top row */
          else if (j > m) j = 0;
                    /* beyond the rightmost column */
          else if (square[i][j] != 0)
                             /* cell already filled */
          {  i += 2;   /* go to the row below last
                               number placed */
             --j;   /* go to the column of last
                            number placed */
          }
       }
       square[i][j] = k;
    }
}

void printmagic(int square[NMAX][NMAX], int n)
{
    int i, j;

    printf("\nMagic square of order %d\n\n", n);
```

```
    for (i = 0; i < n; i++)
    {
        for (j = 0; j < n; j++)
            printf("%4d", square[i][j]);
        printf("\n");
    }
}
```

The following is a sample run of Program P11.2.

```
Size of magic square (up to 13)? 8
Must be positive, odd and not bigger than 13
Size of magic square (up to 13)? 7

Magic square of order 7


    30  39  48   1  10  19  28
    38  47   7   9  18  27  29
    46   6   8  17  26  35  37
     5  14  16  25  34  36  45
    13  15  24  33  42  44   4
    21  23  32  41  43   3  12
    22  31  40  49   2  11  20
```

Arrays of higher dimension (>2) can be declared in C, similar to two-dimensional arrays. For example

```
float salesfigures[10][5][3];
```

declares a three-dimensional array salesfigures. Suppose a company has 10 salespeople, each of whom sells 5 products, each of which comes in 3 models, then we could use:

```
salesfigures[i][j][k]
```

to refer to the sales made by the i th salesperson from product j, model k.

### 11.4 Enumerated types – enum

ANSI C allows the programmer to declare a new data type using the keyword enum. It is called an enumerated type and is simply a list of legal values which a variable of that type may have. For example,

```
enum {red, orange, yellow, green, blue, indigo,
      violet} shirt, blouse;
```

declares two variables shirt and blouse. The only valid values these variables can assume are from the 'enumerated' list of colours enclosed in braces and separated by commas. Each item in the list can be thought of as a symbolic constant – just a name for an integer value. Given the above declaration, C assigns integer values as follows:

```
red      -   0
orange   -   1
yellow   -   2
green    -   3
blue     -   4
indigo   -   5
violet   -   6
```

that is, the first item is assigned the value 0, the second is assigned the value 1, and so on. The following are valid statements:

```
shirt = blue;
blouse = green;
```

or even

```
shirt = blouse; /* assign the value of blouse to shirt */
```

However,

```
shirt = brown;
```

is invalid since brown is not one of the values which shirt may have.

It is customary to assign a type name to an enumerated type as in:

```
enum colour {red, orange, yellow, green, blue,
             indigo, violet};
```

and then use the name to declare variables as in:

```
enum colour shirt, blouse;
```

We could also declare variables at the same time we define the type name, as in:

```
enum colour {red, orange, yellow, green, blue,
             indigo, violet} shirt, blouse;
```

Finally, we could use a typedef to simplify things further, as in:

```
typedef enum {red, orange, yellow, green, blue,
              indigo, violet} Colour;
```

followed by (for instance):

```
Colour shirt, blouse;
```

enum variables are treated as if they are of type int. In particular, they can be used as subscript expressions and as operands of all arithmetic and relational operators.

Enumerated types are used primarily for improving the readability of a program. For example, the colour names are more readily understood than using a code (e.g., 1 = red, 2 = blue) for each colour. In the latter case, we have to keep remembering which colour a particular code stands for.

A major restriction of an enum variable is that its value cannot be input or output directly. For instance, we may be tempted to write:

```
printf("%s \n", shirt); /* this is wrong */
```

thinking that blue, say, would be printed. But remember that the value of an enum variable is really just an integer; we could write:

```
printf("%d \n", shirt); /* this is okay */
```

but, in this case, (assuming shirt = blue), the integer 4 would be printed. To print the symbolic value of a variable of type Colour, we would need to use a function similar to the following:

```
void printColour(Colour item)
{
    switch (item)  {
        case red:    printf("red");
                     break;
        case orange: printf("orange");
                     break;
        case yellow: printf("yellow");
                     break;
        case green:  printf("green");
                     break;
        case blue:   printf("blue");
                     break;
        case indigo: printf("indigo");
                     break;
        case violet: printf("violet");
                     break;
    }
}
```

Now, if shirt = blue, a call such as

```
printColour(shirt);
```

will print blue.

Another way to write the above function is to set up an array of strings and use the integer value of the enum variable as a subscript to extract the correct string. The following illustrates this approach:

```
void printColour(Colour item)
{
    static char *colours[] =
                    {       "red",
                            "orange",
                            "yellow",
                            "green",
                            "blue",
                            "indigo",
                            "violet"
                    };

    printf("%s", colours[item]);
}
```

The array is declared `static` to ensure that it is set up once only and remains in existence for the duration of the program.

As another example, suppose we wanted to store information about four makes of cars – Nissan, Ford, Mazda and Toyota. Each of these four comes in three models – sedan, station wagon and pickup. For each make and model, we wish to store the price. We could use a $4 \times 3$ array, `carPrice`, declared as:

```
float carPrice[4][3];
```

where

```
carPrice[0][0] holds the price for the Nissan sedan;
carPrice[0][1] holds the price for the Nissan station wagon;
carPrice[0][2] holds the price for the Nissan pickup;
carPrice[1][0] holds the price for the Ford sedan;
            etc.
```

To make this more readable, we could declare enumerated types thus:

```
enum {Nissan, Ford, Mazda, Toyota} make;
enum {Sedan, StationWagon, Pickup} model;
```

and then refer to the array elements using the enumerated types as subscripts, as in:

```
carPrice[Nissan][Sedan] or
carPrice[Ford][StationWagon]
```

or, in general,

```
carPrice[make][model]
```

Normally, C assigns integer values starting from 0 to items in an enumerated list. However, this default assignment could be overridden as in the following example:

```
enum colour {red = 1, blue, green, yellow = 12,
             orange, indigo, violet};
```

An explicit value could be assigned by following the name with = and the value desired. The value must be a constant expression of type int and can be negative. Unless initialized explicitly, subsequent items are assigned consecutive values greater than the previous explicit value. Thus the above statement assigns values as follows:

```
red      -    1
blue     -    2
green    -    3
yellow   -    12
orange   -    13
indigo   -    14
violet   -    15
```

The following is also valid:

```
enum {right = 4, wrong = -1, none = 0} reply;
```

Other points to note are:

- Two or more items in an enumeration list could be associated with the same value. For example, the following is valid:

```
enum colour {red = 1, blue = 1, green = 1,
             yellow, orange, indigo, violet};
```

Here, the names red, blue and green are assigned the value 1, yellow is assigned 2, etc.

- The identifiers in an enumeration list must be distinct from other identifiers with the same scope. This includes ordinary variable names and identifiers in other enumeration lists.

## 11.5 The goto statement

This statement has the form

```
goto <label> ;
```

where <label> is an identifier used to label a statement in the same function as the goto statement. A statement is labelled with an identifier followed by a colon, as in

```
identifier : statement
```

A goto statement transfers control directly to the statement with the specifed label. Labels within a given function must be distinct.

Given all the available control structures in C, good programmers almost never find it necessary to use goto statements.

## 11.6 const and volatile

ANSI C provides two new type modifiers not available in traditional C.

The type modifier const is used to declare an object that cannot be modified except for an initialization. It can be applied to a simple type (int, char, etc.), a pointer, an array or a structure. If applied to an array or structure, no element of the array or structure may be modified. For example,

```
const int cashlimit = 10000;
```

declares that cashlimit cannot be changed to another value by the program. It also informs the compiler that, if possible, this 'variable' could be placed in a read-only portion of memory. Another example is:

```
const char password[] = "abracadabra-sesame";
```

Here, `password` is a character array whose initial value cannot be changed by the program.

The type modifier `volatile` is used to declare an object whose value may legitimately be changed by something not under the direct control of the program. The compiler uses this information to ensure that the variable is used exactly as the programmer intends. For example, suppose the value of the variable `era` is updated every second by the system clock, and consider the code:

```
for (k = 0; k < INFINITY; k ++)
{   .
    epoch = 2 * era;
    printf("The new age is %d\n", epoch);
    .
}
```

If there is no explicit assignment to `era` inside the loop, the compiler may assume (erroneously) that the value of `epoch` does not change. In optimizing the code, it may evaluate `epoch` once, before the loop is entered, and remove the assignment from the loop. Obviously, this will not give the intended results. The declaration

```
volatile int era;
```

would prevent this optimization from taking place.

## Exercises 11

(1) Define a macro `exchange` which interchanges the values of its two arguments.
(2) Define a macro `max` which finds the larger of its two arguments.
(3) Define a macro `toupper` which converts its argument to uppercase if it is lowercase and leaves it unchanged, otherwise.
(4) Define a macro which takes three arguments $a$, $b$ and $c$, and returns the root of $ax^2+bx+c=0$ obtained by taking the positive square root of $b^2-4ac$.
(5) Given the declaration

```
#define message(x) printf(#x " ! " #x)
```

what is the expansion of the following?

```
message(Hello);
message("Hello");
message('Allo);
message('Allo 'Allo);
message(50% is too high);
```

If, in addition, we have

```
#define cube(a) ((a) * (a) * (a))
```

give the expansion of:

```
message(magic cube);
cube(magic);
message("magic " cube);
message(magic cube \n);
```

(6)   Write a utility program to copy one file to another. It is invoked by the command line statement:

```
copy fromfile tofile
```

where `fromfile` is the source file and `tofile` is the destination file.

(7)   Write a function which, given a variable of type `enum colour`, reads the input and assigns the next 'colour constant' to the variable. Return an error indication if the next data item in the input is not a valid 'colour constant'.

(8)   Write an `enum` declaration for variables whose values are the signs of the zodiac.

(9)   Write `enum` declarations for describing the 52 cards in a standard deck.

(10)  There are 20 teams in a football league and teams play each other on a home-and-away basis. (Assume that the teams are numbered from 1 to 20). A two-dimensional array `results` is used to keep track of the results of matches. If team `i` is at home to team `j` then `results[i][j]` is set to

and

2 if team `i` wins;
1 if the game is drawn;
0 if team `i` loses.

Write a program to read the results of matches and store the appropriate values in `results`. Choose a suitable format for the input data.

Write a function which, given a team number, returns the number of points earned by that team. Hint: rows gives results of home matches and columns give results of away matches; also if `results[i][j]=k`, then team `j` earned $2-k$ points for the away game to team `i`.

(11)  An $n \times n$ array `distance` is used to store the distance between any two of

*n* towns. `distance[i][j]`, $i \neq j$ is the distance between towns i and j. Obviously, `distance[i][i]` = 0, and `distance[i][j]` = `distance[j][i]`.

Devise a scheme for storing the information in `distance` is a one-dimensional array so that storage is conserved as much as possible.

Write a function which, given the one-dimensional array and the integers i and j, returns the distance between town i and town j.

# Appendix A

# List of C keywords

The following is the complete list of C keywords. Keywords are always written in lowercase.

| | | | |
|---|---|---|---|
| auto | break | case | char |
| const | continue | default | do |
| double | else | enum | extern |
| float | for | goto | if |
| int | long | register | return |
| short | signed | sizeof | static |
| struct | switch | typedef | union |
| unsigned | void | volatile | while |

# Appendix B

# Major differences between functions in ANSI C and traditional C

Our discussion of functions in this book is based on the ANSI C standard. However, for compatibility, many compilers support both the new standard and traditional C. The following cites the major differences between the two standards.

For illustration, consider the following program taken from Section 3.1:

```
main()
{
    int factorial(int n), num;

    printf(" n      n!\n\n");
    for (num = 0; num <= 7; num++)
        printf(" %2d %4d\n", num, factorial(num));
}

int factorial(int n)        /* function definition;
                               no ';' after ')'. */
{
    int nfac;               /* local variable declaration */

    if (n < 0) return 0;        /* return 0 for an
                                   invalid argument */
    for ( nfac = 1; n > 0; n-- )
        nfac *= n;      /* equivalent to nfac = nfac * n */
    return nfac;                /* value returned to the
                                   calling function */
}
```

- In traditional C, the function definition heading would be written as:

```
int factorial(n)
    int n;
{ etc.
```

In general, only the names of the formal parameters are written in brackets after the function name; the types of the parameters are specified after the right bracket. The type of value returned by a function may be omitted, in which case it is assumed to be int. Since this function returns int, it could be shortened to:

```
factorial(n)
    int n;
{ etc.
```

However, it is good style to state explicitly the type of value a function returns.

Another example is:

```
int search(name, first, last)  /* no semicolon after ')' */
    char name[];
    int first, last;  /* int does not have to be repeated */
{ etc.
```

This is equivalent to the ANSI C declaration:

```
int search(char name[], int first, int last)
                            /* int must be repeated */
{ etc.
```

- In traditional C, the calling function does not **have to** declare a called function if the latter returns int. (However, good programming practice dictates that it should be declared, anyway). If the function returns anything other than an int, it must be declared in the calling function. When declared, only the return type, the function name and the brackets after the name are required, for example:

```
int factorial();
```

Another example is

```
char *search();
```

This declares search as a function which returns a character pointer. Note that there is no way to determine from this, the arguments required by search.
- The above program would be written in traditional C as:

```
main()
{
    int factorial(), num;

    printf("    n          n!\n\n");
    for (num = 0; num <= 7; num++)
        printf("   %2d      %4d\n", num, factorial(num));
}

int factorial(n)                /* function definition;
                                   no ';' after ')'. */
    int n;
```

```
{
    int nfac;                    /* local variable declaration */

    if (n < 0) return 0;    /* return 0 for an invalid
                                argument */
    for (nfac = 1; n > 0; n--)
        nfac *= n;           /* equivalent to nfac = nfac * n  */
    return nfac;             /* value returned to the calling
                                function */
}
```

where the declaration

```
    int factorial();
```

in main is not required (but recommended). If omitted, main will be able to deduce from the context in which factorial is used that it is a function.

- In traditional C, if a function is used for effect and not to return a value, the type is usually omitted in the function definition, for example:

```
    printresults(table)
        int table[][MAXSIZE];
    {
        etc.
```

In ANSI C, such a function heading would be written

```
void printresults(int table[][MAXSIZE])
```

- In traditional C, if a function does not take an argument, nothing is written within the brackets in the function definition, for example:

```
    double random()
    {
        etc.
```

This declares random as a function which takes no arguments and returns a value of type double. It is called as in:

```
    x = random();   /* brackets required */
```

In ANSI C, a function which takes no arguments would use void within the brackets to indicate this, as in

```
    double random(void)
```

# Appendix C

# ASCII character set

The following are the character codes used in the ASCII character set. Codes 0 to 31 (and 127) are used for control characters. Some common control characters are

| | |
|---|---|
| 0 | NULL |
| 8 | backspace (BS) |
| 10 | line feed (LF) |
| 12 | form feed (FF) |
| 13 | carriage return (CR) |

The other characters from codes 32 to 127 are:

| Decimal | Binary | Char | Decimal | Binary | Char |
|---|---|---|---|---|---|
| 32 | 010 0000 | space | 55 | 011 0111 | 7 |
| 33 | 010 0001 | ! | 56 | 011 1000 | 8 |
| 34 | 010 0010 | " | 57 | 011 1001 | 9 |
| 35 | 010 0011 | # | 58 | 011 1010 | : |
| 36 | 010 0100 | $ | 59 | 011 1011 | ; |
| 37 | 010 0101 | % | 60 | 011 1100 | < |
| 38 | 010 0110 | & | 61 | 011 1101 | = |
| 39 | 010 0111 | ' | 62 | 011 1110 | > |
| 40 | 010 1000 | ( | 63 | 011 1111 | ? |
| 41 | 010 1001 | ) | 64 | 100 0000 | @ |
| 42 | 010 1010 | * | 65 | 100 0001 | A |
| 43 | 010 1011 | + | 66 | 100 0010 | B |
| 44 | 010 1100 | ' | 67 | 100 0011 | C |
| 45 | 010 1101 | − | 68 | 100 0100 | D |
| 46 | 010 1110 | . | 69 | 100 0101 | E |
| 47 | 010 1111 | / | 70 | 100 0110 | F |
| 48 | 011 0000 | 0 | 71 | 100 0111 | G |
| 49 | 011 0001 | 1 | 72 | 100 1000 | H |
| 50 | 011 0010 | 2 | 73 | 100 1001 | I |
| 51 | 011 0011 | 3 | 74 | 100 1010 | J |
| 52 | 011 0100 | 4 | 75 | 100 1011 | K |
| 53 | 011 0101 | 5 | 76 | 100 1100 | L |
| 54 | 011 0110 | 6 | 77 | 100 1101 | M |

| Decimal | Binary   | Char | Decimal | Binary   | Char |
|---------|----------|------|---------|----------|------|
| 78      | 100 1110 | N    | 103     | 110 0111 | g    |
| 79      | 100 1111 | O    | 104     | 110 1000 | h    |
| 80      | 101 0001 | P    | 105     | 110 1001 | i    |
| 81      | 101 0010 | Q    | 106     | 110 1010 | j    |
| 82      | 101 0010 | R    | 107     | 110 1011 | k    |
| 83      | 101 0011 | S    | 108     | 110 1100 | l    |
| 84      | 101 0100 | T    | 109     | 110 1100 | m    |
| 85      | 101 0101 | U    | 110     | 110 1101 | n    |
| 86      | 101 0110 | V    | 111     | 110 1110 | o    |
| 87      | 101 0111 | W    | 112     | 110 1111 | p    |
| 88      | 101 1000 | X    | 113     | 111 0000 | q    |
| 89      | 101 1001 | Y    | 114     | 111 0001 | r    |
| 90      | 101 1010 | Z    | 115     | 111 0010 | s    |
| 91      | 101 1011 | [    | 116     | 111 0011 | t    |
| 92      | 101 1100 | \    | 117     | 111 0100 | u    |
| 93      | 101 1101 | ]    | 118     | 111 0101 | v    |
| 94      | 101 1110 | ^    | 119     | 111 0110 | w    |
| 95      | 101 1111 | _    | 120     | 111 0111 | x    |
| 96      | 110 0000 | `    | 121     | 111 1000 | y    |
| 97      | 110 0001 | a    | 122     | 111 1001 | z    |
| 98      | 110 0010 | b    | 123     | 111 1010 | {    |
| 99      | 110 0011 | c    | 124     | 111 1011 | \|   |
| 100     | 110 0100 | d    | 125     | 111 1100 | }    |
| 101     | 110 0101 | e    | 126     | 111 1101 | ~    |
| 102     | 110 0110 | f    | 127     | 111 1110 | DEL  |

# Index